T0305124

Organizations and Activism

Series Editors: **Daniel King**, Nottingham Trent University and **Martin Parker**, University of Bristol

---

Organizations and Activism publishes books that explore how politics happens within and because of organizations, how activism is organized, and how activists change organizations.

Forthcoming in the series:

Organizing Food, Faith and Freedom:
Imagining Alternatives
By **Ozan Alakavuklar**

Organising for Change:
Social Change Makers and Social Change Organisations
By **Silke Roth** and **Clare Saunders**

Out now in the series:

Co-operation and Co-operatives in 21st Century Europe
Edited by **Julian Manley, Anthony Webster and Olga Kuznetsova**

Reimagining Academic Activism:
Learning from Feminist Anti-Violence Activists
By **Ruth Weatherall**

Anarchist Cybernetics:
Control and Communication in Radical Politics
By **Thomas Swann**

Guerrilla Democracy:
Mobile Power and Revolution in the 21st Century
By **Peter Bloom, Owain Smolović Jones** and **Jamie Woodcock**

Find out more at

bristoluniversitypress.co.uk/organizations-and-activism

Organizations and Activism

Series Editors: **Daniel King**, Nottingham Trent University and **Martin Parker**, University of Bristol

---

International advisory board:

Find out more at
bristoluniversitypress.co.uk/organizations-and-activism

FOOD POLITICS, ACTIVISM AND ALTERNATIVE CONSUMER COOPERATIVES

Beyza Oba and Zeynep Özsoy

BRISTOL
UNIVERSITY
PRESS

First published in Great Britain in 2023 by

Bristol University Press
University of Bristol
1–9 Old Park Hill
Bristol
BS2 8BB
UK
t: +44 (0)117 374 6645
e: bup-info@bristol.ac.uk

Details of international sales and distribution partners are available at bristoluniversitypress.co.uk

© Bristol University Press 2023

British Library Cataloguing in Publication Data
A catalogue record for this book is available from the British Library

ISBN 978-1-5292-2003-2 hardcover
ISBN 978-1-5292-2004-9 ePub
ISBN 978-1-5292-2005-6 ePdf

The right of Beyza Oba and Zeynep Özsoy to be identified as authors of this work has been asserted by them in accordance with the Copyright, Designs and Patents Act 1988.

Cover design: blu inc
Front cover image: Mustafa Çakırtaş/The terrace garden Postane İstanbul
Bristol University Press uses environmentally responsible print partners.
Printed and bound in Great Britain by CPI Group (UK) Ltd, Croydon, CR0 4YY

FSC
www.fsc.org
MIX
Paper | Supporting responsible forestry
FSC® C013604

Contents

Series Editors' Preface

Daniel King and Martin Parker

Organizing is politics made durable. From cooperatives to corporations, Occupy to Meta, states and NGOs, organizations shape our lives. They shape the possible futures of governance, policy making and social change, and hence are central to understanding how human beings can deal with the challenges that face us, whether that be pandemics, populism or climate change. This book series publishes work that explores how politics happen within and because of organizations and organizing. We want to explore how activism is organized and how activists change organizations. We are also interested in the forms of resistance to activism, in the ways that powerful interests contest and reframe demands for change. These are questions of huge relevance to scholars in sociology, politics, geography, management and beyond, and are becoming ever more important as demands for impact and engagement change the way that academics imagine their work. They are also important to anyone who wants to understand more about the theory and practice of organizing, not just the abstracted ideologies of capitalism taught in business schools.

Our books offer critical examinations of organizations as sites of, or targets for, activism, and we will also assume that our authors – and hopefully our readers – are themselves agents of change. Titles may focus on specific industries or fields, or they may be arranged around particular themes or challenges. Our topics might include the alternative economy; surveillance, whistleblowing and human rights; digital politics; religious groups; social movements; NGOs; feminism and anarchist organization; action research and co-production; activism and the neoliberal university, and any other subjects that are relevant and topical.

Organizations and Activism is also a multidisciplinary series. Contributions from all and any relevant academic fields will be welcomed. The series is international in outlook, and proposals from outside the English-speaking global north are particularly welcome.

There could hardly be a more essential subject to human life than the focus for the fifth book in our series: food. We buy it, cook it, consume it every day. It is essential to survive, and also plays a pivotal role in our overall health and wellbeing. Yet food is more than this. Food is not merely sustenance; it is a source of pleasure, cultural identity and social connection. From birthdays to weddings, holidays to festivals, food takes centre stage in commemorating these important moments in our lives. Food matters.

But how much do we think about how it is produced, organized or distributed? How much do we consider the issues of social justice, ecology and economic sustainability in how we produce and consume food? Can we think differently about food, and how it reflects the world around us?

This book invites us to explore the politics of food, and particularly the activism involved in organizing differently. It argues that the current industrial food production system is influenced by neoliberal policies, in which food is viewed primarily as a commodity traded within global markets where big agro-food companies hold dominant positions. They control production, distribution, machinery and even fertilizer and seeds. These companies operate with a capitalist market logic focused on efficiency, economies of scale and performance indicators like profits and return on investment. However, this logic overlooks the challenges posed by externalities such as natural resource degradation, deforestation, desertification and pollution. Although these companies within the industrial food system can offer cheap food, it comes at a cost to people and the planet.

This book explores alternatives. *Food Politics, Activism and Alternative Consumer Cooperatives* weaves together history and contemporary politics. Through a fascinating account of the Alternative Food Network in Turkey, this book invites us to reflect that how we organize food could be otherwise. It explores how the production and consumption of foodstuffs can be guided by social justice, ecological and economic sustainability, built around the values of solidarity, responsibility, decommodification, non-profit and strategic questioning of the existing economic order. The organizations that Oba and Ozsoy describe are attempts at direct democracy, challenging existing power relations, and bringing in decision-making processes such as consensus-based decision-making, minimum hierarchy and volunteer work.

This book provides a close up view of these Alternative Consumer Cooperatives (ACCs). The authors' first encounter with ACCs was as consumers, residents of the districts in which they operate. In this they bring first-hand knowledge and personal connection with these coops and the places they are embedded in. Alongside interviews they participated in the weekly decision-making, attended workshops and sought to understand the everyday practice of the coop.

With a deep understanding, the authors show these consumer cooperatives as a model form of activist organization. They strive to create a different food system by eliminating intermediaries in supply and distribution, empowering rural women, supporting small farmers, promoting sustainable traditional agriculture and experimenting with non-capital-accumulation-focused surplus distribution. Unlike the industrial production system, they aim to reconnect rural producers and urban consumers, fostering direct social and spatial relationships. Through activities like site visits, workshops and shop encounters, they seek to demystify food, raise awareness about production conditions and reshape perceptions of healthy and high-quality food. This sort of organization is thus an alternative organization with a prefigurative stance, a diverse economy experiment with different forms of food provision. Because if food can be democratised and localised, then it might show that we can take back the economy in many other areas too.

We hope you enjoy this book. If you want to discuss a proposal yourself, then email the series editors. We look forward to hearing from you.

1

Introduction: Experimenting with Direct Democracy

In recent years the Turkish political domain has witnessed a multitude of solidarity initiatives such as consumer cooperatives, women-owned producer cooperatives and neighbourhood assemblies formed by citizens in an effort to express their discontent with the hegemonic neo-liberal project and the tone of its implementation. These initiatives, in response to full-blown neo-liberalism and the increasing drift towards authoritarianism, can be taken as enclaves of 'hope' where, through direct democracy and solidarity among various constituencies, excluded groups can be repositioned within the political and economic realm and citizens can have a voice in politics. Activists involved in these initiatives demand a 'just' distribution of resources within society and claim that by realizing their capabilities, by pursuing their ideals and by offering their time and labour they can shape power relations at the local level. Participants from diverse social and economic backgrounds – workers, professionals, university students, the unemployed – question the predominant norms of the existing political system and develop alternatives that can lead to change. In this book we focus on one of these initiatives: the alternative consumer cooperatives (ACCs) as spaces for prefigurative food politics.

In Turkey, the ACCs are different to conventional consumer cooperatives (CCCs), which have been instrumentalized either by the state or by companies for private gain. The ACCs proliferated after the 2013 Gezi Park protests as a reaction to the hegemony of capitalist relationships in the production and distribution of foodstuff. They are governed by activists who disregard managerialist logic and experiment with alternative ways of governance such as a zero hierarchy and consensus-based decision-making. The daily activities of the ACCs are carried out by consumers who offer their labour voluntarily and who provide examples of non-marketable forms of economic transactions such as reciprocity and social obligation. Given all these features, in this book we view ACCs as spaces of prefigurative politics where politically positioned consumers not only experiment with and gain insight into alternatives to the capitalist logic, but also reshape the existing power relations in and around the ACCs. In so doing, we expose the strategies employed by the government in the construction of a globally oriented capitalist production/consumption nexus in agriculture and explore how ACCs develop counter-strategies to resist and challenge the status quo. In this respect, the book addresses three major issues: (1) how ACCs create a public sphere that fosters prefigurative politics and a new form of activism; (2) how ACCs develop an alternative to the capitalist food provisioning system; and (3) how the practices, in the governance of ACCs, lead to the development of an alternative organizational form.

The underlying premises of food politics in Turkey

Gibson-Graham, in *The End of Capitalism (as We Knew It): A Feminist Critique of Political Economy* (1996a) and *A Postcapitalist Politics* (2006), highlights the importance of alternative spaces and the practices employed by them as a move for underlining the premises of a post-capitalist future. Alternative spaces, by focusing on and experimenting with non-capitalist forms of production, workplace relations and labour conditions, provide examples that promote a politics of possibilities for post-capitalism (Gibson-Graham, 1996, 2006). Capitalist enterprise is based on a capitalist form of organizing where surplus value is generated, appropriated and distributed on the basis of private ownership, wage labour, market transactions and finance models operating with market logic (Gibson-Graham, 2010). With a 'capitalocentric' approach, if capitalism is taken as the only and dominant form of economic structuring, then the 'alternative' and 'non-capitalist' forms of organizing will be either treated as marginal or will be masked. However, alternative capitalist (such as state-owned or non-profit organizations) or non-capitalist (such as worker-owned cooperatives) organizations coexist with capitalist enterprises. Furthermore, Gibson-Graham in *A Postcapitalist Politics* (2006) emphasizes the role of such economic experimentation projects and 'local action' in the making of a different economy that confronts the prevailing capitalist logic. In so doing, the book focuses on the politics of the subject, the politics of collective action and the politics of language. The 'politics of the self' discusses how subjects created by the dominant capitalist logic can be (re)created as communal economic ones through a 'process of 'resubjectivation' – the mobilization and transformation of desires, the cultivation of capacities, and the making of new identifications with something as vague and unspecified as a 'community economy' (p xxxvi). The 'politics of collective action' refers to the conscious and collective efforts of the subjects to build alternatives as a different economic reality and this project deems

2

an economic language that is not incorporated in the prevailing ways of seeing and understanding the economy.

Based on our research data, we position ACCs as a non-capitalist form of organizing, operating with a non-capitalistic form of work, shaped by values of solidarity and responsibility, and deliberately questing for ways to dislocate from hegemonic capitalist relations. Activists involved in their founding and development take an oppositional stance and refute the capitalist and managerialist logic, and instead deliberately experiment with an alternative food provisioning and governance system. Activists want to re-socialize the production and consumption nexus in the food provisioning system by adopting an 'ethics of solidarity', acknowledging the interdependency of the rural petty commodity producers and the urban consumers. As discussed by Gritsaz and Kavoulakos (2016), ACCs are embedded in alternative food networks (AFNs); they are cases of diverse economies that aim to overcome inequality in food provisioning so that healthy foodstuff can be available to, and affordable for, all income groups; they seek to support small local producers who have lost their position within the mass-produced capitalist food provisioning system; and believe that the production and consumption of foodstuffs should be guided by social justice, ecological and economic sustainability (Renting et al, 2003; Whatmore et al, 2003; Holloway et al, 2007; Maye et al, 2007; Jarosz, 2008; Goodman and Goodman, 2009; Maye and Kirvan, 2010; Goodman et al, 2012; Wilson, 2013). Studies on the emergence and diffusion of AFNs in Turkey show that such initiatives began in 2004 (Özden, 2020; Ayalp, 2021) and gained momentum after the Gezi Park protests. The earliest examples of AFNs in Turkey, Tohum İzi Derneği and Anadolu'da Yaşam, were founded in 2004, Bir Umut was founded in 2005 and BÜKOOP (a consumer cooperative founded by the members of Boğaziçi University) in 2008. Due to the absence of a single, unifying source of data about AFNs in Turkey, it is difficult to provide a detailed explanation of the numbers and spatial distribution of AFNs. Instead, we rely on a limited number of studies conducted by academics and data sources such as the online ecological network EkoHarita, a data base developed by volunteers (Özsoy and Oba, 2022). As of 2020, Ayalp (2021) identified 80 civic food initiatives – a subgroup of AFNs – and most of them were located in three big cities – İstanbul, İzmir and Ankara. On the other hand, EkoHarita provides information about 237 AFNs mainly located in the western regions of the country (Marmara, Aegean and Mediterranean). The major difference between these different data sources can be explained in relation to the classification system adopted; for example, Ayalp's (2021) study focuses on civic food initiatives (CFIs) which is a subgroup of AFNs and is comprised of food communities, consumer cooperatives, producer cooperatives, cooperative initiatives and community supported agriculture. EkoHarita's database, in addition to the CFIs, includes collective urban gardens, grow-your-own groups, botanical gardens, eco-enterprises, alternative education and training organizations, and data banks. Based on these diverse sources, the Food Networks Platform provides a tentative list of 48 AFNs operating in Turkey (see https://gidatopluluklari.org/).

No matter the classification and the number of AFNs, similar social, economic and political conditions underlie their emergence in Turkey: the unrest among citizens regarding the neo-liberal policies implemented by the government in relation to environmental issues, which have caused irreversible damage and led to the depletion of natural resources; opposition to the commodification of labour, shaped by the weakening of the labour unions by legislation and worsening work conditions; and discontent among health-concerned citizens over industrially produced foodstuffs (Kadirbeyoğlu and Konya, 2017). Furthermore, the experiences of the early examples of AFNs, and the efforts of Çiftçi-Sen (the Farmers' Union), have been influential in the proliferation of such initiatives. BÜKOOP, Anadolu'da Yaşam, Tohum İzi Derneği and Çiftçi-Sen collaboratively organized workshops and conferences where experiences and ideas were shared. Additionally, Boğaziçi University members, academics from the Middle East Technical University in Ankara and Ege University in Izmir were actively involved as founders of the AFNs (Özden, 2020; Ayalp, 2021). In other words, a group of consumers, the precariat and middle-class professionals, who share concerns about the neo-liberal policies, the hegemonic capitalist logic, the commodification of nature and the impoverishment of their social life, and representatives of the petty commodity producers, who have lost their position in the dominant industrial agricultural form of production, have been the driving force in the initiation and development of AFNs in Turkey.

We consider alternative consumer cooperatives, the focus of this book, as a sub-group of AFNs and explain how their practices are shaped by the premises and concerns of the AFNs. The ACCs claim to develop an alternative food provisioning system, which aims to bypass intermediaries in supply and distribution, empower rural women, support small farmers, promote the de-fetishization of agricultural products, support eco-friendly traditional agricultural production methods, and experiment with a different type of surplus distribution that does not target capital accumulation by the founders. In contrast to the industrial production system, the ACCs aim to re-socialize and re-spatialize food by establishing direct links between rural petty commodity producers and urban consumers. It is anticipated that direct communication links such as site visits, workshops delivered by the producers in the cooperative shops and shop encounters will de-fetishize food, raise awareness about production conditions, and change perceptions of healthy and good quality foodstuff. Furthermore, by transforming the consumption habits of the urban consumers, petty commodity producers who have lost their position in the industrial production system can be re-positioned.

The industrial food production system shaped by neo-liberal policies treats food as a commodity exchanged in global markets that are dominated by big agro-food companies. These companies operate with a capitalist market logic that is based on efficiency, economies of scale and performance indicators such as profits and return on investment. This type of logic fails to solve the problems of externalities, that is, the degradation of natural resources, deforestation, desertification and pollution. Furthermore, while the companies embedded in the industrial food system are able to provide cheap foodstuff due to increasing economies of scale and expanding market shares, such a system leads to dispossession and the extinction of peasantry and traditional farming knowledge (McMichael and Schneider, 2011). Thus, taking food as a commodity subject to market logic marginalizes petty commodity producers as a political agency. Against this neo-liberal food provisioning system that positions food as a commodity, the food sovereignty movement perceives food as 'political' and aims to reconstruct a production–consumption nexus that is just, democratic and egalitarian. In line with the principles of the food sovereignty movement, ACCs do not consider commercial concerns as a goal, rather they opt for a system where having access to healthy food is a 'right' for all citizens. In so doing, they claim that a 'just' food policy should take into consideration the livelihoods of petty commodity producers and that they should be included in the decision-making process. The food sovereignty movement acknowledges the role of local production and short supply chains in promoting accountability on the side of the small producers. Such a system also enables the preservation of traditional farming know-how and reduces environmental degradation by minimizing the use of chemicals and pesticides. As discussed throughout the book, ACCs are devoted to these principles and clearly state them on their social media accounts and share them with the public during meetings. At this point it must be noted that one of the most important actors in the promotion of the food sovereignty movement in Turkey and among the ACCs is Çiftçi-Sen, the Confederation of Farmers' Union, and its founding president Abdullah Aysu. The union was established in May 2008, but due to legal limitations farmers were not given a right to form a union; however, after a long series of court cases in 2020 Çiftçi-Sen was officially established. In contrast to the International Labour Organizations' and United Nations' conceptualization, farmers were not recognized as workers, thus, initially Çiftçi-Sen was established as a labour union, which in turn led to a long legal and political struggle. During this process, Çiftçi-Sen, as a member of the European Coordination Via Campesina (ECVC) in Turkey, was actively involved in promulgating the premises of the food sovereignty movement through organizing and participating in local and international conferences and workshops (Çiçek, 2017). Also, through a digital platform, karasaban. net (the plough), Çiftçi-Sen created a space for politics where politicians, academics and specialists in agriculture share information and express opinions about alternative ways of organizing the economy and agriculture while promoting the ideals of the food sovereignty movement.

ACCs are shaped by the ideals and premises of the food sovereignty movement and are characterized by some practices that challenge the capitalist forms of organizing: they are based on values of solidarity, reciprocity, decommodification, non-profit-making (that is, they reject efficiency and profit motives) and the inclusion of marginalized groups (mainly women, small farmers and refugees). However, these alternative organizations are also spaces where imagined futures are realized 'right away, now, so that direct democracy at the local can be an example and lead to new ways of resistance' (Yılmaz et al, 2020, p 49). They are spaces where activists, collectively, with their own will, try to transform their daily lives and envision a future based on their current practices. ACCs manifest an aspiration for and an experiment in direct democracy. They experiment with direct democracy by the inclusion of local petty commodity producers in the decision-making process, about what is to be produced and how it is going to be produced. They also challenge the power relations that shape management and labour practices within their organizations. In so doing they provide an example of an alternative form of organizing, developed around the idea of democracy, and implement practices such as consensus-based decision-making, a minimal hierarchy and volunteer work. ACCs provide a space for the creation of a public sphere which nurtures vigorous political debate and prefigurative politics where a discourse on and practices for food sovereignty is drafted. ACCs provide an example of prefigurative politics which is based on action rather than planning. Placing food provisioning as its central concern and being positioned in AFNs, alternative cooperatives represent the emergence of a new form of activism. They are spaces for the creation of an issue-specific public. Although there are numerous examples in other countries, this is a new form of resistance in Turkey.

The political and economic concerns that fostered food politics in Turkey

The rise of ACCs in Turkey coincided with some social, economic, and political anxieties. Although the first ACC was founded in 2008, these cooperatives proliferated after the Gezi Park protests in 2013. Gezi was marked by the demands, discourse and prefigurative style of the middle class (Tuğal, 2013, 2015). Most of the movement members were white-collar employees, free-lance professionals and students (Konda, 2014), and approximately 32 per cent of them resided in the three middle-class districts of İstanbul: Kadıköy, Beşiktaş and Şişli. They were precariat (Civelekoglu, 2015), facing labour insecurity and also an uncertain social life as a consequence of the policies implemented by the AKP (the Justice and Development Party) government that aims to reorganize social life and labour markets. The Gezi Park protests were not only a resistance to the commodification of a public space, they were also against the neo-liberal, conservative regime (see, for example, Çelik, 2015; Alonso, 2015) and brought together a wide range of social groups such as religious groups, the LGBT community, ethnic groups, football fans, youngsters, the elderly, and different professional groups. Thus, Gezi was an inclusive movement that promoted a milieu where coalitions were built among these diverse and excluded segments of society. Groups representing different socio-economic backgrounds convened around similar demands – participation, direct democracy and just and equitable relations in and around the workplace. These diverse groups, leaving aside previously encountered tensions among themselves, tried a new (for Turkey) way of doing politics. Gezi provided a space for experimenting with a counter-hegemonic struggle shaped by the expectations of direct democracy and for seeing that such claims could be realized. After the police evicted the Gezi protestors, its prefigurative style persisted in park forums and neighbourhood initiatives in Kadıköy, Beşiktaş and Şişli, and the inhabitants of the same districts founded the ACCs. Gezi marked a turning point in Turkish politics: a non-partisan advocacy involved in prefigurative politics that challenges neo-liberal policies on issues such as gold mining, deforestation, nuclear power and the commodification of public land for private concerns. Gezi was influential in the rise and shaping of the values of the ACCs by providing an opportunity for diverse groups of people, sharing similar concerns, to interact and experience solidarity, collective work and mutuality. In interviews with the founders of the ACCs it was underlined that the relations they established during the Gezi protest were influential in the making of their alternative cooperative movement (Oba and Özsoy, 2020), with its premises, values and practices. Also, Gezi opened up the possibility of seeing that through direct democracy people can be actively involved and have a voice in the transformation of the prevailing power relations. In a way, Gezi invigorated a public sphere where a counter-hegemonic struggle around food politics is shaped. The emergence of ACCs as a grassroots initiative claiming to deconstruct the prevailing hegemonic market-driven nexus of production and consumption and trying to establish an alternative food provisioning system based on the ethics of solidarity is rooted in the values, practices and the spirit of Gezi.

As well as developments in the political domain, as a consequence of the populist neo-liberal policies, the Turkish economy currently faces a severe financial crisis, rising unemployment rates, a rising disparity in income/wealth distribution, uncontrolled devaluation and high inflation. One of the sectors suffering most during this crisis is agriculture. Turkey currently faces an acute food crisis. Agriculture in Turkey is dominated by a few big transnational companies that are vertically and horizontally organized. Small farmers who are dependent on foreign supplies cannot cope with increasing costs and have lost their purchasing power due to the devaluation of the Turkish lira. Furthermore, due to financialization, small farmers have become dependent on credit to purchase supplies (seeds, machinery, and so on), which in turn leaves them vulnerable to debt repayments. The current crisis in Turkish agriculture and the food shortages are rooted in the capitalization and liberalization policies implemented by successive governments. Efforts to support agriculture and transform villages and villagers by Köy Enstitüleri and Land Reform during the state-led developmentalist period (1930–1950) were steered more by political than economic concerns. In the following years agriculture went through a pervasive wave of mechanization prompted by Marshall Aid and the premises of the Green Revolution. Consequent increases in agricultural productivity during this period (1950–1975) attracted both foreign and local large-scale producers. However, these emerging actors were more interested in the input segment of the value chain than the production of foodstuff, which in turn left the smallholders more reliant on the inputs provided by big capital. The neo-liberal turn in 1980, by limiting support purchases, along with the power of the state-owned agricultural sales cooperatives, prompted de-peasantization; petty commodity producers who were left to free-market operations and who could not compete migrated to the cities, forming an informal labour force. The decrease in village populations also changed labour relations: since the young male population moved to the cities, farming was left to women and older members of the households. This transformation process deepened after 2001 with the implementation of the Agricultural Reform Implementation Project (ARIP) that was drafted by the World Bank, the Treasury and the Ministry of Agriculture and Rural Affairs. In the following years, with the implementation of this project and the neo-liberal policies pursued by the government, Turkish agriculture went through a comprehensive restructuring where subsidies and support purchases by the government were repealed, parastatals and state-owned agricultural sales cooperatives were privatized, and contract farming was invigorated (Aysu, 2008; Aydin, 2010; Kandemir, 2011; Keyder and Yenal, 2011; Değirmenci, 2021). Thus, the liberalization of agriculture had deep-rooted, irreversible consequences on the production relationship, the ownership patterns and the power position of the actors involved in the system. The system led to dispossession (Atış, 2022), the dissolution of traditional farming, the proletarianization of the petty commodity producers by the pervasive implementation of contract farming, and, furthermore, a shift from the production of subsistence crops to high-value industrial crops. In an effort to overcome these problems in agriculture and as a counter to the dominance of the big agro-food companies, the ACCs experiment with an alternative system that enables the inclusion of petty commodity producers in the food provisioning system by encouraging people back to the land, experimenting with a different surplus generation and distribution system, and by demystifying foodstuff, raising awareness among urban consumers when considering their purchasing habits by de-fetishizing foodstuff.

An evaluation of the cooperative movement in Turkey

ACCs differ from other types of consumer cooperatives in Turkey and other locations. Particularly since the 2007 crises, which led to deep-rooted economic and social problems, there has been an increasing interest among academics and informed, responsible citizens to study and experiment with alternative forms of organizations that operate with a non-capitalist logic. Cooperatives are alternative organizations (Parker et al, 2007); they are expected to develop innovative solutions to the problems of capitalism in relation to unemployment, housing, food provisioning and energy, as well as providing examples that challenge existing ownership patterns, profit motives and governance mechanisms. One avenue of academic study has focused on worker cooperatives as examples of a special type of surplus management and social economy (Gibson-Graham, 2003; Gradin, 2015). In the same vein, other research has studied the challenges faced by worker cooperatives and considered how the issues of ownership, profit distribution and participation in the decision making process could be resolved (see, for example, Cheney et al, 2014; Fletcha and Ngai, 2014; Heras-Saizarbitoria, 2014; Lambru and Petresu, 2014; Fonte and Cucco, 2017; Pancera and Ritzi, 2018). Cooperatives engaged in distribution and initiated by consumers have also been a focus for academic studies (see, for example, Brunori et al, 2012; Knupfer, 2013; Mais, 2013; Rakopoulos, 2014; Bilewicz and Śpiewak, 2015; Grasseni et al, 2015; Zitcer, 2015; Moragues-Faus, 2017; Zitcer 2017; Barros and Michaud, 2019; Grasseni, 2020; Kociatkiewicz et al, 2021). These studies stress the political character of consumer cooperatives, take them as 'communities' involved in political activism, ascribe an activist role to consumers and provide an explanation of how differently owned and governed organizations develop organizing practices grounded in direct democracy. It is envisioned that food cooperatives initiated by consumers and embedded in AFNs will transform the conventional, industrialized production–consumption nexus by providing a diversity of arrangements and the inclusion of marginalized groups such as small producers and women. Also, consumers with relatively less purchasing power will have access to 'healthy' foodstuff at reasonable prices. However, in practice, experimenting with ideals can be difficult: consumer food cooperatives are criticized for adhering to market-based solutions, reproducing neo-liberal arrangements (Lockie and Halpin, 2005; Busa and Guthman, 2007; Gardener, 2015) and diverging from their initial ideals. They are criticized for their exclusivity in terms of class, income, colour and gender, and inaccessibility in terms of price and the selection of food items offered (Zitcer, 2017). Also, it is claimed that the solutions developed by food cooperatives fail to address the problems of those groups marginalized by the industrial food system and, furthermore, have 'reinforced imaginaries of self-interested consumers as the primary agents of social change' (Figueroa and Alkon, 2017, p 206).

The difference between the ACCs and consumer cooperatives in different locations can be explained in relation to the Turkish context. The conventional cooperatives (CCCs) in Turkey are either established by the state or with the support of the state. In other words, conventional cooperatives, as opposed to the ACCs, are not self-help, voluntary organizations. They are not open to all who would like to use their services; they are 'closed' cooperatives, limiting their services to their members. Members of conventional cooperatives do not participate in the daily operations of the cooperatives, neither do they participate in the decision-making processes. In conventional cooperatives decisions are made by the board of directors. Furthermore, in contrast to consumer cooperatives in other countries, Turkish CCCs are founded and managed by companies or unions which in turn get financial support from the state for their establishment. Thus, in Turkey the conventional cooperatives are state-led, state-dependent and thus open to impeding levels of state intervention.

The Turkish cooperative movement has been marked by tensions between governments and ruling parties and oppositional groups such as intellectuals, labour unions and political parties. Given the dominant role of a centralized and highly bureaucratic state and normalizing its superiority in the social, economic and political realms, a state-led cooperative movement has been the dominant model in Turkey. Experiments with alternative cooperative models have been either marginalized or terminated by various types of state interventions. The earliest examples of cooperatives that underline the dynamics of the power struggles in and around consumer cooperatives in Turkey, which were founded by the efforts of statesmen for solving the problems of the peasants in being exploited by commercial retailers, date back to 1900, the Ottoman Empire period. In the following years, between 1908 and 1918, the intellectual basis for establishing cooperatives was provided by intellectuals Mustafa Suphi, Ethem Nejat and Ahmet Cevat, the founders of the Turkish Communist Party. Ethem Nejat supported the idea that for economic progress the road to be followed should be founded on agriculture and trade rather than industrialization. In his writings he stressed the transformation of village life and the training and schooling of villagers for the promotion of an agriculture-led economic development.

In his writings Mustafa Suphi, influenced by the cooperative philosophy of the French economist Charles Gide, supported the idea that a more 'humane capitalism' was possible if the working and living conditions of the workers were improved, an agricultural system that empowered the peasantry was developed and cooperatives were established. The founding of consumer cooperatives operating in line with the Rochdale cooperatives in the UK was brought about by Ahmet Cevat Emre. Emre, in his book *İki Neslin Tarihi* (1960), explains in detail how he was inspired by the Rochdale cooperatives during his visit to England and how he later realized this idea among the inhabitants of Fatih, a district in İstanbul, followed by three other cooperatives in other districts of the city. These cooperatives were taken as alternative development models that were different to liberal and socialist development models. They were open to all citizens in terms of ownership and participation and were operated by the locals. However, as explained by Ahmet Cevat, with the intervention of the ruling party İttihad ve Terakki, they were closed down and, instead, under the patronage and financial support of the state, in collaboration with a few tradesmen, ten new consumer cooperatives in different districts of İstanbul were established. These experiences are important in underpinning the dominant role of the state and the tensions between the ruling cadre and the intellectuals, and provide an explanation on how cooperatives are instrumentalized by the state.

The cooperative movement during the early days of the Turkish Republic was shaped by similar tendencies. Cooperatives were mainly initiated by the state for state officials or by state-owned banks and factories (for example, Ziraat Bankası, Cumhuriyet Merkez Bankası, Devlet Demir Yolları, Elektrik ve Havagazı İşletmesi, Bakırköy Mensucat, Merinos). They were consumer cooperatives, organized by and managed under the patronage of the government with the aim of providing affordable foodstuff to their members only and to leverage price rises for the benefit of their members. Later, during the 1950s, as government policies were modified for the implementation of an economic programme based on liberal policies and the capitalization of agriculture, the cooperative movement lost its momentum and the preferences of state cadres changed from consumer cooperatives to retail chains such as Migros-Türk and Gima. Meanwhile, legislation for the cooperatives was revised and accordingly cooperatives were recognized as closed-door workplace organizations governed and controlled by the state (Rehber, 2000; Bilgin and Tanıyıcı, 2008; Aksoy and Günay, 2018). In order to build alliances in the political realm, various incentives such as financial resources and physical assets were provided by the state cadres to the privately owned companies and unions. Based on secondary data and interviews, two different examples of cooperatives were identified that diverged from the state-led CCCs in Turkey during this period: MİPAŞ and Halk-Koop. MİPAŞ (The Workers' Bazaar) was established and owned by a labour union, Maden-İş, to combat price rises. In so doing the cooperative utilized a system where items (foodstuff and clothing) sold at their shops were produced by other cooperatives or factories owned by the same union (Öngel, 2020a). Besides establishing and operating its own shops, Maden-İş also encouraged and was engaged in the establishment of workplace consumer cooperatives in privately owned factories such as Philips and Altın Zincir and neighbourhood cooperatives in various districts of İstanbul that comprised a dense worker population. All these cooperatives, in contrast to the state-led CCCs, followed an open-door policy. The other divergent example, Halk-Koop (Peoples' Coop), was initiated by the Communist Party of Turkey (TKP). The presence of Halk-Koop is mentioned in two sources: Kurtuluş (2019) notes the establishment of the cooperative, while Durukanoğlu (2019) mentions a collaboration between Halk-Koop and DİSK (Confederation of Progressive Trade Unions). For details of the Halk-Koop cooperatives we rely on interviews we conducted with the then cooperative members. Halk-Koops accepted all the people living in a specific neighbourhood as partners and was established in a period that experienced severe shortages and black-market operations, especially in the availability of foodstuff. In such a milieu, the provision of scarce items in the shops of the cooperative, with the support of producer cooperatives and MİPAŞ, was helpful for their scaling-up. Although MİPAŞ and Halk-Koops were different to the state-led CCCs in terms of ownership, and independent from the state in their operations and emphasis on the avoidance of middlemen in food provisioning, they also diverged from the ACCs in their governance, aims and practices.

The year 1980 was a remarkable turning point in the Turkish cooperative movement. With the implementation of the structural adjustment programme and the coup d'état, the operations of the cooperatives were restricted; some cooperatives were closed down by the military regime, their assets were seized and members were imprisoned (Aysu, 2019; Ültanır, 2019; Öngel, 2020a). Gradual steps in the liberalization of agriculture gained momentum after 2001 with the ARIP project and newly drafted legislation (Act 4572); in 2000 the privatization of the cooperatives and the implementation of a managerialist logic in their governance started. The gradual exclusion of cooperatives from the economic and political realm continued until 2008 when the first ACC, BÜKOOP, was established.

Why and how to study alternative consumer cooperatives

Given this background we think that ACCs provide a valuable example of alternative organizations; they differ from other similar cooperatives in other locations with their oppositional position taking, not only to neo-liberal policies but also their enforcement. They are shaped and driven by middle-class consumers who problematize the neo-liberal policies, the hegemonic capitalist logic, the commodification of labour and food, and the marginalization and proletarization of the petty commodity producers by the industrialized food provisioning system. In the Turkish context, ACCs are different from state-led consumer cooperatives that are aligned with the dominant capitalist logic (distribution of profits, managed only by founding members, paid labour, economic performance criteria) in various aspects: in terms of ownership their founders are consumers, and they are not funded by the government. Their services are not limited to their members; they are 'open' cooperatives offering services to all regardless of their membership. Since the government does not financially support them, they are more independent in their internal affairs and are able to develop a unique governance model characterized by no hierarchy, consensus-based decision-making and shaped by the ideals of direct democracy. Also, by experimenting with a different value chain, bypassing the intermediaries, the ACCs aim to reposition peasantry in the economic and social realm, and experiment with a different surplus generation and distribution. Such an experiment, moreover, is helpful in raising awareness among the urban consumers about the labour processes involved in the production process, enabling them to de-fetishize foodstuff and change their consumption habits. Furthermore, since the consumers involved in these cooperatives have a specific political orientation, one which is opposed to the populist neo-liberal policies of the ruling party and managerialism, ACCs are spaces where the premises of an alternative future are drafted. They invigorate a public sphere by the extensive utilization of social media, face-to-face meetings, such as shop encounters, excursions to producer sites, public forums and even the forming of an alternative football league for engaging a wider audience and recruiting members to their struggle. And, finally, ACCs and their experiments as alternative organizations have had a transformative effect in other segments of the economy. Zeynep Özsoy, one of the authors of this book, in a series of articles in *Yeşil Gazete*, documented examples of diverse economies and alternative organizations in different sectors, such as Yaykoop in the distribution of printed material such as books, Troya in the renewable energy industry, Tiyatro Kooperatifi, a cooperative of privately owned theatres, Albatros in software engineering, and Biskoop in providing services to bicycle riders in İzmir.

This book aims to explain how, as alternative organizations, ACCs developed their dominant premises and practices and their transformative capacity in the existing power relations in agriculture. We explore the actions taken and practices developed by the ACCs for confronting the prevailing food provisioning system, managerialist logic and governance models. We provide evidence regarding the responses of the ACCs to the historically constructed power positions of various constituencies embedded in the industrial food provisioning system. Whenever we provide evidence about the solutions developed by the ACCs to reshuffle the production and consumption nexus, and the power and domination relations in governance, we also question their viability. In so doing, we expect to contribute to the discussion that there are alternatives to the organizations driven and shaped by capitalist logic and hope that we can invigorate a discussion about the possibilities of direct democracy in and around organizations even in a context characterized by authoritarianism. When we started our research in 2018 there were only two ACCs, BÜKOOP and Kadıköy Kooperatif; the others had not been founded as cooperatives, but were operating as street coops. There were a limited number of written documents provided by academia and practitioners. Within the last four years the number of ACCs has increased and there has also been an increase in the number of publications. Activists have provided valuable insights by sharing experiences in books and articles. For example, the book *Yeniden İnşa Et* (Yılmaz et al, 2020), written by activists involved in the formation of Kadıköy Kooperatif, offers a comprehensive explanation about why they opted for direct democracy. Meanwhile, as the numbers and interesting experiences of ACCs has increased, we have seen that in universities PhD and MA theses have been written on food sovereignty and ACCs (for example, Al, 2020; Atış, 2022). These studies are valuable contributions in explaining the role of food sovereignty in shaping the practices of the ACCs, the supply chain and the unfavourable effects of neo-liberal policies on agriculture and food sovereignty in Turkey. This book, however, considers ACCs as examples of diverse economies and alternative organizations with a prefigurative stance and aims to extend the role of ACCs beyond the avoidance of intermediaries for the provision of affordable, healthy and good quality food in the cities. In so doing, we provide an integrative explanation about the political concerns of the activists, their struggle in invigorating a public sphere, repositioning peasantry and changing the capitalist logic in surplus generation and governance.

In this book, we also present the experiences of many ACCs rather than a specific case. As the authors of this book, our first encounter with the ACCs was as consumers; we both live in the districts where some of these cooperatives were founded. As residents of the district and citizens concerned with the economic and political conditions prevalent in Turkey, we were interested in their ideas, values and practices, especially the governance practices and attempts to develop alternative solutions to the capitalist form of food provisioning. As academics, we thought that such forms of organizing and their role in the political, economic and social realms needed to be documented. With this impetus, we started our research in the spring of 2018. As mentioned earlier, when we started the research, there were only two ACCs, but the number of ACCs has increased over time. Currently, it is estimated that there are about 15 ACCs operating in different districts of İstanbul and five in other cities (Ankara, Eskişehir, İzmit, İzmir). Since there is no detailed database about cooperatives functioning in Turkey, it is difficult to identify the exact number of ACCs. The data provided by the Ministry of Trade (koopbis.gtb.gov.tr) does not provide detailed documentation of consumer cooperatives in terms of for-profit/non-profit and type of operation (that is, serving only members or everyone). Thus, it is challenging to identify the exact number of ACCs currently operating in Turkey. Our estimates are based on our fieldwork and interviews.

For data collection purposes, we used multiple sources: in-depth interviews, participant observation, social media accounts and secondary sources. Such an approach to data collection is expected to be useful for triangulation purposes that will increase the validity of the concepts studied. We started our research by studying two examples. As new ACCs were founded, we extended our survey so that the opinions of the new activists and practices of the new ACCs were also incorporated into our analysis. To identify the informants, in the initial stages of the research we employed purposeful sampling and approached the founders of the ACCs. In the later stages of our study, we also utilized theoretical sampling to identify, elaborate and build on the emerging concepts in our data. We interviewed volunteers and producers who supply their foodstuff to the ACCs. At this stage, we also interviewed various other constituencies, such as the founders of producer cooperatives, activists involved in Çiftçi-Sen, the AFN platform, the Ecological Farming Association, EkoHarita and members of the alternative producers' network. Approaching these different groups has been helpful in representing both differing and similar opinions around various issues raised by our research. We continued to collect data until the data provided by the informants did not provide new information. In total, we did 51 in-depth interviews which are recorded and transcribed verbatim. We have chosen to anonymise participants, excluding their names and identifying information such as organizations they are linked to, for privacy. Instead we refer to them as 'an activist' or 'a volunteer' or 'an interviewee'.

To conduct participant observation, we did shop visits, which helped us observe the daily routine of the cooperative shops, we participated in the regular, weekly decision-making meetings of some of the ACCs, followed online and offline public meetings organized by different ACCs to explain their values and practices, attended workshops run in their shops, and visited festivals arranged by the ACCs and the municipality. We also participated in various informative events which were organized in these shops (for example, cheese-making at home, the problems of conventional agriculture, and preparing a 'fair' and healthy diet). To identify the scope of activities performed and values communicated to wider audiences, we documented posts on the social media accounts of the ACCs. We classified these posts as: news (providing detailed information about producers, products and the specific ACC), calls (for public meetings that provide information about ACCs, and campaigns in response to the actions taken by the government that would have adverse consequences for agriculture, workshops and meetings), and short articles (on food sovereignty, food safety and alternative cooperatives). Such encounters with the activists provided an understanding of how various forms of food activism are reconciled with the daily operations of the cooperatives. Finally, we also collected and analysed secondary sources like websites, online journals and radio programmes focusing on AFNs, solidarity economy, agriculture and cooperatives in Turkey, which enabled us to collect evidence that would contradict or verify the insights accrued through interviews, participant observation and social media accounts.

Data analysis was carried out in two stages. In the first stage, we aimed to understand why and how the ACCs evolved. Based on the data provided by the informants, we were able to identify the political, social and economic concerns of the activists and problems in Turkish agriculture as the drivers of the ACCs. In this stage, we identified two context-specific issues that enabled the formation of ACCs: the implementation of neo-liberal economic policies in agriculture and the exclusion of certain social groups (mainly the urban middle class and rural petty commodity producers) from decision-making processes. This stage of analysis was complemented with secondary sources to grasp a deeper understanding of the enabling or constraining drivers of the ACCs. In the second stage of analysis, we focused on the activities performed by different cooperatives by using data gathered from interviews, participant observation and social media accounts. The central questions that guided our analysis at this stage were 'what is done', 'how it is done' and 'by whom it is accomplished'. In this way, we identified recurring themes emerging from different data sources, which finally were aggregated into three major groups: experimenting with (a) an alternative governance system, (b) an alternative surplus generation and distribution system, and (c) the development of an alternative public sphere. Such a classification was useful to understand and describe how direct democracy worked within the cooperatives, how petty commodity producers were incorporated into the food provisioning system and, finally, how a space for politics was created. Throughout the research stages, we were careful to retain our observer and researcher position, that is, we were careful to incorporate contradictory views and ideas. Besides the creative solutions developed and experimented with by the activists, we were careful to register problems encountered and instances of failure and refraction. We tried to refrain from judging how various informants perceived and explained the local conditions surrounding them. We were careful not to censor or privilege any comment, idea or action.

Structure of the chapters

Following this introduction, and to provide a deeper understanding of the values and practices of the ACCs, in Chapter 2 we focus on diverse economies, alternative economic spaces, the food sovereignty movement and prefigurative politics. Such an approach enabled us to explain how ACCs, as alternative organizations positioned as examples of diverse economies, experiment with a non-capitalist form of organizing in food provisioning and with governance shaped by the premises of the food sovereignty movement. The background given in this chapter is also helpful to describe the ACCs as prefigurative spaces where activists aiming for direct democracy develop and experiment with the means of implementing direct democracy in the governance of the cooperatives and the inclusion of rural petty commodity producers and the urban middle class in the food provisioning system.

Chapter 3 examines the Turkish political, economic and social context in which the ACCs emerged and function. The chapter starts with the 1980 neo-liberal turn and its full-blown implementation after the 2000s, with a particular emphasis on the role attributed to the state in Turkey. It explains how unconditional commitment to neo-liberal policies after 2002 influenced accumulation, empowered big capital and marginalized formal labour (white-collar, middle-class professionals) and petty commodity producers. To elaborate on the process that led to the rise of a 'new' big capital, inclusion of the urban population labouring in the informal economy to the welfare system, and evasion of urban commons (the market gardens, parks), we explain the policies followed by the government, such as social assistance, supporting civic charity organizations, financialization and gentrification. The main argument developed in this chapter is that while populist neo-liberal policies facilitated some groups' inclusion in the economic and social realms, their outcomes were exclusionary for other groups, such as those who founded the ACCs.

Chapter 4 explores the political economy of consumer cooperatives in Turkey in different periods. In so doing, we aim to juxtapose ACCs to the traditional consumer cooperatives in Turkey that are instigated by the state, managed in a top-down manner, serve only their members ('closed' coops) and function as distribution centres for overcoming supply shortages and price rises. As we note in the last part of the chapter, ACCs, in contrast to these traditional cooperatives, are founded by activists (petty commodity producers and the urban middle class) who oppose the prevailing food provisioning system, are committed to the food sovereignty movement and opt for direct democracy, autonomy, equality and justice. Food activists involved in the ACCs try to reshuffle the food production and consumption nexus, preserve agricultural land from urbanization and regain their lost position in the economic and political realm.

In Chapter 5, we focus on the ACCs and explain how, in response to the legitimacy crises of the neo-liberal hegemonic project and decreasing public participation in politics, they constitute an alternative public sphere that is shaped by a diverse set of institutions (shop, social media, an alternative football league), activities (workshops, talks, film screenings, celebrations, direct meetings, site visits) and critical discourse for raising awareness (discussing and revealing problems in agriculture and in food provisioning). We discuss how this alternative public sphere is a hub for experimenting with direct democracy and aligning the politically and socially excluded groups for transforming the existing food provisioning system.

Chapter 6 explains the alternative food provisioning model developed and experimented with by the ACCs in response to the neo-liberal policies implemented in agriculture. In order to explain the difference of this model, we describe the agricultural policies (the capitalization and liberalization of agriculture) drafted and implemented by governments at different periods with a particular focus on the post-2001 period, which is marked by the full-blown implementation of neo-liberal policies (direct income support, contract farming and the privatization of state-owned sales cooperatives). In the second part of the chapter we describe the alternative food provisioning system experimented with by the ACCs and discuss how an unmediated relationship between producers and consumers and an alternative surplus generation is developed and the de-fetishization of the foodstuff is tried out. In this section, we also discuss the scaling-up problem (for example Reed, 2015; Utting, 2015), which is always raised as a limitation to sustainability. We also provide the alternative view (horizontal and vertical scaling-up) posed by the food activists involved in the ACCs.

In Chapter 7 we explain the alternative governance model experimented with by the ACCs in response to capitalist labour relations, work practices and performance measures. ACCs are non-profit-making and do not aim to scale-up; their performance is not evaluated in terms of growth and profit, instead they are organized around the ethics of solidarity. Decisions on the types of foodstuff to be sold, identification of the suppliers, terms and conditions of payments to the petty commodity producers, allocation of workloads and work procedures are taken with the full participation of all involved in the cooperative. In the chapter, based on our research data, we provide detailed information on how direct democracy is experienced through prefigurative organizing (division of work, rotation, consensus-based decision-making and zero-hierarchy) and how work and work volunteers shape relations. In so doing, we also describe the problems encountered and concerns raised in the trial-and-error process underlying the evolution of these practices.

In conclusion, we provide an overview of the ACCs, focusing on their differences in terms of their values and practices. Faced with dire economic conditions and operating within the capitalist system, we discuss how they have survived as spaces of 'possibility' that nurture hope for the development of new ones.

2

The Politics of Food: Alignment for Solidarity and Resistance

Refute and rebuild ... another world is possible.
Yılmaz et al, *Yeniden İnşa Et*, 2020, p 270;
Kadıköy Kooperatif, 2021

Introduction

Is capitalism the only way to organize the economy and production relations? Is profit the only value that can be created by organizations? Taking capitalism and capitalist forms of organizing as the only possibility for an economic and political system limits our vision; we do not see or try to experiment with alternative forms of organizing. In this book our aim is to show that organizations shaped by non-capitalist forms of production relations and value creation orientations and practices do exist. In so doing, we view alternative consumer cooperatives (ACCs) as an alternative, non-capitalist form of organizing. Activists involved in ACCs refuse to accept the prevailing power relations and experiment with a different surplus generation and governance model; their practice is based on the 'ethics of solidarity' (Gibson-Graham, 2003); rather than opting for profitability they aim to establish solidaristic, unmediated and trust-based ties between rural petty commodity producers and the urban middle class. Their daily practices are prefigurative; they experiment with what they aim for. They envision direct democracy and organizations devoid of hierarchies and inequalities. These are not fantasies, they are, at least to a certain extent, practised.

During our field study and analysis of the secondary data we have seen that the founders of the ACCs are inspired by the works of diverse economies, alternative organizations and are involved in prefigurative politics. Thus in this chapter, in order to provide a background for the underlying premises and practices of the ACCs, we elaborate on the tradition of diverse economies (Gibson-Graham, 2003, 2006, 2008, 2014; Gibson-Graham et al, 2013) and alternative economic spaces (Parker et al, 2014; Parker, 2017) in order to explain how ACCs experiment with a non-capitalist form of organizing and operate with a non-capitalistic form of work, shaped by the premises of alternative food networks and the values of the food sovereignty movement. Activists involved in the ACCs deliberately search for and experiment with practices that will dislocate hegemonic capitalist relations. Such attempts by the ACCs are prefigurative since activists create 'new' within the 'old' (Leach, 2013) with the 'conflation of their ends with their means' (Maeckelbergh, 2014, p 350).

Diverse economies

Gibson-Graham's (1996, 2003, 2006, 2008; Gibson-Graham et al, 2013) theoretical work on diverse economies draws on an approach that, as a step toward post-capitalism, aims to change views on the economy and draw attention to alternative spaces and their practices. Gibson-Graham in *The End of Capitalism* (1996) offers a different way of conceptualizing the economy – the economy as a space of difference rather than convergence. Such a conceptualization is based on the assumption that the economy is intrinsically heterogeneous in form and encompasses various exchange mechanisms, forms of labour and ownership. Taking capitalism as a monolithic entity leads to other forms of economy being unnoticed (Gibson-Graham and Dombroski, 2020; Healy, 2009). These alternative forms can be unpaid labour, volunteer work, cooperatives (producer and consumer), community supported agriculture, voluntary organizations, social enterprises and non-profit organizations (Gibson-Graham, 2008).

Capitalism produces a capitalist state, a capitalist economy and identities such as workers and consumers (Gibson-Graham, 1996). Within this capitalist framework, the perceptions and actions of actors are guided by some beliefs that further reproduce capitalist economic relationships and subjectivities. In a capitalist economy it is believed that growth is good, private ownership of resources is valuable and private enterprises contribute to the wealth of individuals and nations (Gibson-Graham et al, 2013). However, such a conceptualization disregards the voices of marginalized groups and promotes an economy where social and economic inequalities are exacerbated. On the other hand, if we take the economy as a heterogenous space where individual actors have a diverse set of roles (for example, worker, caretaker, activist) and integrate with others in various ways (for example, employment relations, family bonds, ideological similarities) we can reframe the economy, the work, the enterprise and the market.

Gibson-Graham et al (2013), in the book *Take Back the Economy*, claim that if we consider the economy as a machine which operates efficiently without any interference (from environmentalists, concerned citizens, unions) and operates with the premise of growth, we will start to see ourselves as cogs in this machine; our roles will be reduced to paid workers and consumers. However, we have other roles as well: we take care of our households, the elderly, children; we are engaged in activities that aim for the betterment of our community and the protection of our environment. This set of activities, vested in our daily lives, constitutes a wider portion of the economy which is neglected in mainstream studies. A reframing of the economy around these daily practices highlights a diversity of actors and activities in labour, market transactions, ownership, enterprise and finance (Gibson-Graham, 2008; Gibson-Graham and Roelvink, 2011; Gibson-Graham et al, 2013;). Diverse economies also describe some methods of production, ownership, surplus generation and distribution, labour and consumption patterns that are different from the mainstream economy. Studies on various forms of diverse economies emphasize their role in the construction of non-capitalist subjects, re-politicizing the economic realm (Gibson-Graham, 2003) and re-socializing economic relations by building community economies (Gibson-Graham et al, 2013).

The typical capitalist firm is characterized by the provision of inputs for the production of a product/service/knowledge. During this transformation process labour adds value to the raw materials, machinery and equipment, and knowledge and this value is reflected in the price. The efforts of workers are compensated by a fixed wage, managers are rewarded by salaries and also bonus and share options as well, while owners of the means of production appropriate profits. One of the major outcomes of this dominant capitalist logic is reflected in the inequalities in wealth distribution both within a country and among nations. Also, by fuelling consumption and production, by taking growth as the prime indicator of success, by enforcing competition as the only viable strategy, the capitalist logic leads to a state where natural resources are depleted and the ecological system is severely damaged. Market-based logic falls far behind in handling the problem of externalities. Accepting the economy as homogeneous and comprising only a collection of capitalist firms neglects other forms of organizations such as cooperatives and social enterprises. As indicated by Gibson-Graham (2008), consumer, producer and worker cooperatives, operating with the premises of solidarity and practising different surplus generation and distribution methds, provide jobs for a vast number of people. Some of these cooperatives distribute the surplus among their workers, while others, such as the ACCs, experiment with a different approach to surplus generation and distribution. They do not aim to make profit, instead they support practices that are beneficial to all their stakeholders and that are sustainable. These practices enable the inclusion of low-income groups in the consumption of safe, pesticide free, good quality foodstuff and empower small farmers as they are paid a fair price, on time and in cash.

According to capitalist logic the allocation of resources takes place through a price mechanism. As stated by Gibson-Graham et al (2013):

> we are all members of a 'democracy of consumers', free to exercise choice over what we want and free to achieve the highest possible standard of living we can buy. In this democracy, price mediates our encounters with other people and environments that supply what we need to live well. (p 78)

However, the price of a commodity does not reflect, even veil, the working conditions of those involved in its production and the wages paid in return for their labour. Besides labour issues, prices do not provide knowledge about the production process (for example, whether pesticides are used during the production process or whether local seeds are used) and its consequences on the environment. As activists adhering to the premises of ethical consumerism, ACCs try to build long-lasting, trust-based relationships with their suppliers. In so doing, they try to bypass intermediaries and build direct relations with the small farmers. These close encounters with small farmers are useful in controlling prices but, more than that, through these direct transactions, farmers are provided with know-how on agrochemical safe production methods, and they are encouraged to form collaborative networks for equipment and information sharing. Furthermore, consumers' choice for direct transaction is useful in identifying, connecting and supplying foodstuff to disadvantaged and excluded groups in society. One of the underlying premises of the ACCs is the inclusion and empowerment of the disadvantaged groups. In so doing, they develop and experiment with various mechanisms; for example, while identifying their suppliers they give priority to women farmers and women-owned cooperatives. Currently, these groups constitute approximately 35 per cent of the ACC suppliers. Through direct encounters activists are able to sell the products of suppliers who do not use chemicals during the production process, who do not exploit female labour and where conditions for a decent job are provided.

Drawing on Hazel Henderson's 'icing and layered cake' metaphor, Cameron and Gibson-Graham (2003) developed an argument that traditional economics ignores the non-monetized part of the economy and focuses only on the monetized layers. Monetized layers comprise the private sector, operating in line with the free-market logic and its premises such as paid work, cash transactions, growth and profit motives. Such a focus ignores the non-monetized productive economy – the unpaid housework, volunteering, subsistence agriculture, home-based production, sharing and mutual aid. However, without the non-monetized economy it would be difficult to make and maintain the monetized one. Furthermore, as noted by Williams (2014), in advanced economies people spend the same amount of time in paid work and non-exchanged work (work for the elderly or younger family members, formal volunteering, working for a wage in an NGO). People, in their daily lives, are continuously traversing between monetized and non-monetized domains of the economy; they perform various roles (employee, mother, child, citizen, employer) which inscribe their economic and social identities (Gibson-Graham 2006). Thus, the distinction between monetized and non-monetized economic domains as well as the commodified and de-commodified labour is fuzzy (Williams, 2014). By focusing only on the monetized economy and commodified labour we neglect unpaid, uncommodified, volunteer work.

In ACCs, except for a paid accountant (which is a legal requirement), all work is done by volunteers who are local to the district where the ACCs offer their services. Volunteer work enables the cooperative to control costs and offer good quality food at affordable prices. Also, by relying on volunteer work ACCs are able to alter the prevailing surplus generation and distribution system. Furthermore, volunteering promotes a milieu where 'ethics of solidarity' (Gibson-Graham, 2003) can be experienced, and collective identities are developed.

From food security to food sovereignty

Food is political.

Abdullah Aysu, *Kooperatifler*, 2019, p 25

ACCs embedded in alternative food networks (AFNs) are cases of diverse economies (Gritsaz and Kavoulakos, 2016). AFNs predominantly emerged in North America and Europe as a response to the crises caused by the hegemonic conventional, corporate-led food provisioning system (see, for example, Renting et al, 2003; Whatmore et al, 2003; Holloway et al, 2007; Maye et al, 2007; Jarosz, 2008; Goodman and Goodman, 2009; Maye and Kirvan, 2010; Goodman et al, 2012; Wilson, 2013). The major concerns of AFNs are to overcome inequality in food provisioning (healthy, good quality food should be affordable for all income groups), ethical consumerism (social justice and environmental sustainability) and supporting small local producers who have lost their position within the mass-produced capitalist food provisioning system.

ACCs are also advocates of the food sovereignty movement that has been popularized by the peasant movement La Vía Campesina in Central America as an alternative framework for capitalist agriculture systems (see, for example, McMichael and Schneider, 2011; Edelman, 2014; Jarosz, 2014; McMichael, 2014; Alonso-Fradejas et al, 2015; Claeys, 2015; Jansen, 2015; Robbins, 2015). The food sovereignty movement emerged as a response to food security initiatives drafted by the United Nations' Food and Agriculture

Organization (FAO). In 1974, at the World Food Conference, FAO General Director Boerma's plan was adopted as a means of overcoming food shortages and increasing grain prices. Especially, the Sahelian drought, famine, and dislocation between 1968 and 1974 impacted the lives of many people, marginalized agriculture and led to severe food shortages. The Boerma plan targeted food aid from the North to the South, building national reserves and the establishment of a global warning system for famines (Shaw, 2007). The plan approached food security as a national problem and its outcome was large-scale programmes for improving agriculture. These programmes mainly relied on Green Revolution technologies (Jarosz, 2014)such as controlled irrigation, use of agrochemicals and mechanization. A decade later, the World Bank developed a redefinition of food security which changed its scale from the national level to the household level and the scope from self-sufficiency to the ability to purchase. In the following years, although there were opposing arguments, this conceptualization of food security appeared in the reports of the World Bank and the FAO, and, as remedies, structural adjustment programmes and trade liberalization were proposed (Jarosz, 2011). In the mid-1990s the major reason for hunger was taken as poverty that could be reduced by the integration of local markets through trade arrangements. Due to neo-liberal policies and free trade arrangements, the scope of the food security movement was redefined, and the local and national' self-sufficiency premises were replaced by global markets. During this period, in line with the policy recommendations of the World Bank and the FAO, and by the implementation of pervasive structural adjustment programmes and free trade arrangements, the food security movement became embedded in global markets that were driven by neo-liberal policies. Currently, both the World Bank and the FAO reports tackle the food insecurity problem at the individual and household level rather than as a national issue. Also, the scope of food security has been redefined, and the problem is equated with nourishment and healthy dietary requirements. In these reports, hunger and undernourishment are related to poverty; the increase in food insecurity is attributed to climate downturns and economic declines. As noted in the Food Security Report of the FAO et al (2021), the emphasis is on the availability of and access to 'nutritious' food that constitutes a healthy diet. It has been stated that healthcare costs related to the treatment of diet-related diseases (such as stunting, overweight, obesity) will increase as a consequence of undernourishment, labour productivity will decrease, and severe ecological problems will be faced. The policy recommendations offered as solutions to food insufficiency caused by the prevailing food system is to cut down costs of nutritious food by increasing productivity and diversification (for example, producing horticultural products, legumes, nutritious foodstuff) in food production. Furthermore, transportation systems and roads are to be improved so that accessibility to the market will be improved. The protectionist measures such as tariffs and quotas taken by the governments of low-income countries are criticized since they give way to the production of foodstuff that is poor in terms of vitamins and micronutrients and have an 'adverse effect on the affordability of more nutritious foods' (FAO et al, 2021, p 12). Although the scale and scope of food security has been redefined over time, the solutions drafted (trade liberalization, purchasing power, productivity) aligned it with neo-liberal policies, especially in the case of low-income countries. Given this, food insecurity is still prevalent: 34.7 per cent of the world population faces severe and moderate food insecurity, especially in low-income countries and landlocked developing countries. Small farmers are displaced from their land and agriculture and large-scale land grabs in countries that face food insecurity continue to take place.

In contrast to the food security movement driven by supranational organizations such as the World Bank, the FAO and large-scale agro-business corporations, food sovereignty is a grassroots counter-movement (McMichael, 2014). In 1996, La Via Campesina, a peasant movement founded in Belgium in 1993, announced its declaration on food sovereignty, which was in response to trade liberalization and its economic consequences. The declaration, with an anti-globalization stance, emphasized the importance of local and national food provisioning systems in promoting sustainable agriculture and repositioning small farmers who were distanced from the decision-making process by neo-liberal policies, land grabbing and lengthened food supply chains. The displacement of farmers from land and agriculture by free trade had several consequences: the dispossession of land, the loss of agriculture related knowledge and ecological disruption. Also, long supply chains in industrial agriculture distances consumers from knowledge about the foodstuff they purchase and the conditions under which they are produced. This and the following declarations of La Via Campesina are in opposition to the World Bank, World Trade Organization (WTO) and powerful nations and claim that pervasive worldwide hunger and poverty are the outcomes of the global policies drafted and implemented by these organizations. These declarations claim that it is the responsibility of governments to develop and promote small farm-based food provisioning systems rather than industrial agriculture.

The declaration of Nyéléni in 2007 by representatives of 80 countries, included consumers in the food sovereignty movement as well as farmers (Jarosz, 2011; McMichael, 2014). Reform in agriculture can benefit all of society: consumers can have healthy, accessible food that fits their culture; the migration from rural to urban can be prevented; and equality between men and women and different economic classes can be established. Food sovereignty as a counter-movement aims for a democratic redesigning of domestic agriculture to overcome food dependency and de-peasantization.

The main argument behind the food sovereignty movement is that, because of the dominant mass-produced agricultural system, farmers – petty commodity producers – are displaced from agriculture. This displacement has severe consequences such as the displacement of land-related tacit knowledge, the displacement of land for housing, and the isolation of consumers from the environment so that they cannot conceive of the hazards caused by mass production. The movements' main principle is to position food not as a commodity but as a human right. A democratic rebuilding of local agriculture, where land users rather than big corporations and international organizations govern the food systems, shapes the vision of the movement. Both AFNs and the food sovereignty movement emerged as a reaction to free trade, neo-liberal policies and the market logic of the corporate-led food provisioning system, which is characterized by standardization, efficiency and cost minimization.

AFNs have been criticized for being silent on the issues of inclusion and equity (Goodman and DePuis, 2002; Goodman and Goodman, 2009; Allen, 2010; Wilson, 2013). Extant research on AFNs in the USA indicates that they are places of 'white belonging' and produce inequalities of class and race (Slocum, 2006; Goodman and Goodman, 2009). Furthermore, most of the operations in AFNs are carried out by volunteers and the efficient running of the system requires time commitment and knowledge accumulation, which in turn asserts that being part of an AFN requires a significant level of economic and cultural capital (Goodman and Goodman, 2009). These inequalities of class, race, socio-economic status and cultural capital cause a division among consumers. AFNs are also criticized for their emphasis on being 'alternative', which leads to a dichotomy between alternative and conventional food provisioning systems (Maye et al, 2007; Wilson 2013; Le Velly, 2019). This distinction is not applicable in most cases (Holloway et al, 2007; Jarosz, 2008): in some countries AFNs gradually became part of the conventional system in supply and distribution (Goodman and Goodman, 2009; Maye and Kirwan, 2010). AFNs have also been criticized for their emphasis on localism, which can lead to the empowerment of the educated middle class rather than small farmers and less advantaged consumers (Hinrichs, 2000). Finally, AFNs are criticized for providing universal solutions which disregard local conditions; the practices developed and experienced by AFNs can differ depending on the social, economic and political conditions prevalent in a specific context that shape the emergence and development of food systems (Holloway et al, 2007; Jarosz, 2008; Allen, 2010).

The food sovereignty movement, similarly, has been criticized for having a romantic optimism about a local, ecologically safe food provisioning system driven by petty commodity producers (see, for example, Jansen, 2015 and Bernstein, 2014). The movement appears to promote nationalism due to its emphasis on local production in challenging the conventional food production system dominated by vertically integrated global firms. According to Bernstein (2014), by neglecting the productive possibilities of capitalism, the food sovereignty movement also falls short of finding an answer to the following question: how can small farmers, engaged in ecologically safe farming, using local seeds and local knowledge, compete with the big farms that can afford the new technology?

Given these debates on AFNs and the food sovereignty movement, we discuss how, in a different context characterized by different political, economic and social conditions, consumer cooperatives embedded in AFNs can develop different practices. In the Turkish context, ACCs strive to be inclusive; in their counter-hegemonic struggle, being inclusive enables them to exercise their citizenship rights and challenge the dominant power relationship. Following the premise of localism, AFNs in Turkey try to bridge the gap between rural petty commodity producers and urban consumers. As stated on their social media accounts and web pages, one of the major goals of these networks is to develop a trust-based relationship between consumers and producers. Producers are small farms and producer cooperatives (especially those owned and managed by women) located in different parts of the country. The identification and inclusion of small producers to the network is done collectively by the members of an AFN. Producers engaged in ecologically safe, traditional farming practices use heirloom seeds and do not exploit female labour in the production process. On the consumption side, AFNs serve consumers located in a specific district that are inhabited by middle-income groups who are interested in good quality, reliable foodstuff and concerned with the way this foodstuff is produced. The inclusion of both concerned consumers and petty commodity producers to the network is promoted by various face-to-face events such as workshops, festivals and talks. AFNs do not set the price while purchasing from the small producer, instead it is assumed that the price requested by the producer will be a fair amount to safeguard their livelihood and the good quality food at a reasonable price demands of the consumers. Since intermediaries are bypassed and profits are not the goal, the price of foodstuff sold in the AFNs is lower than ecologically safe food sold via the conventional food distribution system. Given this background we can say that AFNs in Turkey attain their goal of being inclusive and local.

In contrast to examples in other countries, the ACCs have also preserved their 'alternativeness' in Turkey by providing examples of short supply and distribution chains where middlemen are bypassed (Akyüz and Demir, 2016). In so doing, the ACCs use their own shops or methods such as box schemes and pre-order deliveries for the distribution of their foodstuff. Especially during the COVID-19 pandemic, the AFNs, by establishing WhatsApp groups, communicated with their customers on a regular basis; information about the arrival of foodstuff was shared and, in return, orders were taken and delivered. During the same period, most of the shelves of the conventional food distributors, such as supermarkets, were often empty due to logistical problems. Furthermore, by promoting a milieu where producers and consumers are in direct contact, the AFNs also enabled small producers to take orders directly from the urban consumers and deliver them as well. This has been useful for urban consumers as they have faced less food shortages and it has enabled the rural petty commodity producers to sell their products. Abiral and Atalan-Helicke (2020), based on their experiences during COVID-19 in the USA and Turkey, provide ample evidence that shorter supply chains like the ones in Turkey are more resilient. This insistence on using alternative distribution channels bears some risks to scaling up; some cooperative shops operate only few hours a day, but currently, in line with the increasing interest in the services of the ACCs and the commitment of citizens for volunteer work, we have seen that some of them have started to offer their services for much longer.

Prefigurative politics in alternative consumer cooperatives

Living the word.

Yılmaz et al, *Yeniden İnşa Et*, 2020, p 48

We conceptualize ACCs as prefigurative 'spaces' (Haug, 2013) where the activists involved try to develop a new alternative model within the predominant system by continuously crafting strategies and experimenting with them. Prefigurative politics seeks to develop 'new' within the 'old' (Leach, 2013) and enact a desired future in the present. Activists involved in a social movement, by experiencing and experimenting, develop new structures and practices that challenge the prevailing power relationships (Maeckelbergh, 2011). The concept of prefiguration, as applied to political movements, was developed by Carl Boggs. In 'Marxism, prefigurative communism and the problem of workers' control', published in the journal *Radical America,* Boggs defines the term as 'the embodiment, within the ongoing political practice of a movement, of those forms of social relations, decision-making, culture and human experience that are the ultimate goal' (1977, p 101). The article focuses on council movements in Italy, Russia and Germany and discusses their commitment to democratization, which is promoted by local and collective structures. In contrast to the instrumentalism of bureaucratic power struggles, these small, local collectives can develop structures that overcome the division of labour, generate a leadership that emerges from the local and facilitate the inclusion of a wider set of issues to the political struggle. According to Boggs (1977), prefigurative structures are important because the Leninist political strategy in Russia, with its overemphasis on bureaucratic methods and techniques, failed to realize its goals and reproduced the prevalent power relationship. Hierarchical authority relations, authoritarianism, centralized forms, and the separation of mental and physical labour in the workplace for the sake of efficiency and productivity turned out to be instruments for worker control. The prefigurative model with its emphasis on new participatory forms established by workers themselves can be useful in eliminating subordination and alienation. Boggs (1977) also problematizes the separation of politics as a separate sphere and explains that prefigurative structures will create a new type of politics where the division of labour between everyday activity and political activity will be broken down.

Wini Breines (1989), in her studies on Students for a Democratic Society (SDS), a grassroots movement embedded in the New Left, described the society as decentralized, activist and involved in direct action. In explaining the characteristics of the movement, she used the term *prefigurative politics* to express its personal and antihierarchical values. According to Breines (1989) participatory democracy and the notion of community are the central concepts of prefigurative politics. Community, as opposed to the formal relations underlying the functioning of the state, is explained as a more direct and personal network of relationships where, on an equal basis, individuals participate in the decisions that affect their lives. Participation of all members in the decision-making process and direct action is taken as being political, which denotes an equivalence between means and goals. Breines (1989) takes prefigurative politics as an attempt to develop a new society by implementing the premises of participatory democracy, which are supported by the values and processes of counter-institutions.

In the 1990s, studies on new social movement theory emerged, and analysis of movements organized around issues such as environmentalism, sexism and human rights provided evidence that political processes are organized around multiple sources of power which are both material and symbolic (Armstrong and Bernstein, 2008). As a counter-argument to institutionalist studies that perceive the environment as a resource provider (see, for example McCarthy and Zald, 1977; Tilly, 1978), these studies emphasize the role of culture and the importance of cultural contexts in promoting organizational creativity for the mobilization of existing resources. This approach tries to provide an answer to the question of how actors imagine new solutions in the case of an institutional crisis and view culture as a 'powerful and constraining force' (Armstrong and Bernstein, 2008, p 82), claiming that structure is constituted by cultural meanings. In an effort to overcome the dualism between structure and actors in social movement studies, Alberto Melucci (1985) views social movements as action systems. Accordingly, social movements have structures for providing unity among members and allocating resources for action. These structures in turn are developed and maintained by the aims, beliefs and decisions of the movement participants. These movements, by challenging the prevailing cultural codes and confronting political systems, stimulate innovation, create new patterns of behaviour and new models of organizations (Melucci, 1985, p 813). They represent an 'intermediate autonomous public space' between the state and civil society that aims to reflect their claims to society (Melucci, 1985, p 815). Envisioning social movements as 'spaces' is useful for overcoming the dualism of structure/actor agency. Prefiguration and 'free spaces' as part of the new social movements (see Polletta, 1999) are formed by the voluntary participation of individuals; they are usually small in scale and lead to the development of an oppositional culture (Polletta, 1999). Free spaces provide a physical setting and a cultural milieu where participants can reflect on the future; they provide opportunities for solidarity. They also contribute to the formation and maintenance of collective identities, a shared sense of 'we' and associated frames, or mental representations that enable shared understanding and response to specific events. Prefigurative free spaces are characterized by symmetric ties; in other words, they develop and maintain a cultural milieu where relations are developed around norms of reciprocity and governance. These ties and their form shape the collective identities and emergence of new organizational forms. Thus, free spaces are built on and shaped by these ties, showing that the impossible can be done and taboos can be discussed. The idea of free spaces, as discussed by Polletta (1999), emphasizes the role of community, culture and the formation of collective identities during or after mobilization.

Marianne Maeckelbergh (2011a) acknowledges the political legacy of the 1960s movements in altering social movement praxis. In her studies on alter-globalization movements and participatory democracy within these movements she explains the shift in social movement praxis – a shift towards prefiguration, conceptualizing social movement as a continuous learning process rather than a revolutionary struggle. This shift is reflected in practices like participatory democracy and inclusive forms of decision-making that shape 'the struggle towards a predetermined goal, but also in the process of determining goals' (p 302). Accordingly, prefiguration, 'enacting one's ideals in the present moment' (p 331) is the best strategy for those movements that value inclusive, non-hierarchical, egalitarian and participatory democracy. Maeckelbergh's (2011b) explanation of prefiguration eliminates the distinction between goals and ends and positions strategy as an activity.

Building on David Graeber (2002), Maeckelbergh's work (2011a, b) emphasizes that prefiguration is inspired by anarchist tradition especially with its emphasis on decentralized, non-hierarchical democracy, consensus-based decision-making and direct action. In explaining the efforts of activists in reinventing democracy, David Graeber (2002) states that they are, 'all aimed at creating forms of democratic process that allow initiatives to rise from below and attain maximum effective solidarity, without stifling dissenting voices, creating leadership positions or compelling anyone to do anything which they have not freely agreed to do' (2002, p 9). These activist groups have also experienced what they have said, that they prefer action to planning since the only way to see how a practice or form works is by doing it (Graeber, 2002; Maeckelbergh, 2011). As explained by Franks (2010), for the anarchists, direct action as part of the envisioned goal encompasses balancing power relations and thus creating non-hierarchical social relations. This requires the involvement of those who are directly influenced by a specific problem to the decision-making process. This is in contrast to the involvement of mediators like politicians and consultants, who will be instrumental only in enlarging their own power base.

From the mid-2000s on there has been a proliferation in studies related to prefiguration, especially in relation to the Occupy movements (Yates, 2021). These studies emphasize three aspects of prefiguration: temporality, 'means and ends equivalence' (Yates, 2015) and experimentation. Prefiguration with its emphasis on experimenting with a future alternative in the present bridges the future with the present. This bridging of 'here and now' with an 'alternative future' creates a possibility of experimentation for social transformation. Uri Gordon (2008), Van de Sande (2013) and Raekstad and Gradin (2020) write about the concept of direct action derived from the anarchist tradition in explaining how prefiguration bridges the temporal distinction between 'now' and 'future'. Prefiguration is taken as a process where the distinction between ends and means dissolves, a situation described as 'means–ends equivalence' by Yates (2015). Governance practices like consensus oriented, participatory decision-making, task rotation and developing horizontal structures are aligned with the goals of a more inclusive, egalitarian democracy. Furthermore, these practices are to be designed in such a way that informal inequalities and hierarchies arising from differences in education and gender should be eliminated (Raekstad and Gradin, 2020). As suggested by Yates (2015), these evolving practices are politicized as they are shaped by and reflect the values of the activists, and, furthermore, they are politicizing as they are shared with others (Yates, 2015). Since what is being envisioned as an alternative is experienced by the activists, prefiguration is taken as a process of experimentation (Van de Sande, 2013) and learning (Maeckelbergh, 2011b). Both envisioned, alternative future and means are tested, debated, reformulated and redeveloped based on real-time, first-hand experiences.

Prefigurative politics has its criticisms as well. It has been argued that it lacks an analysis of society, that it lacks a theory, does not lead to a societal change, does not solve the problem of informal inequalities, lacks planning and tactics, and lacks capacity to grow in terms of constituents engaged (Smucker, 2013, 2014, 2017; Srnicek and Williams, 2015a; Reinecke, 2018;

Soborski, 2018). Smucker (2013, 2014, 2017) claims that prefigurative politics is expressive and lacks instrumentality, and by focusing too much on internal matters neglects wider societal change. Based on his observations of Occupy Wall Street (OWS), Smucker claims that it was the major reason for the failure of the movement, which otherwise could have generated long-lasting social change. For Smucker, prefiguration lacks political strategy, that is, actions taken by activists are not tactics but manifestations, expressions of their vision. He admits the value of prefigurative elements like the People's Kitchen, the People's Library and 'mic checks' in OWS that were inspirational in building cohesion and solidarity. However, he questions the impact of such practices in bringing societal change. Srnicek and Williams (2015b), in *Inventing the Future*, view prefigurative approaches as part of 'folk politics': 'a set of strategic assumptions that threatens to debilitate the left, rendering it unable to scale-up, create lasting change or expand beyond particular interests' (2015b, p 9). They claim that 'folk politics' lacks analysis of society and the economy, and fails to develop an alternative project; also, by emphasizing and living in the present, it disregards the past and neglects the future. Practices such as horizontal consensus-based decision-making are symbolic and are not effective; they even weaken the Left.

Reinecke (2018), in reference to Occupy London, shows that over time these spaces can deteriorate in the handling of their initial concerns. Initially the activists created an exceptional communal space that enabled them to express their concerns and develop practices that were aligned with these concerns. The means developed were expressive of their ends and enacted a change in their daily practices. However, over time, the inequalities that prompted the movement re-emerged in the camp. Reinecke (2018) claims that prefigurative organizing supposes a balance between expressive and strategic politics, and if the balance between these two politics is tilted towards either side the movement can fail, as was the case in Occupy London. Soborski (2018) in *Ideology and the Future of Progressive Social Movements* claims that prefigurative commitments lack an ideology, a theoretical foundation, and are characterized by individualism. Analysing the critical studies on World Social Forum summits and Occupy, Soborski (2018) argues that these movements ignored the informal inequalities that hinder a fully democratic and inclusive system. In these movements, only the better-off groups in terms of wealth and education had a voice and, furthermore, since too many people tried to have a voice in the decision-making process, it was nearly impossible finalize a decision. Similarly, Polletta (2005) discusses that the insistence on decentralized organization, consensus-based decision-making and rotating leadership runs the risk of alienating new participants.

Given these criticisms, we reconsidered the position taken by activists involved in the ACCs in terms of the emphasis on wider societal change, analysing the economy and questioning scaling-up. Members of the ACCs have created a space and practices that confront and negate the existing power structures in the production and consumption of foodstuff, but they are also involved in the problems of Turkish society and aim for societal change. The ACCs' public announcement on the 8th anniversary of the Gezi Park protest indicates their position taking: 'Gezi is the light that gives us direction in these dark and depressing days that we are going through … We will bring democracy to this country by our own revolt, by our own actions and struggle.'

Alternative cooperatives extend their egalitarian practices beyond the inner governance of the cooperative. For example, knowing that women are distanced from public life by cultural norms and treated as unpaid family workers, activists develop practices that enable women farmers to be economically autonomous. Alternative cooperatives prioritize the foodstuff produced by women farmers; in those cases where they purchase from family farms, the women are paid separately and they are encouraged to have their own bank accounts (Oba and Özsoy, 2020). In the last couple of years, a group of professionals, especially academics, have become distanced from their jobs and occupations because of their involvement in anti-government politics, and some of them have chosen a rural life. Alternative cooperatives, in an effort to support them, are keen to supply their products and seek to promote this information to these potential customers. These are efforts to transform the status quo, and we have seen that, gradually, some culturally and politically imprinted behaviour patterns in society are changing. For example, male farmers that supply alternative cooperatives have begun to accept that women can have a voice in financial matters at home and in business. The practices developed by activists reflect their norms, values and ideologies, and their strategic choices are expressive – they express the priorities, frames, claims and norms of those who are involved. Members of the ACCs, in pursuit of their goal(s), do not ask for the support of other organizations but instead directly experiment with alternative practices and forms that will transform the prevailing power structure.

In response to the criticisms related to informal inequalities and the reproduction of prevailing power relations, we can argue that the activists are drawing in those members of society who do not have prior experience with participative democracy. Turkish culture is characterized as authoritarian, patriarchal and possessing a high power distance, where the opinions of those who occupy a higher position in the organizational hierarchy have more weight in the decision-making process. In such a cultural context, implementing the basic premises and practices of participation is difficult and loaded with problems, but somehow useful in showing that alternatives are possible. The cooperative is a space which provides a chance of experimenting with consensus-based decision-making, raising concerns and listening to the opinions of others. We have seen that many young new members experienced such practices for the first time; they were excited to do so, although it meant long hours of discussion on trivial issues or even sometimes never concluding meetings. Informal inequalities exist; for example, women activists complain that they cannot attend these meetings since they have to look after their children. In response to the criticisms related to scaling-up, we can say that the activists involved in the ACCs do not aim to scale-up; they deliberately aim to limit their operations to a specific district. In return they aim to scale-up the movement by founding replicas in other districts. The founding members that we interviewed clearly stated that they are willing to provide know-how and support to those who aim to set up an alternative cooperative. In the last six months new initiatives have started in other cities – Ankara, Eskişehir, İzmir and İzmit – and in some other districts of İstanbul (Yeldeğirmeni, Maltepe, Bostancı, Kozyatağı, Arıköy, Kuzguncuk). ACCs scale-up vertically and horizontally: for horizontal scaling-up they enable the establishment of replicates in other districts of İstanbul and in other cities; and for vertical scaling-up they develop alliances to facilitate bulk purchases from small producers and producer cooperatives that produce environment friendly, ecologically safe foodstuff.

In conclusion

Capitalism and capitalist forms of organizing have been so hegemonic that to imagine and experiment with an 'alternative' form of organizing is usually considered 'romantic' and a 'fantasy'. Within the capitalist logic, organizations are expected to perform for profit and growth; they have to scale-up and be efficient by developing hierarchical structures where superiors (managers) are equipped with full authority to make decisions. In such organizations solidarity between various stakeholders is overtaken by competition in the name of betterment and improvement of the organization itself. Furthermore, as discussed by Parker et al, (2014), capitalism produces subjects who are willing to consume the products produced by its organizations and be producers in such organizations.

However, there are alternatives, as is the case with ACCs. ACCs, by providing a diversity of arrangements based on 'the ethics of solidarity' (Gibson-Graham et al, 2013) and the inclusion of marginalized groups like petty commodity producers and especially women producers, have the capacity to transform the prevailing industrialized production–consumption nexus in food provisioning. By adhering to the values and premises of the food sovereignty movement ACCs can democratize the food provisioning system by realigning the interests of the urban middle class and the rural petty commodity producers. It is not a movement for repositioning the marginalized small farmers only, but also for repositioning the urban middle class as partners rather than simply consumers. We have seen the

ACCs' experiments, in alternative surplus generation, governance and non-commodified work, challenge the prevailing power structures, foster a more inclusive, egalitarian food provisioning system, and show a different way of organizing. They are non-profit-making, do not aim for growth, are run by volunteers, and experiment with non-hierarchical organization and consensus-based decision-making. ACCs are also prefigurative spaces where direct democracy is implemented, societal change is aspired to, authoritarianism is questioned, and capitalist logic and capitalist forms of organizing are challenged.

Given this background, which underlines the role of the economic decisions and political choices of the government cadres that led to inequalities in distribution, polarization shaped around inclusion/exclusion and social fragmentation, we argue that ACCs are spaces where excluded groups (such as the urban middle class and rural petty commodity producers) convened around the AFNs and the food sovereignty movement. Petty commodity producers divorced from their land and means of livelihood through the implementation of neo-liberal policies, such as revoking of subsidies and support purchases, privatization of agricultural sales cooperatives and contract farming, are distanced from farming, their main income activity. Similarly, the urban middle class are separated from their occupation (that is, for the sake of getting a job they work in positions that are not related to their occupation), marginalized in the labour market through labour legislation and driven away from their main livelihood activity. Thus, we claim that the ACCs provide a space where these excluded groups co-opt for repositioning in the economic, social and political realms by experimenting with inclusive, solidarity-based food activism that challenges the existing power configurations.

3

Against Neo-Liberalism and Authoritarianism: The Background to Food Politics in Turkey

Introduction

How did alternative consumer cooperatives (ACCs) emerge and how do they function within a context characterized by an exit from democracy, the rise of political Islamism and the populist neo-liberal policies (see, for example, David and Toktamış, 2015; Toktamış and David, 2015; David, 2016; Öktem and Akkoyunlu, 2016; Özden et al., 2017; Çalışkan, 2018; Adaman et al, 2019; Toktamış, 2019; Adaman and Akbulut, 2020)? In a political and economic milieu characterized by the dominance of a strong state tradition and a commitment to the premises of neo-liberal policies, affecting various aspects of social and economic life as well as the daily practices of citizens, how did a non-capitalist form of organizing emerge from those excluded from the political and economic realm? What were the major factors that mobilized the urban middle class to build networks of solidarity with other excluded groups and the petty commodity producers?

Although the neo-liberal turn in Turkey started with the 1980 structural adjustment programme, its full-blown implementation happened in the early 2000s when the ruling party, with the guidance of international organizations, instigated a political project to refashion Turkish society by combining neo-liberal economic policies, democracy and Islam (Çelik, 2015; Tuğal, 2015; David, 2016; Tansel, 2018). The model, usually described as 'passive revolution' in Gramscian terms (Tuğal, 2009), was implemented in a top-down fashion by the appointed bureaucrats and elected politicians. This neo-liberal Islamic model was successful in facilitating the inclusion of some groups (pro-government entrepreneurs, journalists, academics, bureaucrats) to the economic and political domains of society. The model also had a neo-liberal populist character in its capacity to include the new urban poor and informal sector workers by addressing their needs for housing and social assistance (Özden and Bekmen, 2015; Batuman, 2019). The government took certain initiatives (gentrification, low interest rates) to solve the informal housing (*gecekondu*) problems which later gave way to urban exclusion and the occupation of public spaces by mosques and shopping malls (Alonso, 2015). This neo-liberal populist, political Islamist project with its emphasis on the inclusion of the urban poor with the pro-AKP factions was, at the same time, exclusionary (Tuğal, 2015).

After 2002, in line with the political choices and economic decisions of the ruling party, the urban poor and migrant villagers, located in the *gecekondu* districts of the big cities and comprising the informal labour market, were included in the economic and social realm with social assistance programmes and civic charity projects. These moves encouraged migration from the rural areas, which in turn led to a rural transformation shaped by detachment from the land, distancing from agriculture and the proletarization of the petty commodity producers. While the inclusion of informal labour was supported, formal labour and its organizations were weakened with the adoption of a labour law framed with the premises of flexible, temporary work, part-time work and government policies that limited collective bargaining. These changes in the labour regime, while empowering the owners of capital in the workplace, marginalized the white-collar workers that comprised the urban middle class. The government policies were supportive of some selected industries such as construction and media and led to a concentration of ownership and the development of a few big conglomerates operating in both of these industries. One of the devastating effects of such support has been the implementation of large-scale gentrification projects by a state-controlled and operated agency, TOKİ (Mass Housing Development Administration), which led to the marketization of urban land and the demolition of market gardens – the *bostans*. The *bostans*, which for centuries supplied the cities with fresh vegetables and fruit, produced using traditional farming methods, were gradually replaced by luxury housing developments. The gardeners were left to the mercy of municipalities who were given the right to evict them at any time by the government agencies. The discontents of this deepening system – the consumers engaged in alternative food networks (AFNs) and small farmers dedicated to the principles of food sovereignty – collectively set the ground for prefigurative food politics in Turkey, with the actions taken and strategies developed by the leading figures giving rise to the initiation of the ACCs. The Gezi Park protests were an occasion where excluded groups convened, shared their concerns, expressed their distress, and had an opportunity to experience alternative forms of communal life. Gezi, and the park forums that followed, a few of which are still held in some districts of İstanbul, triggered the development and perseverance of a non-capitalist form of organizing, based on the values of social benefits and the elimination of social and economic inequalities, and shaped by mutuality, collective work and solidarity.

This chapter is organized as follows: in the first part we provide a detailed account of the populist neo-liberal turn in Turkish politics, with a particular emphasis on the role attributed to the state in Turkey. In this part we also discuss how the implementation of these populist neo-liberal policies by state cadres influenced accumulation, led to the rise of big capital and the marginalization of formal labour for the urban, mainly white-collar professionals and the petty commodity producers in the rural areas. The second part of the chapter focuses on the tensions between the ruling party and the urban middle class and how the demands and concerns of the Gezi protesters were reconciled with the values that shape the policies of the AFNs and the food sovereignty movement, which aim to develop an emancipatory and inclusive political system in food provisioning and promote justice, equality and democracy.

The state and politics in Turkey

> The Turkish state has played a role of utmost importance. This role has at times been so overwhelming that a certain mystique has grown up around the state which might even justify the use of the Gramscian term 'statolatory' to explain this phenomenon. Such has been the power of this mystique that the state has come to acquire an identity which seems to set it outside and above society as though it has no social basis. This mystique has been captured in modern literature, most notably by Kemal Tahir in *Devlet Ana [Mother State]*, as well as in folklore where *Devlet Baba [Father State]* is often portrayed as the ultimate arbiter, at least in this world.
>
> Ahmad, *From Empire to Republic*, 2008, p 1

The Republican state in Turkey, as well as its predecessor, the Ottoman empire, has been patrimonial and interventionist. As Ahmad (2008) explained, until the 1980s, the role of the state in economic affairs had always been on the agenda of political groups and parties and was centred around whether there should have been statist capitalism that did not rely on private capital, or a state-controlled and supervised economy that retained private initiatives. Moreover, the dominance of the state did not change during the rule of those political parties that adopted a liberal discourse. Turkey has a tradition of accommodating a centralized and highly bureaucratic state that has been ascribed a role above society. The Turkish state has been a prominent actor in the economic and political realm either by providing legal and economic support or drafting regulations to restrain the activities of different constituencies. Although the state-led developmentalism, which covered approximately a 50-year period, showed variations in terms of its emphasis on the decisive implementation of an import substituting industrialization policy, the Turkish state employed a central role in society by implementing economic and distributive policies. Until 1980, Turkish economic policy was shaped by a mixed economy model where the state promoted the development of big capital by implementing a protectionist trade policy and the provisioning of subsidies to various groups. At the same time, the state, by assuming the role of an investor, established state-owned enterprises (SOEs) in most industries (for example, banking, agriculture, steel, and heavy machinery). Around the state-created uncertainties (for example the change in fiscal policies and the prioritization of industries in terms of investment support) (Buğra, 1994, p 23), coalitions were formed between bureaucratic elites, big bourgeoisie-owned conglomerates located in the western part (especially in the Marmara region), the secular urban middle class, formal labour and big landowners (Güven, 2019).

The neo-liberal turn and socio-economic transformations

The major transformation in the political, economic and social history of Turkey occurred in 1980 with the initiation of the structural adjustment programme on 24 January and the military coup d'état on the 12th of September. Under the tutelage of the military regime, Turgut Özal and the Anavatan Partisi (ANAP) initiated and implemented a structural adjustment programme based on a formula from the World Bank. Moreover, a space for implementing the practices of neo-liberal authoritarianism was created by the 1982 Constitution. In a referendum, 91 per cent of the voters backed the constitution, which incorporated issues such as the centralization of economic decision-making and the supremacy of the executive over the legislative (Özden et al, 2017). The neo-liberal turn in Turkey was prompted by the 1979 crises, characterized by a high inflation rate and the emergence of commodity shortages and the black market, and was not independent of similar transformations in other countries (Başkaya, 2011; Önder, 2011; Yaman-Öztürk and Ercan, 2012). It was a comprehensive model that transformed the social structure, distribution relations and the major institutions in Turkish society, and the coup was instrumental in its pervasive realization. During this transformation the Left was decimated, the long-established economic strategy changed from import substitution industrialization to one based on exports (Akçay, 2018), the labour movement was weakened, and the peasantry was phased out of the economic and political realm. As stated by Boratav (2019), the programme was the 'counterattack of big capital' and it was welcomed and supported by business groups which were uneasy with the political and economic developments of the late 1970s, characterized by the development and initiation of a social security system, an increase in wages, unionization and strikes (Önder, 2011; Yaman-Öztürk and Ercan, 2012; Boratav, 2019). The military coup suspended unions, brought court cases against union leaders and drafted legislation to repress wages (Başkaya, 2011; Önder, 2011; Yaman-Öztürk and Ercan, 2012). A similar development was seen in agriculture, which in the late 1970s enjoyed a rise in prices due to the support purchases from the government. The implementation of populist policies such as government support and base prices during the late 1970s tilted the industry/agriculture balance towards agriculture and especially small producers. After 1980, support purchases were regressed, cooperatives (both production and consumption) were banned, and cooperative administrators were convicted (Boratav, 2019).

During the first phase (1980–88) of structural adjustments, the national economic policy based on import substitution was shifted to a policy of trade liberalization. Accordingly, exports were supported with subsidies, capital movements were regulated and floating exchange rates were implemented. Consequently, agricultural support mechanisms declined, the Turkish lira was devaluated and wages fell significantly (Yaman-Öztürk and Ercan, 2012; Boratav, 2019). State Economic Enterprises (SEE), which assumed the roles of investor and producer, were closed down. These policies had a severe impact on agriculture and the peasantry: the scale and scope of agricultural support mechanisms declined, subsidies for agricultural inputs were reduced and the support purchases from agricultural cooperatives were reduced. With the implementation of the structural adjustment programme, small producers of agricultural products that were on the agenda of governments up until the 1980 were left at the mercy of market forces. In an economic milieu characterized by continuous devaluations and export substitutions, farmers facing a drastic price decline were driven out of the economic and political realm. The decline in prices during this period was the most drastic in the history of the Turkish Republic (Boratav, 2019). In particular, with the abandonment of cooperatives that bought agricultural products from petty commodity producers and the provisioning of subsidies to exports, large-scale food exporters evolved as powerful actors and the peasantry declined (Boratav, 2016).

At the beginning of the second phase (1988–97) of the structural adjustment programme, the Motherland Party (ANAP) government lost elections and labour protests (especially by the workers of SEEs) and mass mobilizations against neo-liberal policies became pervasive. With the revival of populist policies (wage increases, increase in support prices for agricultural products), the implementation of the neo-liberal formula was disrupted. The resulting high public deficit and high inflation rates were curbed by capital account liberalization. Although earlier moves towards financial liberalization ended in scandals, such as the collapse of the money brokers (known as 'bankers'), who used the Ponzi system, and some small banks (Boratav and

Yeldan, 2006; Boratav, 2019), establishing a liberalized financial system was always on the agenda for the government. With the liberalization of the capital account in 1989, the Turkish economy was integrated into the international financial system (Boratav and Yeldan, 2006; Boratav, 2019). The Turkish bourgeoisie, being discontent with the populist policies, convinced the coalition government to sign an agreement with the International Monetary Fund (IMF), despite the fact that there was no need for foreign credit (Boratav, 2016, 2019). In the following years, stand-by agreements, signed in 1999, 2002 and 2005, IMF programmes and structural reforms designed by the World Bank shaped the Turkish economy. Political parties of both Left and Right factions supported these programmes. The coalition government comprised of the Democratic Left Party (DSP), the Nationalist Movement Party (MHP) and ANAP, by drafting various laws, prepared the legal foundation for a neo-liberal economic system. The structural reforms were promoted with a slogan claiming that 'the state should withdraw from the economic realm' and, in order to avoid populism, wages, agricultural products and input prices were left to the market mechanism and private investments in health and education were encouraged by changes in the relevant legislation. The legal background for the privatization of the telecommunications and energy (natural gas) sectors was prepared.

In summary, the neo-liberal policies adopted for the liberalization of the commodity markets and the capital account led to a deterioration of macroeconomic indicators, a rise in the informal economy, a huge income disparity between the urban poor and the urban rich, the rise of Islamic capital and the weakening of the peasantry. During the transition period, the state had an active role as a regulator and the sole decision-maker. Roads taken by the state always favoured big capital and led to the creation of conflict in the distribution of wealth (Cizre-Sakallıoğlu and Yeldan, 2000). In 2002, before the elections, there was a pervasive reaction to the IMF and the austerity measures: while small tradesman, villagers, white-collar workers and the urban poor lost their position and economic power, owners of big capital, emerging rentier and finance capital gained power. Given this background, in the early elections of 2002, a new party, the Justice and Development Party (AKP), which adopted a conservative, Islamist political stance, came to power.

Unconditional commitment to neo-liberal policies

The new government, formed by the AKP, took over the IMF and World Bank recovery programmes that had already been put into operation by the previous coalition government. These programmes, besides monetary and fiscal measures, covered institutional reforms such as banking regulations, transparency, good governance and anti-corruption measures that complemented the market-related policies of the neo-liberal transformation

(Güven, 2019). The fiscal policies of the government were carried out in line with the IMF recommendations. As an outcome of the World Bank structural adjustment programme, the position of farmers, to a great extent, was determined by market forces, flexibility dominated labour markets, outsourcing and sub-contracting became a prevalent way of doing business, and state-owned enterprises were privatized. The unionization rate, especially within privately owned companies, declined drastically (Boratav, 2019). The pricing mechanism for agricultural products was re-framed in relation to the conditions of international markets (Kandemir, 2011; Boratav, 2019; Şazmaz and Özel, 2019). After a pervasive privatization, the telecommunication system was sold to a United Arab Emirates company, the energy sector was totally privatized, and the privatizations of the state-owned raw paper producer SEKA and the alcohol and tobacco monopoly TEKEL mainly contributed to the budget of the government. Furthermore, from 2003 onwards the AKP started preparation for full European Union (EU) membership and drafted related legislation. These economic and political moves by the AKP government had full support from all segments of the bourgeoisie and liberal-oriented intellectuals at home and finance capital internationally.

This neo-liberal populist model implemented in the early 2000s was successful in facilitating the inclusion of some groups into the economic and political domains of society: entrepreneurs were supported with low interest rates and loans provided by state-owned banks, big capital in the construction and media industry was supported by enabling conditions that led to a high-level concentration, and the urban poor comprised of informal sector workers were supported by the social assistance programmes. On the other hand, the same programmes, while empowering certain groups in Turkish society, were exclusive in their implementation, so that with the adoption of the new Labour Law (4857) in 2003, formal organized labour and the unions were weakened. This transformation in labour conditions marginalized the labour force comprised of educated middle-class citizens. They had to work without job security under demanding working conditions. With the gentrification projects carried out by a few big construction companies, market gardens that supplied the city with fresh foodstuff were demolished. Gardens were replaced by luxury housings complexes; petty commodity producers were displaced from their land; and farming traditions were eroded. The following sections provide a detailed explanation of this social and economic transformation by explaining the conditions that drove the emergence of the ACCs.

Social assistance and inclusion in the welfare system

The new model possessed a neo-liberal populist character in its capacity to include the new urban poor and informal sector workers by addressing their needs for housing and social assistance (Özden and Bekmen, 2015; Batuman, 2019) and for drafting mechanisms for financial inclusion. This neo-liberal populist, political Islamist project, with its emphasis on the inclusion of the urban poor and informal sector workers in pro-AKP factions, was, at the same time, ethnically and religiously exclusionary (Tuğal, 2015). The populism of the AKP, similar to that of Özal and the ANAP during the first phase of the structural adjustment programme, was aimed at the urban poor located in the *gecekondu* districts of the big cities. One way of doing this was to revise the existing welfare regime, which only provided benefits (health care and retirement) for formal sector workers and civil servants. By expanding the health care benefits of Green Card holders, which was initiated in 1992, the new system was able to provide all sorts of health benefits to those who were not insured through a social security system, those who did not get a retirement payment, and those who were not taxpayers or farmers. Later, in 2012, Green Card holders were transferred to the General Health Insurance system. Another step taken by the AKP in line with the inclusive transformation of the welfare system was the initiation of the Conditional Cash Transfer (CCT) programme endorsed by the World Bank. The programme aimed to provide financial resources to those households living in poverty in order to support the education and healthcare of their children (Bergman and Tafolar, 2014; Akçay, 2018; Şener, 2016). The programme allocated cash on a regular basis to mothers for sending their children to school and for having health checks. The aim of the programme was to facilitate the lowest income groups' participation in education and health care. The programme was launched in 2004, and in 2007 the responsibility for the implementation of the programme was transferred to the General Directorate of Social Assistance and Solidarity, an organization operating under the Office of the Prime Minister (Bergman and Tafolar, 2014; Akçay, 2018). Although the programme was instrumental in increasing the enrolment rates and confidence of the beneficiary mothers, there were criticisms related to gender and its utilization for political purposes. Although the programme emphasized the empowerment of women, the way it was structured and implemented reinforced the traditional roles attributed to women (Şener, 2016), and women were considered not as active participants of the labour market but as caregivers and housewives (Bergman and Tafolar, 2014). Moreover, since the programme was carried out by a government office, it was used by the AKP to exercise political power and was presented as a result of the 'benevolence of the AKP' not as a social assistance programme (Bergman and Tafolar, 2014). Consequently, the programme has been instrumental in deepening the support for AKP cadres during the elections (Akçay, 2018), since it gave credence to the idea that the government cared for the poor (Özden and Bekmen, 2017).

Poverty, civic charity and the inclusion of the urban poor

As shown by the Gini coefficient (0.410 in 2020), Turkey faces a persistent income inequality and relative poverty, where the average income of the poor is below the poverty line. Until the 1960s, through various strategies (such as supporting small farmers, not taxing agricultural products), governments confined poverty to the rural areas. After the 1960s, with the move towards industrialization, big cities hosting factories became attractive for the rural poor looking for seasonal jobs. The rural poor moved to the fringes of the cities, forming shanty towns (*gecekondu*) and governments of all political factions instrumentalized the urban poor as a voting pool by granting amnesties for legal ownership of their *gecekondu*. Especially after the structural adjustment programme of the 1980s, which marginalized the peasantry, the movement from the countryside to the cities saw an upsurge and urban poverty became a pervasive issue (Pinarcioğlu and Işık, 2008). With the implementation of open-market policies, domestic firms, in an effort to compete in international markets, implemented a competitive strategy based on cost cutting, either through low labour costs or by outsourcing and sub-contracting (Buğra and Keyder, 2006). Both of these strategies gave way to the rise of the informal economy where the urban poor became part of an informal labour force or self-employed entrepreneurs in micro-organizations. Thus, the informal economy in Turkey emerged and was strengthened as an outcome of neo-liberal reforms that reduced the effectiveness of the state in 'policing' the economic actors (Kuş, 2014). The rise of the informal economy gave way to two alternatives for the urban poor: job opportunities as unskilled, informal labour, located on the fringes of the cities and living below the poverty line without any social security, and entrepreneurship opportunities in forming micro-organizations in labour-intensive sectors.

When the AKP became the governing party in 2002 the problem of poverty and the social inclusion of the urban poor was an issue that could not be disregarded and the party integrated 'neo-liberal benevolent ethics' into its programme (Tuğal, 2017, p 439). This was a turn in Turkish politics, as until then combatting poverty was carried out by voluntary organizations. This change in governmental policy was also related to the implementation of pro-market neo-liberal policies and Turkey's aspirations to be accepted into the European Union (EU). In line with the accession process and the directions of the supranational organizations, voluntary philanthropy initiatives based on private benevolence were assumed by the government. In so doing, two complementary sets of policies were implemented in relation to poverty alleviation: providing financial resources to self-employed entrepreneurs and developing a network of benevolent associations. As discussed by Tuğal (2017), these associations were receptive to neo-liberal expectations under leadership with a religious bias. Although Islam motivated their approach, they accepted neo-liberal organization as a model in shaping their practices.

The AKP, in an effort to include those groups that were excluded from the existing social security programme, articulated a model in cooperation with religiously motivated civil society associations and municipalities that were governed by elected AKP members (Buğra, 2007; Buğra and Candan, 2011; Tuğal, 2017). These examples of 'neo-liberal benevolence' (Tuğal, 2017) were funded by wealthy families and from donations collected by television programmes, and were carried out with the support of the municipalities and the government. Municipalities provided in-kind assistance and support for the needy by collecting money and goods from companies, which most probably received benefits in return (Buğra and Candan, 2011). Neither the selection of the cooperating companies nor how the funds are allocated has been transparent. As was the case with other welfare initiatives, this model gave discretionary power to municipalities and, as stated by Buğra and Candan (2011), 'they reinforced the traditional clientelist forms or patronage of the political relationship between the state and the citizens' (p 523). The other strand of social inclusion of the urban poor was realized through creating financial resources and the empowerment of self-employed entrepreneurs through micro-financing (Buğra and Keyder, 2006; Buğra and Candan, 2011; Tuğal, 2017). Micro-financing gained popularity among government members who claimed that the cause of poverty was a lack of capital. Accordingly, micro-financing was introduced as a means of poverty alleviation and a way of social inclusion. It was stated that through micro-financing, dependence on support from the government and civic organizations would be replaced by the provision of capital to be used for starting a small business and being an entrepreneur. According to Buğra and Keyder (2006), the popularity of micro-financing, besides its attempt to alleviate poverty, can be attributed to its capacity for bridging finance companies and civic society organizations. Consequently, there has been a proliferation in the number of microcredits granted (Buğra and Candan, 2011) and, as stated by Tuğal (2017), the neo-liberal Islamic charity based on the partnership between government and civic charity organizations governed by professionals, 'tended to replace the formal welfare system' (p 436) either by distributing grants or seed capital.

Financialization and financial inclusion

Although the financialization process in Turkey started in 1989 with the liberalization of the capital account after the 2002 elections, the scope of the process was widened to allow low-income groups into the consumer market. Expanding consumer credit as a populist neo-liberal mechanism was a way of including the lower income groups during a period when wage increases were suppressed due to de-unionization (Akçay, 2018). In an economy where wages are squeezed, unemployment rates are high and, due to privatization, public services are expensive, indebtedness is necessary to achieve a basic standard of living (Akçay 2018, 2021).

Between 2002 and 2008, the government, using various mechanisms that reshaped the labour regime, prevented wage increases, which in turn led to productivity increases in the manufacturing industry. During this period, the Turkish finance sector experienced an increase in the number of foreign banks that were interested in investing in manufacturing as well as in making deals with Turkish banks. Especially after the 2001 economic crises, and following regulations in the banking sector, a wave of mergers and acquisitions between international and domestic banks was realized. Given the competitive forces of the period and expectations for the expansion of the consumer credit sector, most banks changed their target from government securities to household consumption and invested in retail banking (Kuş, 2016). Consequently, there has been an upsurge in credit usage, especially by low-income groups for upgrading their living standards. The wage squeeze was counterbalanced by using credit and being in debt, and consequently consumer demand was boosted by household indebtedness. Kuş (2016) claims that this is a 'debtfare system' where the vulnerability of the household is masked by the ability to consume. The usage of credit and indebtedness is not only an economic issue, but also involves social control (Akçay, 2018) and redistribution of wealth, and can be used a political instrument. Lower income groups can improve their living conditions and material wealth through indebtedness, but at the same this increases their dependency on the actions taken by the government.

Inclusion of the big new capital: gentrification and the construction industry

One of the major criticisms related to the capital accumulation process after the 1980 neo-liberal turn is related to the revalorization of urban land. The government single-handedly took certain initiatives (gentrification, low interest rates) to solve the informal housing problems which later gave way to urban exclusion, displacement, the erosion of market gardens and the occupation of public spaces by mosques and shopping malls (Bartu-Candan and Kolluoğlu, 2008; Lovering and Türkmen, 2011; Melis and Tok, 2011; Alonso, 2015; Tuğal, 2021). From 1980 onwards, in line with the implementation of the structural adjustment programme, there was a transformation in the social structuring of cities, especially in İstanbul. During the early 2000s, with the dissolution of the peasantry due to measures taken in agriculture, there was an expansion (6.42 per cent in 8 years) of urban working-class households (Ercan and Oğuz, 2015) and the informal economy (Tuğal, 2021), while the percentage of petite bourgeoisie and landed peasants declined by 7.25 per cent (Ercan and Oğuz, 2015). One of the consequences of this transformation in the social structure of Turkish society was the transformation of urban spaces.

The reshaping of the city projects was empowered by a series of new laws and governance means that equipped local municipalities with more authority while expanding the scope of their operations. The law of 1984 brought agencies such as Water Supply and Sewerage and The Master Plan, which were formerly attached to various ministries, under the control of the municipalities. Consequently, the municipalities, operating with a market logic, privatized various services (such as housing and natural gas supply) and, with urban space being commodified, revenue generation concerns dominated social and ecological interests (Bartu-Candan and Kolluoğlu, 2008; Bezmez, 2008; Melis and Tok, 2011). After the AKP took over big city municipalities, specifically the İstanbul municipality, and with the 2004 and 2005 legislations, a remarkable neo-liberal turn was realized. These laws further increased the power of the municipalities by giving them the sole authority to plan and implement urban transformation projects. Thereafter, a deep-rooted transformation of the landscape and social fabric of big cities such as İstanbul, İzmir and Ankara took place. Indeed, one of the so-called mega-projects aimed to reshape İstanbul by building recreational areas, luxury hotels and private marinas. These projects, while being attractive to high-income groups, destroyed the social and historical fabric of the city, and by revaluing public spaces (such as the beaches and seaside) and limiting access, were exclusionary to lower-income groups. Another group of projects aimed to transform the *gecekondu*, which led to the demolition of these districts, the displacement of the residents to the periphery of the city, the marketization of the urban land (Bartu-Candan and Kolluoğlu, 2008; Lovering and Türkmen, 2011; Tuğal, 2021) and the demolition of *bostans*. This transformation process was carried by TOKİ, the only agency regulating the sale of state-owned urban land (Kuyucu and Unsal, 2010) and directly controlled and administered by the prime minister. TOKİ, a state agency, carried out its regeneration of state-owned land projects in partnership with privately owned construction companies and, when a specific project was finalized, the profits or properties were distributed among the partners (Unsal, 2015). Besides dispossession, social exclusion and the erosion of public spaces in the city, TOKİ projects created and included new actors and power relations in the reshaping of the city. While the involvement of locals in the decision-making process (at least with their votes) was minimized (Bezmez, 2008) and became inefficient, the state, the municipalities and the big construction firms emerged as the dominant actors in shaping the culture, social fabric and landscape of the cities.

One of the most devastating effects of the urban transformation projects in İstanbul was the demolishment of the *bostans*. These gardens, which have supplied fresh vegetables to the urban population for more than three hundred years, are currently owned by the municipalities and the Directorate of National Estate (Milli Emlak Genel Müdürlüğü), which is organized under the Ministry of Environment and Urbanization. Municipalities charge a 'recompense for land occupation' (*işgaliye bedeli*) which renders gardeners as occupiers of the land rather than tenants (Turan, 2015) and equips the municipality with a right to evict them from the land. Market gardens are sources of good quality, cheap foodstuff as they use traditional methods of production and irrigation and reduce transportation costs. However, municipalities operating with a market logic and empowered by related legislation revalorized market gardens. Currently, most of these gardens have been replaced by expensive development projects, housing complexes, car parks and 'greenwashing projects' (hobby gardens, recreation areas, sports complexes) that are run by private or state-owned companies (White et al, 2015; İstanbul Kent Bostanları Çalışma Grubu, 2021). The consequences of such revalorization led to a shortage of good quality foodstuff, the destruction of farming traditions, the displacement of families involved in agriculture and the loss of farming know-how.

Inclusion of the big new capital: the media industry

When the AKP won the elections and came to power in 2002 the media industry was controlled by a few conglomerates (such as Doğan and Doğuş). A clientelist relation between media owners and politicians was common practice, and censorship and poor working conditions were dominant features of the Turkish media industry (Çoşkun, 2020). The AKP did not challenge this neo-liberal order; on the contrary, it accentuated the neo-liberal project that was imprinted in the post-1980 period. Particularly after its second term in 2007, the party, with its strong commitment to market logic and adhering to statist imperatives, intensified neo-liberalism. As part of this process, the media industry was a tool for promoting conservative, nationalist, Islamist values (Farmanfarmainan et al, 2020) and controlling information to ensure government success (Coskun, 2020). In so doing, a pro-government media was created by seizing existing media conglomerates, controlling advertising revenues and providing incentives to new media conglomerates. Existing media conglomerates, by tender offers and tax sanctions, changed hands. Currently, 90 per cent of the mainstream media is owned by a few families or individuals known to be close to the government.

Currently, the Turkish media industry is characterized by being highly concentrated, with high cross-media ownership and vertical and horizontal integration (Yeşil, 2018; Tunç, 2018; Çoşkun, 2020). In terms of ownership, out of 40 media companies, four conglomerates (Turkuvaz, Demirören, Ciner and Doğuş) control 71 per cent of the cross-media audience. These vertically and horizontally integrated conglomerates operate in various other sectors, are involved in public projects contracted by the government and enter into public tenders such as those for İstanbul's third airport, urban redevelopment projects and subway construction (Media Ownership Monitor in Turkey, 2021). Due to the prevalent pyramidal ownership structure in Turkey, family members own the shares of these companies. Consequently, entry barriers to the media are very high. Furthermore, the detrimental effects of high ownership concentration are reflected in labour conditions and the lack of unionization of media workers: wages are low in the industry, employment contracts are waived (Yeşil, 2018) and unionized employees are threatened with the loss of their jobs (Tunç, 2018; Çoşkun, 2020).

The ruling party's efforts to include previously excluded social groups through redesigning the welfare system, developing civic charity networks, supporting self-employed entrepreneurs by micro-finance schemes, promoting big capital (especially in the construction industry) through mega gentrification projects, and creating vigorous consumer markets through financialization has created tensions between these groups (the urban poor, informal labour, micro entrepreneurs) and those that are excluded by these populist neo-liberal policies, that is formal labour, the urban middle class, professionals, civil servants and farmers. Furthermore, these policies are carried out in a milieu that is characterized by a departure from democracy and a drift towards authoritarianism which is affecting various aspects of social and economic life and leading to a redistribution of wealth (see, for example, Toktamış and David, 2015; David, 2016; Öktem and Akkoyunlu, 2016; Özden et al., 2017; Çalışkan, 2018; Adaman et al, 2019; Toktamış, 2019; Adaman and Akbulut, 2020).

Exclusion of formal organized labour and petty commodity producers

One of the major policies of the AKP, in line with neo-liberalism and the demands of big capital, was the liberalization of the labour markets. With the adoption of a new Labour Law (4857) in 2003, flexible work, part-time, temporary and contract labour and sub-contracting was legalized (Ercan and Oğuz, 2015; Akçay, 2018) and many pro-labour practices established by the previous legislation were modified (Çelik, 2015). Furthermore, the new legislation, by increasing the powers of the employer, was instrumental in changing working conditions and thus subordinated workers. According to Özdemir and Yücesan-Özdemir (2006) an employer can determine the weekly working hours, can increase the daily work period up to 11 hours, can determine the starting hour and break times, and has the right to lay-off workers in times of crises. Job security provisions are applicable to organizations that employ 30 or more workers (previously this number was ten or more employees), leaving workers in micro-organizations outside the scope of its coverage. Similarly, in cases of dismissal the amount of compensation to be paid has been reduced to 4–8 months where formerly it was 6–12 months (Çelik, 2015). The new labour law, besides positioning work as a commodity, has weakened formal labour and its organizations (Çelik, 2015; Akçay, 2018). The government has also limited collective labour bargaining: according to OECD 2019 data, only 9.9 per cent of employees are registered with a trade union, only 8.5 per cent of employees have the right to bargain, and work councils representing employees are rare. Union density declined from 11.2 per cent in 2003 to 9.9 per cent in 2019, with the lowest percentage (6.39) in 2012 and 2013. Providing data related to public employees, Çelik (2015) suggests that the AKP has created unions that have symbiotic relationships with the party so that their operations can be controlled. For example, Memur-Sen, a pro-Islamist union for civil servants, increased its coverage by 1,586 per cent in 11 years (from 2002 to 2013) whereas the membership of KESK, a left-wing union, was reduced by 10 per cent over the same period.

In line with neo-liberal understanding, the government took drastic steps to lessen the role of the state in the economy by privatizing public services, which led to the proletarianism of public employees (Ercan and Oğuz, 2015). The consequences of this vast privatization move were two-fold: goods and services produced by state economic enterprises (SEEs) became more expensive and became a burden on the household budget; and the adoption of managerialist practices commodified the labour of public employees. With the privatization of public services in health, energy and education the price of the services produced in these industries were left to the market mechanism. These services became available to wider consumer groups but at a price that could only be acquired through consumer loans (such as for higher education) or private insurance schemes (such as for health services). Operating in line with a market logic and in an effort to reduce costs and increase revenues, these organizations introduced managerialist practices such as performance criteria, performance-based wages, specialization, flexible and contractual work. This approach had a devastating effect especially on professionals: doctors, nurses, teachers, academics, lawyers, engineers and architects were faced with being employees working in precarious conditions (Akbaş, 2013; Bahçe, 2013). Given the premises of the Labour Law (4857) they were forced to work without job security, with short-term contracts or sometimes as part of a temporary workforce – they became the precariat. These social groups that are assumed to constitute the middle class had to struggle with unemployment (Bora, 2021), devalorization and the commodification of their labour, which was mainly the outcome of the neo-liberal policies. Neo-liberal policies, by empowering big capital, marginalized white-collar workers in the economic realm and excluded them from the economic and political domain.

As discussed in detail in Chapter 6, with the pervasive implementation of neo-liberal policies, especially after 2001, the petty commodity producers were left to free-market operations. With the implementation of the Agricultural Reform Implementation Project (ARIP) that was drafted by the World Bank, the Treasury and the Ministry of Agriculture and Rural Affairs, Turkish agriculture went through a comprehensive restructuring where subsidies and support purchases by the government were revoked, parastatals and state-owned agricultural sales cooperatives were privatized, and contract farming was implemented. Consequently, the petty commodity producers lost their competitive position. Furthermore, with the dominance of big agro-food companies in food processing and packaging, small producers were driven out of agriculture and traditional farming and moved to the cities where they comprised the informal labour force situated in the *gecekondu* districts. Those who stayed in the rural areas were proletarized by the pervasive implementation of contract farming.

Food activism for repositioning the urban middle class and rural petty commodity producers

A decade after the AKP came to power in 2002, the results of the populist neo-liberal policies, which displaced the peasantry, positioned labour, especially professionals, as precariat, and provided an economic space for the rise of the big new capital, led to the dispossession of public land through mega gentrification projects. The consequent redistribution of wealth created discontent and social polarization, evidenced by the Gezi Park protests. Gezi and protests in other cities were a reaction to the AKP government that aimed to reorganize social life by instigating changes such as a prohibition on abortion, promoting the idea of three children per family, limitating entertainment (with travel restrictions) and regulating the sale of alcohol (banning the sale of alcohol between 10 pm and 6 am), while tolerating policies that caused discrimination against and violence towards women. The Gezi protestors not only objected to the interference in their lifestyles, but they also had other concerns and doubts about the violation of women's rights, urban restructuring projects, ecological disruption, populist neo-liberal policies and also capitalism (see, for example, Alonso, 2015; Çelik, 2015). The Gezi protests were not only a resistance to the commodification of a public space, but they were also against the neo-liberal, conservative regime of the government.

After the evacuation of the park by armed government forces, protests carried over to different districts of the city in 'park forums' and, as winter approached, protestors moved on to Occupy houses in the same districts. The Gezi protests, neighbourhood forums and Occupy houses provided an arena for the gathering of activist groups, collectives and citizens who were not previously involved in politics. The Gezi protests were a true test of the government's commitment to democracy and pluralism. The government's attempts to build consent through a pro-democratic, pro-growth and pro-capitalist discourse was betrayed by its own practices (Tuğal, 2016). The beginnings of the ACCs can be traced back to the Gezi protests, and their underlying values and practices were developed in the 'park forums' and Occupy houses. Furthermore, the Gezi protests provided the first opportunity for the discontents of the hegemonic neo-liberal project to convene and propagate the seeds of a counter-hegemonic struggle. Gezi had two major impacts on the rise of the ACCs: firstly, it provided an opportunity for diverse groups of people, sharing similar concerns and worldviews, to meet, interact and discuss. Secondly, participants had a chance to develop interpersonal ties without any expectation of an economic return (see, for example, Tuğal, 2013) and experience a daily life shaped by solidarity, sharing, collective work and mutuality that later shaped the dominant values of the ACCs (see, for example, Örs and Turan, 2015).

The major actors of the Gezi protests were educated, white-collar professionals who were proletarianized due to the new labour regime. They were precariat, facing labour insecurity and also a precarious social life as a consequence of the policies implemented by the government (Civelekoglu, 2015). As stated by Boratav (2013), the participants of Gezi were waged labour groups such as lawyers, engineers, architects and academics. According to Uysal (2017), 90.8 per cent of the participants earned a salary that was below the poverty line. A further survey conducted among the participants of the Caferağa and Yeldeğirmeni initiatives, which later formed one of the earliest ACCs, supports this observation. Two thirds of the participants in these initiatives were women, 77 per cent waged labour, 70 per cent were not unionized, 20 per cent were jobless and 3 per cent were self-employed. Among the waged group only a very few were blue-collar workers, and the others were teachers, academics, engineers, public relation specialists, script writers and architects, and the majority of them were not union members nor were they formally affiliated with a political party. However, nearly all of them were members of professional organizations. Many of these people had to work overtime without being paid and most of them were forced to work more than 45 hours a week, as well as at the weekend (Yılmaz et al, 2020).

Although the first ACC was formed before the Gezi protests by the academic and administrative staff of a university in İstanbul, Gezi influenced the proliferation of similar initiatives. A group of activists describe the vestiges of Gezi as: solidarity instead of competition, diversity instead of homogeneity, sharing instead of greed, respect instead of prejudice, opposition instead of oppression, participation instead of hierarchy, common spaces instead of boundaries, green instead of concrete. Moreover, as explained by a group of activists, "with the self-confidence of the Gezi protests they moved to the local so that they could go back to the centre". During this period, some of the major concerns were how to be part of the decision-making process about the common spaces of the district, how to build solidarity among various constituencies in the district and how to create a better living space for all of its inhabitants. Consequently, they organized campaigns against the governmental agencies; they aimed to rejuvenate the parks and public schools through gentrification projects, *bostans* were revived in some districts, libraries were built, and workshops were organized for improving the skills of the locals. Events were organized for rebuilding ties with the local small shop owners and minorities (Yılmaz et al, 2020). Besides being active at the local level, the activists were also interested in similar movements and developments in other areas. In this vein some local initiatives organized panels with the participation of Greek, Italian, German, Dutch and Bulgarian activists (Yılmaz et al, 2020). These interactions with the 'local' and the 'international' were instrumental in identifying a common problem and searching for solutions. Basically, it was a learning process. Gradually, a single issue – food provisioning – was identified as a problem and the experiences of the food sovereignty movement and alternative food networks were taken as examples for developing solutions.

Both movements, food sovereignty and the AFNs, aim to develop an emancipatory and inclusive political system in food provisioning, which is expected to promote justice, equality and democracy. By engaging in these movements activists expected to express their dissension with the existing economic system and the authoritarianism underlying the implementation of these policies. Engagement in these movements enabled activists to exercise their citizenship rights; to be part of a decision-making system which influences the allocation of resources and wealth and facilitates the inclusion of marginalized groups. The AFNs and the food sovereignty movement in Turkey enabled the unification of those groups who were excluded by the populist neo-liberal policies. Furthermore, by being part of these movements, activists were able to express their discontent and create a free space in which to practise their worldviews: participative decision-making, reshuffling relations between producers and consumers, giving voice to marginalized actors (for example, women, academics and civil servants whose contracts had been cancelled by the government), reworking gender relations, being autonomous and independent.

In conclusion

This chapter aimed to elaborate on how the economic decisions and political concerns of the government in Turkey influenced the emergence of the ACCs. In so doing, we have provided an explanation of how certain groups were empowered and included in the political decision-making process. The neo-liberal policies implemented after 2001 were instrumental in including both the urban poor, mainly the dispossessed small farmers, and big capital in the economic and political realm. With an unconditional commitment to the premises of neo-liberal policies, the government deliberately drafted mechanisms such as social assistance programmes and civic charity projects that enabled the inclusion of the urban poor in the political domain. The outcome of these measures, although useful in alleviating urban poverty, contributed to the problems that shaped the formal labour market and prompted the de-peasantation of petty commodity producers. Furthermore, through financialization, the indebtedness of petty commodity producers and urban households grew worse, leading to a redistribution of wealth and a dependency on the political and economic decisions of the government. On the other hand, the inclusion of big capital, especially in the construction industry supported by gentrification projects, also distanced small producers located in *bostans* from farming. The neo-liberal project was successful in including urban poor, informal labour (such as micro-entrepreneurs) and big capital in political and economic realms. However, the same project was exclusionary for rural small producers (small farmers) and urban middle class (such as white collar workers and professionals). In particular, with the changes in the labour law that legitimized flexible work, temporary work and sub-contracting, these groups were marginalized, faced economic insecurity and unemployment, and their work was devalorized.

Given this background, which underlines the role of the economic decisions and political choices made by government cadres, and which has led to inequalities in distribution, polarization in the form of inclusion / exclusion, and social fragmentation, we argue that the ACCs are spaces where excluded groups (the urban middle class and rural petty commodity producers) were able to convene around the AFNs and the food sovereignty movement. Petty commodity producers divorced from their land and means of livelihood through the implementation of the neo-liberal policies, such as the revoking of subsidies and support purchases, the privatization of agricultural sales cooperatives and contract farming, are distanced from farming, their main income activity. Similarly, the urban middle class, separated from their occupations and marginalized in the labour market through labour legislation and the privatization of state economic enterprises, are driven away from their main livelihood activity. Thus, we claim that the ACCs provide a space where these excluded groups co-opt for repositioning in the economic, social and political realms by experimenting with inclusive, solidarity-based food activism that challenges the existing power configurations.

4

The Political Economy
of Consumer Cooperatives
in Turkey

Introduction

During the last two decades, with the implementation of populist neo-liberal policies, Turkish agriculture has gone through a comprehensive restructuring which has led to economic and social transformations. Petty commodity producers have become distanced from agriculture, the peasantry has declined, and a majority of the young rural population has moved to the cities, and comprise an informal labour force. Those who stayed in the rural areas have became proletariat on their own land with the pervasive implementation of contract farming by the agro-food companies. These transformations on the production side are coupled with the food crises, namely price rises and low-quality foodstuff, in the cities. Alternative consumer cooperatives, (ACCs) with their alternative provisioning system, governance model shaped by direct democracy and a commitment to the premises of the food sovereignty movement, can provide a solution in reconfiguring the prevalent production–consumption nexus. Especially after 2013, as awareness of the social, political and economic effects of capitalism grew, we began to witness the progression of alternative cooperatives in Turkey. In the Turkish context, alternative consumer cooperatives, besides forming a site for the development of an alternative to the capitalist forms of organizing, provide a remarkable example in terms of divergence from the conventional consumer cooperatives (CCCs).

The cooperative movement in Turkey is rooted in the examples that were developed during the decline of the Ottoman Empire. These early examples provide the background to understanding the evolution of the CCCs; they were established by the deliberate efforts of statesmen in an effort to provide a solution to the problems faced by villagers. Secondly, although there were some initiatives for a cooperative model based on the example in Rochdale, their operations were terminated by the ruling party. These grassroots initiatives, shaped by the ideas of the intellectuals Mustafa Suphi, Ethem Nejat and Ahmet Cevat, were expected to by-pass the middlemen and support the consumers to be their own producer. These experiences are important in underlining the dominant role of the state and the tensions between the ruling cadres and the intellectuals, and provide an explanation of how cooperatives are instrumentalized by the state. Similar tendencies shaped the cooperative movement in the early days of the Republic; cooperatives were mainly initiated by a state-owned organization (for example, a bank or factory) with the aim of providing affordable foodstuff to their members and to control price rises. They were managed under the patronage of the founding organization in a top-down manner. During the early 1950s, with the implementation of an economic programme based on liberal policies and the capitalization of agriculture, the cooperative movement slowed down and instead the government supported the establishment of retail chains. Initially, Migros-Türk in 1954 and then Gima in 1956 were established as alternatives to consumer cooperatives. Migros, a consumer cooperative in Switzerland, was established in Turkey as a corporation owned by private individuals and a private and state bank at the special invitation of the mayor of İstanbul and the Minister of Economics and Trade (Oluç, 1954). Two years after the founding of Migros-Türk, Gima was established in Ankara with the same ownership and governance model. Towards the end of the 1960s, with the implementation of new legislation, cooperatives were defined as closed-door, that is workplace organizations strictly controlled by the state (Rehber, 2000; Bilgin and Tanıyıcı, 2008; Aksoy and Günay, 2018). The state provided various incentives to privately owned companies and unions to establish workplace cooperatives, which in turn were instrumental in building alliances for political means. During this period, two divergent and remarkable examples of consumer cooperatives were MİPAŞ and Halk-Koop, where different ownership and provisioning was implemented. In 1980 the implementation of the structural adjustment programme and the coup drastically influenced the consumer cooperatives; some cooperatives were closed down by the military regime since they were considered places of mass activity (Aysu, 2019; Ültanır, 2019; Öngel, 2020a), their assets were taken over and members were taken into custody. The final blow for consumer cooperatives was realized in 2000 with the Cooperative Act (4572), which enabled the privatization of their fixed assets and enforced the implementation of managerialism. Thus, the cooperative movement and the CCCs in Turkey, unlike other countries, have been heavily influenced by the political and economic choices of the ruling cadres and operated under the close control of governments. Except for a few divergent examples, CCCs functioned as distribution centres for overcoming supply shortages and price rises. Since they offered their services only to their members their scope was limited, and the major beneficiaries of this system were the cooperative members and the founding organization.

With the initiation of the alternative consumer cooperatives in 2008, the Turkish cooperative landscape experienced a different model of ownership, governance and surplus generation. ACCs in contrast to CCCs are founded by food activists committed to the principles of the food sovereignty movement, experimenting with a non-hierarchical governance model. They are non-profit organizations trying to create social value and are open to all. Members of the ACCs share a worldview that emphasizes freedom, autonomy, equality and justice as values and try to implement practices that will give voice to excluded groups, reshuffle the production and consumption of food provisioning, defend agricultural land from urbanization and gentrification, and regain their lost position by building communities of solidarity.

In this chapter we focus on the history of consumer cooperatives in Turkey. In so doing we aim to develop a background for contrasting conventional and alternative consumer cooperatives so that a comparison can be made and the ACCs positioned in a political and economic context. The chapter is composed of three parts: the first part describes how, drawing on the Rochdale principles, the consumer cooperatives were initiated by intellectuals during the decline of Ottoman Empire. The second part discusses the state-led cooperative movement and conventional consumer cooperatives in Turkey, and the third part explains the emergence of the ACCs, followed by a comparison of conventional and alternative cooperatives in Turkey. In each part, after discussing the local consumer cooperative movement, a comparison with movements in other countries is provided.

The Ottoman period

Early examples

The earliest examples of cooperatives in the Ottoman Empire date back to 1863 when Mithat Paşa, the mayor of Niš, established the first Memleket Sandık (The National Vault). Seeing the success of the first example, Mithat Paşa later drafted a statute and presented it for the approval of the government (Fındıkoğlu, 1967). In 1867, after the approval of the statute, the establishment of a Memleket Sandık was delegated to the mayors of the Empire (Mülayim, 1999). Memleket Sandık was a combination of producer and credit cooperatives (Mülayim, 1999; Kocabaş, 2003; Bilgin and Tanıyıcı, 2008). Initially, the project was shaped around collective work and collective production. Financial resources were provided in the form of credit. Accordingly, based on the *imece* tradition (a system for collective production and revenue generation), villagers worked together (planted, harvested, built irrigation systems) on the state-owned land, and the yield was collectively transported to towns and sold under the supervision of the government officials. After reaching a specific amount of capital (two hundred gold Ottoman lira) and becoming financially strong, a Sandık ('homeland funds' – the first financial organization founded and operated by the state for supporting producers of agricultural products) was entitled to give short-term credit with a low interest rate to the villagers (Mülayim, 1999). In this way it was expected that the exploitation of the villagers by usurers would be avoided. However, over time, the *imece* system was replaced by a taxation scheme due to incidences of exploitation of less powerful members of the village by those more influential villagers (Mülayim, 1999).

A typical Memleket Sandık was managed by four unpaid staff who were chosen through a majority vote by the locals. The only paid staff member was an appointed accountant. The statute defined an upper limit for the expenses of each Sandık. The major revenue sources were interest collected and a once-only fee charged for joining the Sandık. On a yearly basis a committee was established for the evaluation of the financial statements and the distribution of the profits. The committee was comprised of the local officials, Sandık managers and prominent residents of the town, and was chaired by the highest government official within the estate. One third of the profits were distributed to the members and the other two thirds were used for the construction of schools, roads and water systems (Mülayim, 1999). In 1883, two decades after their establishment, and in response to the problems encountered (inability to collect debts, deficiency of capital, lack of auditing), major changes were made in the management and financial structure of the Memleket Sandık. In order to solve the problems related to capital accumulation Aşar (a tax in the Ottoman empire), taxes taken from the villagers were increased. The rationale for this was explained as the need to increase the benefit for the public, and the name Memleket Sandık was changed to Menafi Sandık (organizations for the public benefit) and their governance was taken over by the state. Five years later, in 1888, all the Menafi Sandıks were closed, and their functions were assumed by a state-owned bank, Ziraat Bankası (Agricultural Bank) (Fındıkoğlu, 1967).

Although the Raiffeisen cooperatives were founded around the same time as the Memleket Sandık, there is no evidence about the possible influence of the Raiffeisens on the formation of Memlekt Sandık. In one of the most comprehensive studies on the sociology of cooperatives, Fındıkoğlu (1967) asserts that due to local social conditions (for example, the absence of a bourgeoisie class) it is evident that cooperative movements (such as Raiffeisen) in different countries could not be transferred and realized in the Ottoman Empire. In a recent study, Soydemir and Erçek (2022) develop the argument that 'the organizational configurations and normative aspirations' of Raiffesisens and Memleket Sandıks 'significantly diverged due to contextual differences' (p 18). Both of these rural and agricultural credit cooperatives were established by public servants in order to help small farmers overcome their problems relating to the provision of financial resources. Both of them identified debts to the usurers as a major problem for the villagers. The Memleket Sandık and Raiffeisen cooperatives were expected to be instrumental in combatting the dominance of the usurers by relying on the principle of self-help, where rural people, by utilizing their own capacities, could develop a new credit system. Frederick Wilhelm Raiffeisen claimed that by strengthening the village community through solidarity, it would be possible to overcome poverty and lessen the financial burden on the small farmers (Fairbairn, 2017). Mithat Paşa's initial model additionally depended on solidarity in production and the *imece* system. The scale of operations in both cases was limited to a specific rural area, in the case of Sandık to an estate and in the case of Raiffeisen to a local parish. In terms of governance both cooperatives showed similarities. In Raiffeisen cooperatives, and in line with the legal requirements of the local cooperative law, two different bodies existed for administrative purposes: a management committee for daily operations and a supervisory committee (Prinz, 2002). The management committee evaluated loan applications and the supervisory committee, on a quarterly basis, assessed the management (Goglio and Leonardi, 2010). Similarly, Memleket Sandık were governed by two bodies with similar responsibilities, as previously noted.

The major difference between the Memleket Sandık and Raiffeisen cooperatives was related to the capital accumulation and surplus distribution. In Raiffeissen cooperatives the capital was secured by loans from the banks and individuals, whereas in Sandık, at least in the earlier period, capital was accumulated by the collective work of villagers (Mülayim, 1999). Accordingly, Memleket Sandık was a cooperative that can be classified as a producer and a credit cooperative. In the case of Raiffeisen profits were not distributed to the members but reserved in an 'indivisible fund' which was allocated for charitable purposes, such as schools or support for the elderly (Prinz, 2002), and as a guarantee for capital borrowings (Goglio and Leonardi, 2010). In the case of Memleket Sandık, a specific percentage of the profits were distributed to the members.

The interest in *consumer* cooperatives in Turkey initially appeared in 1900 when the governor of İzmir, Kamil Paşa, took steps to organize collectively owned 'village grocers' to combat the power of grocers owned by individuals. In so doing, it was expected that peasants would be protected from itinerant traders, peddlers and usurers who used to sell on credit with high interest rates. The idea of village grocers was announced in a local newspaper, *Ahenk*, alongside a questionnaire and a competition; readers were asked to develop ideas that could be useful for the development of these grocers (Arıkan, 1989; Kocabaş, 2003). These initiatives were named Teavün Şirket (solidarity company), but in later years the term cooperative was used. Various articles sent to the newspaper explained how the existing individually owned grocers charged high prices and exacted high interest rates (a 100 per cent interest rate was charged for sales on credit) for essential items and how this system led to the poverty of the villagers. As a solution it was proposed that villagers could collectively form a Teavün Şirket, a consumption cooperative that would compete with the existing grocers (Arıkan, 1989). Some of these articles stressed that managing such a cooperative venture required know-how and business knowledge, and thus there should be schools in the villages for the education of the younger generations. These early examples of the cooperative movement were useful in raising awareness among the villagers and drafting the scope of possible consumer cooperatives (Bilgin and Tanıyıcı, 2008; Arıkan, 1989).

The Second Constitution period (1908–18)

A more comprehensive approach that also incorporated the philosophy of consumer cooperatives in the Ottoman Empire was seen after 1908 (Fındıkoğlu, 1967), with the proclamation of the Second Constitution. In the following years, intellectuals who had fled the country because of their political standing against the authoritarianism of the Sultan returned to İstanbul and shared their experiences and observations on cooperatives. Between 1908 and 1918, the intellectual background for consumer cooperatives was provided by Ethem Nejat, Mustafa Suphi and Ahmed Cevat (Emre), socialist intellectuals who moved to the Left during the First World War. In 1920 Mustafa Suphi established the Turkish Communist Party and Ethem Nejat was the General Secretary of this party (Kardam, 2020). Sharing similar political concerns and being in opposition to the ruling party, they advocated a political system where local organizations with the involvement of workers would directly participate in the political decision-making process. In line with their ideas and initiatives during this period, consumer cooperatives functioning in line with the principles of the Rochdale cooperatives were established in the Ottoman Empire. Most of these cooperatives were in İstanbul and local consumers had a dominant role in their founding (Toprak, 1995). Although the cooperative movement of this period was influenced by the Rochdale example, the social, economic and political conditions that promoted them were different.

The 1908 constitutional revolution or the 'Young Turk Revolution' in the Ottoman Empire brought a change in the political regime. As a response to the deep-rooted state intervention in the economic realm and its negative outcomes in terms of intrigues, peculation and inefficiency, the Young Turk movement favoured a liberal economy, decentralization and individual initiative. The patrimonial, interventionist and centralized state role needed to be replaced by a state that would strengthen the economic structure and provide a milieu for individual initiative (Toprak, 1995). Between 1908 and 1912, the Empire enjoyed a pluralistic liberal period: unions and associations were established, the labour movement became visible, boycotts were organized, and the first feminist movement started. Specifically, after the abandonment of the guild system, small producers, mainly of Muslim origin, lost their economic power within the free trade system. The Muslim Ottoman small producers were less educated, lacked capital and shared a mentality that was against competition. As will be explained in the following paragraphs, the Ottoman intellectuals who proposed cooperatives as part of an alternative economic model stressed the need for education in trade and agriculture and saw cooperatives as a means for capital accumulation for the small producers.

The 1914 crises in Europe had severe impacts on the Ottoman Empire. Young Turks, by imposing various control mechanisms, impeded the operations of organizations owned by foreigners; the İstanbul and İzmir bourses that were controlled by foreigners were closed, shipping companies suspended their services and insurance companies either did not insure or charged high premiums. Consequently, prices, especially food prices, increased dramatically and shortages increased (Ahmad, 1968). The government started to import essential items such as sugar (from Austria) and wheat (from Romania) and the efforts of the government to regulate prices and block hoarding were insufficient. During this period urban consumers and peasants suffered the most: the consumers paid high prices for low-quality products and a new class of tradesmen (named as merchants of 1916 or 332 tüccarı), profiteering from the extreme war conditions, emerged (Ahmad, 1968; 1988). The peasantry was conscripted, their animals were seized by the government for the war and thus there was a shortage of labour, productive assets and land for cultivation. Once again these conditions affected mostly the petty commodity producers, and a new class of 'middle peasants', benefiting from drastic price increases, emerged. Given these conditions, the Young Turks, who aimed to create a capitalist economy through free enterprise and individual initiative, revised their policy and the state started to intervene in various aspects of social and economic activity. The ruling party Ittihad ve Terakki, adhering to the German example pioneered by Friedrich List, recognized the need for state intervention in the economic and social realm and developed a new economic model 'Devlet İktisadiyatı' (State Economy) which was state capitalism (Ahmad, 1968; Toprak, 1995; Ahmad, 2008). The emergence of consumer cooperatives during the First World War was inspired by the Rochdale principles and shaped by the ideals of a national economy, empowerment of the small peasantry and protection of urban consumers. As will be explained in the following paragraphs, the intellectuals who were actively involved in the development of these cooperatives envisioned them not only as an economic tool but also as a means to restructure the society.

Imprints of the Rochdale movement

One of the earliest writers on consumer cooperatives was Ethem Nejat, an authority on education and a contributor to the Ottoman National Economy School. In contrast to the other members of this school, Ethem Nejat emphasized the role of agriculture and trade rather than industrialization on the road to economic progress (Erkek, 2010; Özveren et al, 2016). His writings in *Toprak* (Earth), a rural magazine, and *Osmanlı Ziraat ve Ticaret Gazetesi* (Ottoman Agriculture and Trade Newspaper) supported the idea that development should begin in the village and, for that, villagers had to be trained, rural elementary schools had to be opened and teachers had to be trained according to the needs of agriculture. Another problem mentioned by Ethem Nejat was related to the absence of national corporations due to the lack of capital accumulation (Toprak, 1995). Ethem claimed that the cooperative companies, where owners were the customers, could be instrumental in overcoming capital shortages in the Ottoman Empire (Erkek, 2010; Özveren et al, 2016; Dural, 2017). Given the economic conditions, capital shortages and the moral grounds of the Empire, these cooperatives would provide tailor-made solutions for the locals (Erkek, 2010). In 1908 local people started to form 'district companies' that were considered examples of consumer cooperatives (Toprak, 1995). These cooperatives were similar to grocers and their functions were limited to a district. However, in an effort to develop a framework for economic development, Ethem Nejat, in his writings, asserted that these initiatives should extend their scope by getting involved in the production of the things they sold, and also that district cooperatives in close proximity to each other should merge their activities in order to increase the scale of thir activities (Toprak, 1995).

During the same period, another intellectual, Mustafa Suphi, was influenced by publications about the cooperative movement by the French economist Charles Gide and claimed that a more humane capitalism could only be attained by the betterment of both the working and living conditions of the workers through a social security system, by the development of an agricultural system that would empower the peasantry and by the establishment of cooperatives. Earlier in his career, Mustafa Suphi stated this position in the programme of the political party Milli Meşrutiyet Fırkası, of which he was one of the founders. The programme stated that villagers, small farmers and artisans should be supported through government subsidies and legislation, and cooperatives should be immediately established in villages (Suphi, 2021, p 1). Accordingly, as recounted by Kocabaş (2011), with the cooperation of villagers and small producers, the Tesai Cemiyeti (Society

Cooperatives) for production and consumption were established. One of the major goals of these cooperatives was to distribute profits to the producers and it was expected that the disparity between small producers and big capital holders would be minimized. By having a shop where they could sell their own goods, these cooperatives could bypass the grocers and middlemen and their profits would be given to the participants in the cooperative. Mustafa Suphi was one of the first people to criticize the individual entrepreneur concept favoured by Ottoman liberals (Toprak, 1995); he believed that the Ottomans lacked not only the individual entrepreneurial capacities but also collective entrepreneurial capacities as well. He claimed that individual entrepreneurship could tilt social equilibrium and only cooperatives (Tesai Cemiyetleri) formed by workers and small producers could redress the imbalance in wealth distribution (Toprak, 1995). The Samsun Kardaşlar Istihlak Şirketi (Samsun Brotherhood Consumption Company) was one of the earliest examples of a consumer cooperative (Toprak, 1995) established to eliminate the middleman.

During the same period, Ahmed Cevat (later, in the Turkish Republic he took Emre as his family name), a lecturer of linguistics at the Darülfünûn (University of İstanbul) and an intellectual who joined the leftist movement, promoted the idea of consumer cooperatives based on the Rochdale principles. His book İktisatta İnkılâp: İstihlak Teavün Şirketleri (Revolution in Economics: Consumption and Solidarity Companies) was published in 1913 after his visit to the Rochdale cooperatives in England (Ahmet Cevat Emre, 1960) and is considered to be the first local book on cooperatives (Fındıkoğlu, 1967; Toprak, 1995; Kocabaş, 2003). The book provides examples from different countries based on the author's observations. The major ideas developed in the book are centred around the idea that the power struggle between labour and the owners of capital can only be resolved by cooperatives. Ahmed Cevat believed that cooperatives represented an economic revolution where the problems stemming from private ownership would be resolved. According to him, cooperatives would avoid the middleman and enable consumers to be their own producer and tradesman (Ahmet Cevat Emre, 1960); by forming an alliance among district cooperatives and purchasing directly from the producer, the middleman would be bypassed, prices would be reduced and economic stability would be established (Fındıkoğlu, 1967; Toprak, 1995). Ahmed Cevat considered cooperatives to be an alternative development tool that was different to the liberal and socialist economic development models. Similarly, he perceived cooperatives as a way forward for nationalization: during this period most of the big companies in the Empire were owned by foreigners and the Ottomans lacked capital for establishing corporations, so cooperatives (for production, consumption, housing and credit) could be a solution for capital accumulation.

The ideas of the Rochdale movement attracted the interest of other intellectuals as well: in 1914 Cemal Bey drafted the first cooperative law (Kooperatif Şirketler Kanunu Layihası ve Esbab-ı Mucibesi), İsmail Rıfkı Bey prepared a collection of papers about cooperatives in other countries and, under the leadership of Aynizade Hasan Tahsin, an association for promoting cooperatives *(Kooperatifçilik Cemiyeti)* was established (Kocabaş, 2011). The goal of the association was to restructure the economic system and make cooperatives an integral part of the economy; in order to publicize this idea, courses were to be designed and books were to be published. All professors and teachers were taken on as members of the association with the expectation that special lectures and courses on cooperatives would be incorporated into the curricula. The first legal draft aimed to ensure that (1) consumer cooperatives would eventually also be involved in production, (2) capital should be collectively accrued, (3) the cost of products sold should be minimal, (4) an organization for collective purchasing should be formed, and (5) involved parties should be trained and educated (Fındıkoğlu, 1967).

In line with these developments, in 1914, under the leadership of Ahmed Cevat, consumer cooperatives in three different districts of İstanbul were established (Ahmet Cevat Emre, 1960). Ahmet Cevat (1960) in his book *İki Neslin Tarihi (History of Two Generations)* provides some information about these cooperatives and the way they were initiated:

> I thought that Fatih [a district in İstanbul] would be the best location for a consumer cooperative. I visited the coffee houses, talked with some retired army officers, and then delivered lectures about the cooperatives in England to the men and women living in the district. During the third lecture I explained how this could work in Fatih and we started the first cooperative. The shop was not on the main street, but we were careful to choose a place with a modest rent. From among the partners, five people (retired officers and civil servants) were elected as the management committee. They worked on a voluntary basis. A member volunteered for bookkeeping. Paid staff were the cashier and a shop helper. Goods were purchased from the wholesalers and items which were not in demand in the district were not sold. (p 179)

All Ottoman citizens had the right to have a share in these cooperatives, and shares were distributed on a personal basis and could be acquired in instalments which had to be paid within a year. A month later, in the same way, with the participation of the locals, the second (in Karaköy) and then the third cooperative (in Unkapanı) were established. However, given the war conditions, İttihad ve Terakki, the ruling party, resumed the responsibility for the development and structuring of these cooperatives (Toprak, 1995). Ahmet Cevat was called to a meeting by the party where it was declared that his role would be confined to delivering lectures on consumer cooperatives and the cooperatives themselves would be established by the party (Ahmet Cevat Emre, 1960). The first three cooperatives founded and operating in line with the Rochdale example were closed down and, under the patronage of the state with huge investments and in collaboration with a few tradesmen, ten consumer cooperatives in different districts of İstanbul were established (Ahmet Cevat Emre, 1960). However, these state-instigated cooperatives ran at a loss and soon disappeared from the economic realm. This intervention reduced the functioning of the cooperatives to that of being merely distribution centres under the patronage of the state and exemplified exactly the opposite of what of a Rochdale cooperative should have been (Fındıkoğlu, 1967).

By 1918, İstanbul cooperatives that were structured in a top-down manner by the state had approximately 8,243 members and similar consumer cooperatives were established in other cities (Izmir, Çarşamba and Lazkiye) (Toprak, 1995). These cooperatives were useful in providing cheap food to their members and in cooperation with the Ministry of Nutrition (Beslenme Bakanlığı) some rationed foodstuff and kerosene was distributed through their stores. As well as these cooperatives owned by locals and serving the locals, some ministries and companies established consumer cooperatives for their officials. Nonetheless, by 1919 all these consumer cooperatives were closed (Bilgin and Tanıyıcı, 2008). Fındıkoğlu (1967) mentions the Memurin Erzak Kooperatifi, founded in 1921 in İstanbul during the armistice period. The founders of this cooperative also drafted a set of rules for its operations that were designed in line with examples in Europe.

The examples of consumer cooperatives during the Ottoman era were inspired and initiated by intellectuals who were influenced by the ideas of Charles Gide on co-operation and Friedrich List on economic nationalism. Being against a liberal economy they visualized consumer cooperatives organized around the Rochdale Principles as an antidote to the economic problems faced by peasants and small business owners (Bilgin and Tanıyıcı, 2008; Kocabaş, 2011). The major concern was to strengthen the local economy and empower local producers who had lost out because of the competition from foreign importers and overseas companies. Given the conditions in the Ottoman Empire, the lack of a working class and bourgeoisie, and the capital accumulation by the locals and people educated in agriculture and trade, the cooperative movement was led by a group of intellectuals who envisioned cooperatives designed in line with the Rochdale example as a means to a more humane capitalism. They provided the economic, legal and ideological basis for the cooperative movement and tried to mobilize younger generations and peasants through their writings and lectures. They were able to practise their ideals: the consumer cooperatives established during the First World War were initiated by them around their vision. However, in later years with the intervention of the ruling party, İttihad ve Terakki, consumer cooperatives turned out to be distribution centres operating under the patronage of big tradesman (Fındıkoğlu, 1967). Despite the efforts of Ethem Nejat, Mustafa Suphi and Ahmet Cevat, who envisioned an economic development based on agriculture and the mobilization of the peasants, the cooperative movement of the 1908–18 period was instrumental in empowering Turkish-Muslim tradesmen. Toprak (1995) and Ahmad (2008) explain this process as the emergence of a state-initiated national bourgeoisie who later would become influential during the Republican period. Especially in the western parts of the country, by organizing producers around cooperatives, the capital accumulation of local big tradesman was secured. The emergence of a state-promoted tradesman class did not lead to the development of the working class since this new class was involved in value creation by marketing (Keyder, 1993). Consequently, the cooperative movement of this period was not a grassroots movement and was different from the Rochdale-type cooperatives in the UK, USA and Australia (see, for example, Fairbairn, 1994; Knupfer, 2013; Patmore and Balnave, 2018). The Ottoman consumer cooperatives were not initiated by the working class, as they were unable to bypass the middleman and connect urban consumers with rural petty commodity producers.

The consumer cooperatives in Turkey

The state-led cooperative model

With the fall of the Ottoman Empire and the demise of the consumer cooperatives based on the Rochdale principles, the cooperative movement in Turkey was dominated by the state and cooperatives became a political instrument and an economic device. The first consumer cooperative in the early days of the Republic was Ankara Memurları Istihlak Kooperatifi, which was established in 1924–25 in İstanbul for the civil servants and was under the leadership of the government, which paid their partnership fees by giving them a premium (equal to half of his/her salary) (Polat and Tayanç, 1973; Mülayim, 1982). Mustafa Kemal Atatürk and İsmet İnönü (the then prime minister) were the first members of this cooperative. Because of the high demand, the cooperative opened branches in different districts of the city but due to problems related to mismanagement these branches were closed after 1944 and only the headquarters survived until 1950 (Polat and Tayanç, 1973). In subsequent years, similar cooperatives were established in İstanbul, Denizli, Eskişehir, Burdur and Antalya. The two cooperatives established in İstanbul provide an example of the member recruitment and management of the cooperative movement of this period. These cooperatives were established by the municipality for its officers; the first one was unsuccessful, and its members (officers) were forced to pay its debts in instalments which were deducted from their salaries. The second cooperative was established in 1942 and all the civil servants employed by the government were forced to beome members and pay the partnership fees (Fındıkoğlu, 1967). During the same period, in addition to the government and municipality cooperatives, some state-owned companies (for example, Ziraat Bankası, Cumhuriyet Merkez Bankası, Devlet Demir Yolları, Elektrik ve Havagazı İşletmesi, Bakırköy Mensucat and Merinos), operating in the banking industry, railway transportation, utilities and various industrial sectors, established consumer cooperatives for their employees (Fındıkoğlu, 1967). In the late 1940s, Gerard Kessler, studying labour conditions in the Karabük coal basin, mentions a consumer cooperative with 700 partners selling foodstuff and clothing (Kessler, 1948). For Kessler, this cooperative, like others in Turkey, was far from being based on the Rochdale model. The cooperative could not scale-up or serve non-members, partnership fees were very low, pricing of the commodities sold was not done according to market conditions and it did not distribute dividends (Kessler, 1948).

With the initiation of these types of consumer cooperatives, the Turkish cooperative movement shows a divergence from the Rochdale example in its aims, governance, member recruitment, operations and financing. The aim of these state-initiated consumer cooperatives was to provide low-cost items to their members, but none of them were involved in production. Thus, they can be taken as distribution centres for foodstuff and clothing. Especially during the Second World War, the major operation of these cooperatives was limited to the distribution of scarce commodities to their members under the patronage of the state. Consequently, cooperatives were able to profiteer (Fındıkoğlu, 1967),[1] the government was able to establish an alliance base, and urban consumers (civil servants and officers) were able to obtain essential items. These cooperatives were considered 'closed-door' or 'workplace' cooperatives that served only those members who worked in a specific organization (Fındıkoğlu, 1967; Polat and Tayanç, 1973). In some cases, employees were forced to be members and over time the quality and quantity of the products offered declined. They were managed in a top-down manner by the organization (for example, the bank, the factory, the municipality) that owned and initiated the cooperative. They were under the patronage of the founding organization. This patronage was exercised in two ways: first, the founding organization supported the cooperative with credit that had to be used to purchase the products to be sold, and which and later had to be repaid in instalments; second, the products produced by the company (for example, clothing, foodstuff) were sold to the members of the cooperative, that is, the workers of the same company (Fındıkoğlu, 1967). Evidently, the major beneficiary of this system was the organization supporting the cooperative; they developed their loyal customer base, promoted a feeling of belonging among their workers and gained a financial return. One exception to these organization-owned, 'closed-door' cooperatives was Demirtepe Halk Istihlak Kooperatifi that was established in 1942 in one of the districts of Ankara (Polat and Tayanç, 1973). Most of the partners were high-level officials, parliament members and academics and partnership was open to all the citizens living in Ankara. After the Second World War, most of the partners claimed that there were no longer shortages and started to leave the cooperative, and eventually the cooperative was closed in 1950.

The cooperative movement lost its momentum after the period 1950–60, in line with the policies of economic liberalization; consumer cooperatives, which functioned as distribution centres for the government, lost their importance for consumers and government support for essential items such as gasoline and food items was withdrawn. In the political realm, after 1945 a multi-party system was adopted and in the 1950 elections the opposition party, the Democrat Party (DP), took over. The ruling party decided to implement an economic development programme based on liberal policies and aimed to create a commercial and industrial bourgeoisie (Ahmad, 2008). In so doing, measures for an inflow of foreign capital and aid were drafted: some of this foreign aid, provided by the Marshall Plan, was used for constructing highways and roads, agriculture was supported by credit and a market for consumer goods was created. The government had lost its enthusiasm for cooperatives, and instead, with the establishment of Migros-Türk in 1954 (Oluç, 1954; Martin et al, 2013) and the founding of Gima, a state-owned national supermarket in Ankara, in 1956 (Akdoğan et al, 2020), alternatives to consumer cooperatives were created. For the founding of Migros-Türk, the İstanbul municipality, supported by the mayor, contacted the Swiss retail cooperative Migros, and funding was secured by a state-owned bank (Ziraat Bank) and a private bank (Yapı Kredi). Migros, different from the Swiss model which was a cooperative, was established as a joint venture between public and private partners and assumed the legal status of a corporation in Turkey (Oluç, 1954; Franz et al, 2013). This model was followed by another retail chain, Gima, which was established in 1956 through the partnership of Ziraat Bank, the Turkish Grain Board and an insurance company (Franz et al, 2013). Although the cooperative movement slowed down, cooperatives were on the agenda of the state: new legislation was drafted in 1969; a report by a foreign expert was prepared (Memioğlu, 2017);[2] Türk Kooperatifçilik Kurumu (Turkish Cooperative Association) organized congresses on a regular basis; and from 1963 onwards every National Plan stated the importance of cooperatives in the national economy.[3] The 1969 Cooperative Act (1163) contained proposals relating to the unification of consumer cooperatives through a higher organization and solutions for financing and auditing the cooperatives. However, these proposals were not implemented. The 1969 legislation defined consumer cooperatives as 'closed-door', 'workplace' organizations (Polat and Tayanç, 1973). Consequently, consumer cooperatives became reliant on the government office or the private company that initiated them and led to deepening state intervention in their governance. In other words, the state had a dominant role in financing, governing and controlling the cooperatives (Rehber, 2000; Bilgin and Tanıyıcı, 2008; Aksoy and Günay, 2018). Although the political orientation of the ruling parties has changed over time, cooperatives in Turkey have been managed under the strict supervision of the government. Various incentives – payment of partnership fees, subsidies, price support – were provided to the companies, public organizations and labour unions that established cooperatives. These incentives, in the long run, have been instrumental in building alliances with business circles, farmers and union leaders in return for support in elections.

Deviations from the state-led cooperative model

One remarkable example of a consumer cooperative is Maden İş Sendikası İşçi Pazarı (MİPAŞ – The Workers' Bazaar) established by the labour union T. Maden İş in the late 1970s (Öngel, 2020a). Between 1974 and 1977 only a small shop in the union building in Pendik was in operation, but later, in 1979, three big shops, two in the Silahtarağa and Pendik districts of İstanbul and one in the mining town of Ereğli, were established. To combat price rises these shops offered a variety of items – clothing, meat, vegetables, kitchen utensils, household appliances and electronics. MİPAŞ, which was owned by the union, was different than the previously described cooperatives: the prices were controlled by bypassing the middlemen and most of the foodstuff sold was cultivated by MİTES, another producer cooperative owned by T. Maden-İş. Similarly, ready-made clothes sold in the Workers' Bazaar were produced by a company owned by the union (Öngel, 2020a). As well as establishing its own cooperative and shops, T. Maden-İş promoted the establishment of workplace consumer cooperatives in factories (for example, in the Philips and Altın Zincir factories) and neighbourhood cooperatives in various districts of İstanbul (Kuştepe, Sanayi Mahallesi and Levent), which were characterized by a dense worker population. These consumer cooperatives operated in a similar manner: items sold in their shops were provided by the union's producer cooperative and if the demand for a specific item was high they arranged for nearby farmers to produce the foodstuff. Besides their members they served the local people as well (Öngel, 2020a).

Another divergent example is the Halk-Koop (Peoples' Coop), which was initiated by the TKP (the Communist Party of Turkey). At that time, the party was not recognized as a legal organization (Babalık, 2003) and documented information about the Halk-Koop experience is limited. However, there are still a few cooperative members who witnessed its establishment and the scope of its operations. Thus, in this part of the chapter we rely on the notes that were taken during our interviews. In 1973, the party cadres decided to expand their operations into neighbourhoods in cities, mainly in İstanbul, by establishing consumer cooperatives. The TKP considered cooperatives as an instrument with which to contact local people by means of their basic needs. All the people living in a specific neighbourhood were accepted as partners. Consequently, between 1976 and 1978 numerous Halk-Koops were established in İstanbul and many other cities. Each Halk-Koop was an independent legal entity with at least 500 partners who paid 1,000 Turkish lira as a partnership fee, which was used as the seed capital (interview notes). At the end of the fiscal year, instead of distributing dividends of 5 per cent of the profits to their partners, as conventional cooperatives did, Halk-Koops usually distributed products sold in the cooperative. The cooperatives were run by professional staff who were mainly trained by party members. Although the party did not have the majority of seats on cooperative boards, they were able to control the operations of the cooperatives by means of these appointed professionals.

Halk-Koop scaled-up in a short period of time. Within two years, as the number of cooperatives in İstanbul increased, they also established a union in the Marmara region. Moreover, there were many cooperatives in other cities as well. Halk-Koops worked in cooperation with Köy-Koop, which supplied most of the food items such as olives, olive oil and cheese at a reasonable price, sometimes at even half of the market value. However, they were also selling items other than food, such as light-bulbs and soap. During 1977–78, many household items, including oil and other products, were provided by the black market. The aim of Halk-Koop was to circumvent the 'black marketeers'. The party used its relationships with labour unions to supply some products to the cooperative shops, for example, Unilever workers helped them with the supply of margarine. Also, DİSK (Confederation of Progressive Trade Unions) supported Halk-Koop by providing it with assets, such as a union building (Durukanoğlu, 2019). The union cooperative MİPAŞ supported Halk-Koops by delivering some of its stock and some other products were provided directly from producers. As Halk-Koops scaled-up, their credibility among industrial producers increased and in return they were able to forward buy and sell in cash.

In the 1980s two events drastically influenced the consumer cooperative movement in Turkey: the 1980 coup and the structural adjustments programmes initiated by the Özal government. The military regime that came to power in 1980, besides banning all political activity, closed down some cooperatives as they were considered places promoting mass activity (Ültanır, 2019). For example, the MİPAŞ consumer cooperative was closed down and the facilities of MİTES were taken over (Öngel, 2020a).

Köy-Koop, initiated in the mid-1960s to develop agriculture and support farmers, was closed and managers of the cooperative were arrested (Aysu, 2019). Likewise, in April–May 1981, members of Halk-Koop were taken into custody and interrogated. One of the witnesses from this time stated that, "I was taken into custody; they asked me: why did you establish a cooperative? How do you earn a living?" The police did not find any criminal evidence and in the end nobody was arrested. After three years all of the Halk-Koops had disappeared. Similarly, TARKO, the higher organization that coordinated cooperatives that sold agricultural products, was also closed down (Rehber, 2011; Aysu, 2019). Instead, the government instrumentalized these cooperatives to determine purchasing prices, the sales prices of agricultural products and the allocation of sales revenues (Aysu, 2019). These activities were carried out under the patronage of the government, and representatives from two government offices (Ministry of Industry and Trade and Undersecretariat of Treasury and Foreign Trade) and a state-owned bank (Ziraat Bank) were appointed on a temporary basis to oversee the purchasing and sale of the agricultural products (Aysu, 2019). The 1982 Constitution (article 171) stated that cooperatives were under the strict supervision and control of the state and could not be involved in politics or cooperate with political parties (Ültanır, 2019). Later in 1995 this article was changed, and cooperatives, in line with full-blown neo-liberal policies, became targets for privatization and the domains of managerialism. With changes to the Union Law (2821) in 1983, the relationship between the labour unions and cooperatives was limited – unions could support the formation of a cooperative for their own members with credit that was no more than 10 per cent of their current assets (Öngel, 2020b).

The disruption of the cooperative movement

The major transformation of the CCCs in Turkey was realized in 2000. The coalition government of the Democratic Left Party (DSP), the Nationalist Movement Party (MHP) and the Motherland Party (ANAP) passed a new law (Act 4572), that enabled the privatization of the fixed assets and marketing departments of cooperatives involved in the sale of agricultural products. The legislation had been on the agenda of previous governments: in 1985, 1991 and 1993 governments who adhered to different political ideologies worked on the legislation but were not able to realize it. The aim of the law was to develop mechanisms for the efficient and productive operations of the cooperatives and a restructuring committee was created, composed of three members from the Ministry of Industry and Trade, three members from the Directorate of Treasury and one member from the association of cooperatives (this member was to be proposed by the Ministry of Industry and Trade and approved by the cabinet) (Aysu, 2019). With this legislation, farmers were left out of the decision-making process and cooperatives drifted away from their real functions (Aysu, 2019). The production and marketing units of the cooperatives assumed corporation status and, later, shares in these corporations were sold to private companies. With this legislative change, conventional cooperatives were to be governed in line with the principles of managerialism. In the following years, unprofitable assets such as production facilities, buildings and land were sold to private companies and workers were laid off. Governance of the cooperatives was left to professional managers, usually appointed by the government, and decisions were made by these managers rather than by the cooperative partners. Cooperatives retained their character as political instruments, as all practices were carried out with a partisan attitude. After the year 2000, as well as the cooperatives owned by farmers, union cooperatives were also passivized. With legislation (Act 6356) passed in 2012, the formation of cooperatives by labour unions was deliberately neglected and instead they were allowed to invest up to 40 per cent of their equity in companies involved in trade and industrial activity (Öngel, 2020b).

The emergence of alternative consumer cooperatives

From the mid-2020s onwards, and especially after the Gezi Park protests in 2013, a different type of cooperative movement gained momentum in Turkey: the alternative consumer cooperatives. The emergence of alternative cooperatives can be explained in relation to the impoverishment of the CCCs, the dominance of agro-food companies in the production and distribution of agricultural products, the dissolution of peasantry and traditional farming, the unconditional commitment to neo-liberal and managerialist policies by the government in various aspects of the economic realm, but especially in agriculture, and the rise in awareness of ecologically grown (free of pesticides, the utilization of heirloom seeds) foodstuff. Furthermore, during the Gezi Park protests and the forums that followed, it was seen that 'another way is possible', 'solidarity' can be built among various constituencies, and things can be 'changed'. An alternative food provisioning system, shaped by the solidaristic hopes of citizens, sensitive to safe, ecological food, an urban middle class comprised of white-collar workers and professionals, and petty commodity producers, excluded from the political and economic realm by the hegemonic neo-liberal policies, could be experimented with in an attempt to transform the prevailing food provisioning system. The ACCs, embedded in alternative food networks and positioned in the food sovereignty movement, arose with the assertion that they are grassroots organizations that experiment with an alternative governance and surplus generation model.

Various actors have been influential in the emergence of the ACCs. One of these actors is Çiftçi-Sen (Confederation of Farmer's Union), a member of La Via Campesina and European Coordination Via Campesina (ECVC), a regional organization. After a four-year-long legal struggle, Çiftçi-Sen was established in 2008 (Karakaya, 2016) to promote agroecology and family farming. The union opposes the marketization of agriculture and neo-liberal policies (Çalışkan, 2008) and is a devoted follower of food sovereignty principles. Çifti-Sen played a key role in forming alternative food initiatives and consumer cooperatives. Another organization that promotes collaboration between farmers, political parties, consumer organizations and urbanites is the GDO Karşıtı Platform (Anti-GMO Platform) (Kocagöz, 2018).

Furthermore, consumer-led ecological food initiatives, such as EkoHarita and Buğday Derneği, have contributed to the emergence and expansion of the ACCs. With their knowledge and know-how on food production, the members of these initiatives have been influential in promoting awareness on the side of the consumers and supporting small producers by sharing their experiences in agriculture (Al, 2020; Atalan-Helicke and Abiral, 2021). Also, a producer cooperative, Kibele Ekolojik Yaşam, assumed a leading role in the initial phases of the alternative cooperatives. Kibele was a cooperative founded by small farmers involved in ecological production. On the consumer side, Tohum-İzi Derneği, an association aiming to bridge producer cooperatives with consumer cooperatives, had a leading role in forming and shaping the ACCs. The primary concern in the early days of the alternative cooperative movement was to bridge the gap between the petty commodity producers, driven away from traditional farming by the neo-liberal economic policies, and the urban dwellers. Petty commodity producers were at the centre of the movement rather than the urban middle class. In other words, the ACCs became a space where petty commodity producers and the urban middle class exchange commodities, knowledge and information. The following quotes, taken from different actors in the alternative consumer movement, summarize the major concerns behind the formation of the ACCs and some of their underlying premises (koopBülteni, 2011):

> Industrial food and seed and pesticide producers opt to control the food production and distribution chain. Due to the pesticides and chemicals used, foodstuff became a source of poison rather than health … Local producers cannot compete with the imported products: Imported foodstuff is unhealthy and does not provide enough nutrition … In this system, small producers and consumers are the losers while the winners are big companies … It is evident that there is a need for a comprehensive agriculture reform, which can be done only by the small farmers and the conscious consumer. (The president of Çiftçi-Sen)

Within a year after our founding, the number of producers who wanted to work with our cooperative increased … after discussing the issue in our decision bodies, we decided to refuse the big companies and work with only small farmers or farmers' cooperatives after we know them. I have to say that Çiftçi-Sen and their president were very helpful in collecting information about the producers. (One of the founders of BÜKOOP)

For the perseverance of conventional agriculture, we have to register traditional farming know-how and invigorate an agriculture based on the learned and wise farmer. (The founder of Kibele)

As an association, we opt for promoting a just producer–consumer relation … we want to develop sustainable farming, advance women and youngsters' participation in the decision processes, develop direct sales channels between producers and consumers. (The founder of Tohum-İzi Derneği)

Based on our research data, the struggle of La Via Campesina shapes the premises of the ACCs. The contributions of La Via Campesina to the alternative cooperative movement can be summarized as defending food sovereignty, utilizing local heirloom seeds and ecological farming. This is translated into empowering small producers and consumers in the food production and distribution system, evading the middlemen, localization, and supporting farmers that use traditional methods and provide healthy food to the consumer. Two major issues supported by La Via Campesina – food sovereignty and ecological farming – are being developed by farmers and villagers as an alternative to the neo-liberal order and global capitalism. They incorporate practices inclusive in the production and consumption nexus, such as maintaining the culture of villages and farms, the culture of food consumption and the relationship between rural and urban (Kocagöz, 2016).

The ACCs needed to adopt a specific governance or cooperative management model and tried to translate cooperative practices developed in other locations. The development of current practices was a learning process: when a problem was encountered, founders consulted with the other constituencies such as Çiftçi-Sen, the producers, and international organizations to develop a solution. For example, in the early stages of Boğaziçi Mensupları Tüketim Kooperatifi (BÜKOOP), one major problem was the supply of organic food. Organic food was expensive and the certification process empowered organizations that provided the certificate. There were problems implementing proper control mechanisms, and small farmers could not afford the certificate costs. The organic food supply, although ecologically safe, was expensive for the consumer and producer.

BÜKOOP's founders organized a workshop on Participatory Guarantee Systems (PGS) for the provision of sustainable food systems in search of an alternative. Participants included Çiftçi-Sen, Tohum-İzi Derneği, the International Federation of Organic Agriculture Movements (IFOAM) and the producers of various foodstuffs from different regions of the country. This workshop provided an opportunity for both consumers and producers to discuss and learn collectively. One of the principles of PGS is related to participation and horizontal organizing; instead of having certification organizations that conduct controls and checks of the foodstuff, the cooperative members are expected to control each other. Such an approach leads to knowledge-sharing among producers. Providing information about the foodstuff produced (for example, detailed information about the producer, production conditions and also excursions to farms) creates an unmediated relationship between the producers and consumers. The premises of this system guided the ACCs in developing local, pluralistic communities of producers and users based on principles of mutuality, trust and transparent relations (Akyazı and Ertör, 2012).

The earliest ACC in Turkey was BÜKOOP, a university-based cooperative established in 2009 through the collaboration of the academic and administrative staff of Boğaziçi University (BU) and with the support of Çiftçi-Sen, Eğitim-Sen and Tohum İzi Derneği (Karakaya, 2016; Kaya, 2019; Kurtuluş, 2019), which started its operations in a shop – the Barrack – on the university campus. The aim of the cooperative is to reorganize the food production and consumption nexus in an egalitarian and solidarity-based way. The founders of BÜKOOP opted for developing a cooperative model that could be implemented in other universities and neighbourhoods. In the long run, they plan to increase the number of independently owned ACCs and develop a network of producer and consumer cooperatives aligned around the premise of the democratization of the production–consumption nexus (Kurtuluş, 2019; Al, 2020; Öz and Aksoy, 2019). Though BÜKOOP membership is limited to BU-affiliated people, the Barrack and organized events are open to all. BÜKOOP is 'an open-door cooperative' which distinguishes it from earlier examples of consumer cooperatives in Turkey. Creating an alternative, BÜKOOP deliberately stays small and encourages others to establish similar cooperatives by sharing their experiences in food provisioning, governance and retail operations. As noted by Öz and Aksoy (2019), their choice of staying small is rooted in the vision of a 'de-growth economy'. Though BÜKOOP made several attempts to promote their model in other universities, this ideal was not realized until the establishment of Kadıköy Kooperatif in 2016.

The short history of Kadıköy Kooperatif dates back to the Gezi movement in 2013, and the experiences of activists at that time and the succeeding forums and Occupy houses that inspired them to engage in other types of organizations reflecting similar values and beliefs. The activists saw that it was possible to develop alternative ways of living without being subject to the dominant cultural, social and economic framework in Turkey. In the following years, until the cooperative assumed its legal status in 2016, the activists organized various workshops to discuss and learn about the alternative cooperative model from local groups such as Çiftçi-Sen, BÜKOOP, Anadolu'da Yaşam Tüketim Kooperatifi, Tohum-İzi Derneği and international organizations such as La Via Campesina (Özsoy et al, 2018; Oba and Özsoy, 2019; Al, 2020; Kadıköy Kooperatifi Kolektifi, 2020). At this stage, the experiences of BÜKOOP, regarding producer selection, the producer repository (building a database of the selected producers) and the consumer cooperative model, and the guidance of Çiftçi-Sen on the necessity of an ecological transformation for combatting the problems in agriculture, directed their efforts in forming the cooperative (Kadıköy Kooperatifi Kolektifi, 2020). Through such a learning process the idea of founding an alternative cooperative has come to fruition and engagement with other constituencies has been realized (Kadirbeyoğlu and Konya, 2017; Akbulut, 2020; Al, 2020; İnce and Kadirbeyoğlu, 2020). In 2015, a group of activists under the title of Kadıköy Tüketim Kooperatifi Girişimi (Kadıköy Consumer Cooperative Initiative) started to work on the formal establishment of a cooperative. During this period, as a 'street coop', the initiative was able to gain public visibility, experiment with collective decision-making, learn about pricing, make deals with small producers, and develop pre-order box distribution schemes (Oba and Özsoy, 2019; Kadıköy Kooperatifi Kolektifi, 2020). Finally, in 2016 the Kadıköy Kooperatif was legally established and they began their operations in a small rented shop. Although BÜKOOP was the first initiative in Turkey that can be considered as a solidarity-based, grassroots alternative consumer cooperative, the movement gained momentum after the initiation of the Kadıköy Kooperatif. Following the experiences of BÜKOOP and Kadıköy Kooperatif, the activists involved in environmental issues, food and feminist movements started to initiate similar cooperatives in different districts in İstanbul (Yeldeğirmeni, Yerdeniz, Maltepe, Bostancı, Kozyatağı, Kuzguncuk, Ataşehir, Salkım, Nardugan and Arı Köy) and in Ankara, Eskişehir, İzmir and İzmit.

Concluding remarks

Instead of a conclusion, in this part we provide a comparison between conventional and alternative cooperatives in Turkey. We anticipate that such a comparison will be useful in accentuating the political positioning, surplus generation and governance models of the ACCs which will be discussed in the succeeding chapters. The ACCs are different from conventional consumer cooperatives in various aspects: the CCCs were established through the efforts of the state, municipalities, companies and unions in a top-down manner, whereas ACCs are grassroots organizations initiated by locals and food activists. These activists are mostly young, educated, middle-class professionals, a precariat facing job insecurity either because of the managerialist practices of big firms or the exclusionary practices of the ruling party. They oppose the prevailing neo-liberal food provisioning system which empowers the agro-food companies, marginalizes the petty commodity producers, and leads to the dissolution of farmers and traditional farming know-how. In return, activists involved in the ACCs envision and experiment with a model characterized by the provision of ecologically safe, reasonably priced foodstuff by bypassing the middlemen, empowering petty commodity producers and building networks for bulk purchasing.

On the other hand, the CCCs were established for controlling price rises, restricting the black market and to fill a gap in retailing, but were instrumentalized for political support. Their sole function was to provide cheap commodities to their members, whereas in other countries consumer cooperatives have aimed for participatory democracy, community formation, support for local farmers and educating the consumer (see, for example, Knupfer, 2013; Patmore and Balnave, 2018). Conventional cooperatives in Turkey are managed under the patronage of the founding organization such as the state and companies. These cooperatives provide financial resources such as credits to their members, and sell only those items produced by the founding organization. Thus the beneficiaries of these cooperatives are the founding organizations. The instrumentalization of consumer cooperatives by the government and some companies has led to the erosion of trust in such organizations and also the cooperative movement. Except for the examples of Demirtepe Halk Istihlak Kooperatifi, MİPAŞ and Halk-Koop, which were founded by bureaucrats, a labour union and a political party, the CCCs were all 'closed-door' organizations serving only their members.

Although all cooperatives in Turkey adhere to the same legislation, the governance of CCCs and ACCs differs as well. According to Kooperatifler Kanunu (Cooperative Law 1163), in Turkey a minimum of 50 per cent of the revenues can be distributed among the cooperative partners. Thus, the CCCs distribute a share of profits to their partners, whereas the ACCs experiment with a different surplus generation model (as discussed in detail in Chapter 6) and do not look for profits. The ACCs identify themselves as non-profit organizations prioritizing social value creation. Accordingly, prices are set to cover costs and if any surplus is created it is used for the betterment of disadvantaged groups in society (Oba and Özsoy, 2020). Another difference between the ACCs and the CCCs is their reliance on volunteer work. As discussed in Chapter 7, all the operations (finance, technical, organization-building, training, research, relations with producers, communication, finding and including women producers, archiving and social media) in the ACCs are carried out by volunteers. Volunteers participate in the decision-making process and choose which work unit they want to be part of. Volunteers are usually recruited during the public meetings which are regularly held by each ACC or by open calls. On the other hand, operations in the CCCs are carried out by salaried employees at all levels of the hierarchy. Especially after 2000, in line with the changes in legislation and the pervasive implementation of a managerialist logic, the management of the CCCs has been carried out by professionals appointed by the government cadres. Finally, unlike the hierarchical structure of the CCCs, where decisions are made by the partners and professional managers (discussed in detail in Chapter 7), the ACCs experiment with a non-hierarchical governance model shaped around participation, inclusion and consensus-based decision-making.

The ACCs are similar to the consumer cooperatives in other countries and different from the conventional cooperatives in Turkey. The ACCs are sites of food activism: like examples in other countries (Knupfer, 2013; Rakopoulos 2014; Grasseni et al, 2015; Bilewicz and Śpiewak, 2015; Grasseni, 2020), they strive to develop a viable alternative to corporate capitalism; they see food and its consumption as a political process (Brunori et al, 2012; Moragues-Faus 2017; Rakopoulos 2014); and they favour participatory democracy and community formation (Knupfer, 2013). They have positioned themselves as the active advocates of the food sovereignty movement in Turkey. They share similar values and experience and similar practices, such as egalitarian relations among members, gender diversity, direct democracy, collective decision-making, cooperation and solidarity. Adhering to the spirit of the food sovereignty movement, they are against the displacement of local farmers from agriculture and aim to support local producers and producer cooperatives, especially those founded and run by women. Also, as sites of food activism, the ACCs take a critical, oppositional position in challenging the hegemonic neo-liberal project. As discussed in Chapter 5, the ACCs can be seen as an alternative public sphere where a diverse set of practices such as shop encounters, social media posts, workshops and site visits are utilized for the engagement of wider constituencies.

Alternative Consumer Cooperatives in the Making of a Public Sphere

Introduction

In recent years, following the 2013 Gezi protests, citizens across Turkey have expressed their discontent with the prevailing neo-liberal system and political regime by establishing various forms of solidarity initiatives – consumer cooperatives, producer cooperatives and neighbourhood solidarity initiatives. These initiatives, while adhering to the spirit of Gezi, were driven by a claim to take an active role in issues concerning all the citizens in a specific locality. Gezi protesters, while responding to 'the institutionalization of neo-liberalism and centralization of powers' (Akçay, 2021, p 93), also developed a hope that through direct democracy, resistance and solidarity, citizens could have a voice in politics (Öztan, 2013; Parlak, 2013; Sevinç, 2022). In the local initiatives that proliferated after Gezi, through forums and neighbourhood assemblies (Mahalle Meclisleri), public opinion on issues such as food, child abuse, violence against women, betterment of labour conditions and collective action for resolving persistent problems was developed (Doğançayır, 2022; Kahraman, 2022). Mahalle Meclisleri (Olcan, 2020), were later named as district solidarity initiatives and, as noted by Fırat (2022), proliferated during the COVID-19 pandemic. After the announcement of the Coronavirus Support Programme by the government, 17 new solidarity initiatives were established in İstanbul, Ankara, Bursa, Ayvalık and Mersin. In this chapter we focus on one of these initiatives, the alternative consumer cooperatives (ACCs) and elaborate on their work in reclaiming the public sphere with a transformative potential that is shaped through the politicization of consumers and petty commodity producers. In so doing, we investigate how a public sphere concerning food politics in Turkey has been developed, who the main actors are, what types of media they use, and which other constituencies have been drawn in.

Borrowing on the Habermasian (1981, 1987, 1989) concept of the public sphere we see the ACCs as a space for the development and articulation of a special discourse. We consider the public sphere as a formation where groups of activists come together and question normative arrangements. We focus on the discourse, that is, how activists reflexively negate and question prevailing habits, practices and assumptions, and how the ACCs try to re-moralize everyday activities (for example as consumers, as volunteers), re-politicize the politics of food and build awareness for an 'alternative'. In a milieu where politics is delegated to political parties and their allies (big capital, pro-government media), the efforts of the activists involved in the ACCs can be taken as constituting a lifeworld through communicative action that is organized by mutual understanding. According to Habermas (1989) the public sphere is a process where diverse groups of citizens question and contest prevailing traditions, identities, morals and norms that constitute the lifeworld. Such a situation usually arises as the consequence of a 'legitimacy crisis' when the existing 'norms lose their integrative power to a degree that the political system is incapable of dealing with' (Crossley, 2003, p 291). And in a public sphere, through communicative action, diverse groups of citizens, who are part of a common problem, can question and evaluate their established habits and draft solutions to change them. During this process, instead of conforming to the 'taken for granted' norms and actions, citizens, through discourse, question and evaluate them (Habermas, 1989, 2021). Similarly, social norms that provide a base for the development of a 'universal solidarity', where the inclusion of the marginalized is facilitated, are developed by a discourse where each participant, on an equal basis, participates, anticipates and accepts the views of the others (Habermas, 2021). In this sense, we view the 'public sphere' as a process initiated by a legitimacy crisis, shaped by a reflexive discourse and capable of triggering change. In line with such a conceptualization of the public sphere, we argue that the ACCs response to the legitimacy crisis of the neo-liberal hegemonic project and decreasing public participation in politics is crystallized in the 'making' of an alternative public sphere. This public sphere is constituted by urban middle-class consumers, activists for food sovereignty and petty commodity producers, and utilizes a diverse set of institutions (shop, social media, an alternative football league), activities (workshops, talks, film screenings, celebrations, direct meetings, site visits) and a discourse that is critical, oppositional of the prevailing system and inspiring a new one.

The chapter is organized as follows: we first explain the concept of the public sphere and refeudilization as developed by Jürgen Habermas. In this section we also discuss the criticism that it attracted and why we see the ACCs as a public sphere. Then, in order to accentuate the conditions that triggered the making of a public sphere, we provide a snapshot of the political and economic conditions in Turkey. In the third part of the chapter, we provide a detailed account of various institutions utilized by the ACCs in this process, with a focus on the discourse used.

The public sphere

> We humans learn *from one another*. And this is only possible in the public space of a culturally stimulating milieu.
>
> Jürgen Habermas, 'Public space and political public sphere', 2021, p 7

Jürgen Habermas, in *The Structural Transformation of the Public Sphere*, describes the 'public sphere' as a gathering of private citizens assembled to debate issues important to social life and of public concern (1989). As such, the public sphere is a discursive space, shaped around 'critical debate', where citizens assemble freely, discussions about common interests take place without coercion, information and ideas are exchanged freely, and political participation is performed through talk (Habermas, 1981, 1989). The public sphere in politics acts as a separate entity from the state and economy, and enables a specific discourse that criticizes, challenges and influences the operations of the state and economic markets to be produced and articulated. While making a social-historical analysis of the concept and tracing notions of 'private' and 'public', Habermas, in reference to the fully developed Greek city-states, explains that the 'public sphere was constituted in discussion (lexis), which could also assume the forms of consultation and of sitting in the court of law, as well as in common action (praxis), be it waging of war or competition in athletic games' (Habermas, 1989, p 3). Later, the notion of 'public' in feudal society was used in reference to someone who symbolized higher power and the sphere of public authority embodied the courtly noble society. Habermas (1989) identifies this situation as the 'publicness of representation' (p 7), which was an attribute of the power holder – the king, the Church, the prince and the noble. Publicity was staged in dressing, rhetoric and courtly ceremonies where the common people were taken as nonparticipants, purely spectators.

In the transformation to a modern society, the concept of 'public' changed as well. The economy emerged as a separate sphere from the family, based on commodity production, commodity exchange and wage labour. With the advent of capitalism and the modern state, a new bourgeois public sphere arose, one which provided an interface between the economy, state and family, and dominated by the newly emerging middle class. In this intermediate sphere, private citizens, who did not rule, who were once taken as bystanders, came together as a public. The *tischgesellschaften*, saloons, the tea houses and reading clubs began to host private individuals engaged in 'rational-critical' argumentation by reading and reviewing newspapers and artistic works. Later, the focus of argumentation shifted from literary to political issues and critique of the state. As such, the 'bourgeois public sphere' composed of private individuals (the educated and propertied) made demands for democratic representation, a critical publicity as opposed to the representative publicity of the feudal power holders.

Habermas (1989) identifies three institutional criteria that characterize the various forms (*tischgesellschaften*, saloons and tea houses) of this bourgeois public sphere; a social interaction that disregarded status, discussions that problematized issues that were not questioned before and inclusiveness in principle. The public sphere provided a milieu where social interactions were free of social class and economic dependencies. Habermas also adds that 'not that this idea of the public was actually realized in earnest in coffee houses, the saloons and the societies; but as an idea it had become institutionalized and thereby stated an objective claim' (1989, p 36). Furthermore, Habermas explains that private individuals in the public are united by a mutual will for discussing issues that concern them all, rather than by being members of a class. These critical debates on political and economic issues allow the formation of a 'public will' and its conveyance to the public authority – the state. The issues discussed were 'general' in being significant to all and accessible by all. Everyone should be able to participate on an equal basis and with an equal opportunity and autonomy to develop an argument expressing ideas and opinions. Thus, the bourgeois public sphere emerged as a separate realm to the sphere of public authority, as a social and political space between society and state, with a concern for limiting the personal powers of the ruling nobles.

Refeudilization of the public sphere

According to Habermas (1981, 1989), this ideal public sphere, in line with the changes in the media, the culture industries and the evolution of large-scale organizations, went through a transformation. As the public sphere grew in size, with the participation of all engaging in critical debate, dealing with matters of common interest necessitated a means – newspapers, trade journals – for sharing and disseminating ideas. Over time these newspapers and magazines were taken over by large corporations which in turn led to a shift in their purpose and a change in their functionality. With the rise of the business press the dissemination of political ideas by the newspapers was replaced by a sales strategy that guided their operations. Gradually, newspapers, magazines, radio and television became the media of the public sphere. During the course of this transformation the 'public' became a fundamental part of the consumer mass culture, where powerful private interests were disseminated as general concerns through a pervasive usage of public relations, marketing and advertising campaigns. These instruments, by manipulating the opinions of the private citizens, rendered critical argumentation a futile effort. The bonds between private citizens constituting the public weakened and, as stated by Warner (2013), people turned into unthinking mass consumers.

One of the functions of the ideal public sphere was to counterbalance the power of the state. However, as capitalism became more pervasive the recipients of the bourgeois public sphere – the state, political parties and interest groups – started to instrumentalize this sphere for political power. In an effort to increase their votes, these groups approached citizens with the same marketing tools that would enable them to influence and control opinions. As explained by Habermas (1981, 1989) the public sphere, which once had a mediating role between the private citizens and the state, was transformed into a space where different interest groups competed and confronted each other. With the intervention of the state, some of the public functions were transferred to privately owned corporations that could only be secured by political compromises, given in support of the state. Legislation, which would be expected to be drafted according to the 'pressure of the streets', with consensus formed from discussions in the public sphere, increasingly represented the conflicting private interests (Habermas, 1981). Moreover, as the state tended to adopt the interests of a civil society as its own, taking on some functions of the commodity exchange and social exchange realms, a re-politicized social sphere emerged where the distinction between public/ private could not be applied (Habermas, 1981). In other words, as capitalism became organized and liberalism reached a peak, the relation between public and private dissolved and the public sphere eroded due to the efforts of large-scale companies to manipulate it for profit and the efforts of political agencies seeking political power (Habermas, 1981, p 140). The public sphere turned out to be passive, deprived of rational-critical debate where 'consensus developed in rational-critical public debate has yielded to compromise fought out or simply imposed non publicly' (Habermas, 1989, p 179). This erosion of the distinction between public/private and the development of a representative publicity by the state is identified as 'refeudalization of the public sphere' by Habermas (1989). Consequently, citizens concerned with issues germane to all, and through rational-critical debate drafting solutions that were transmitted to public authorities, turned out to be passive followers of the discourse articulated by state and media. During this transformation, from being active political citizens to passive consumers, the populace lost its power for making political and economic decisions.

Discussing the public sphere in the Turkish context

The concept of the public sphere as developed by Jürgen Habermas has been criticized by some studies for being exclusionary, in terms of gender and class, and for overemphasizing the lifeworld. In this section we will focus on these criticisms and try to discuss that, in the case of the ACCs, such claims are not explanative, in the sense that they do not apply to or illuminate the practices of ACCs. In Chapters 3 and 6 we argue that, as a consequence of populist neo-liberal policies and their authoritarian implementation by the government cadres, formal labour, peasantry and the middle class, either organized through unions or individually, are marginalized. In a way, they are excluded from the political and economic decision-making process. With the implementation of the Labour Act (4857) in 2003, work was positioned as a commodity and formal labour, as well as its organizations, was enfeebled (Ercan and Oğuz, 2015; Çelik, 2015; Akçay, 2018). In general, union density dropped and new unions that had a symbiotic relation with the AKP were formed. Furthermore, in line with the privatization wave and the managerialist logic implemented with the premise of the same Labour Law, the professional middle class comprised of doctors, nurses, teachers, academics, lawyers, engineers and architects became precariat. With the liberalization of agriculture and the implementation of tools such as direct income support and contract farming, petty commodity producers were proletarianized.

On the other hand, big capital, which had a pivotal role in the shift to neo-liberal policies in 1980, by accentuating the prevailing clientelist relations with the state, moved yet further to the core of the economic and political realm. While the government accentuated the 'hegemonic neo-liberal' project with its strong commitment to market logic and following statist imperatives, big capital secured its central position through rent-seeking and establishing relations with the government cadres. As these groups, either individually or through their associations, in an effort to secure their economic power, established more connections with the ruling cadres, the main principles around which economic and political decisions are organized changed as well. Favouritism and loyalty became the major basis for being part of the economic realm, the distinction between politics and markets disappeared, and wealth accumulated in the hands of whichever big capital was capable of establishing close relations with the government and voiced pro-government and pro neo-liberal sentiments. As we discussed in relation to the media industry, a pro-government media was created by seizing existing media conglomerates, controlling advertising revenues and providing incentives to new media conglomerates (see, for example, Akser, 2018; Filibeli and İnceoğlu, 2018; Sözeri, 2019; Coskun, 2020). These new media conglomerates are not only effective within the media industry but also operate across various other sectors, being involved in mega projects contracted by the government, for example, İstanbul airport, highways and gentrification projects. With the accelerating problems related to accumulation, wealth distribution and social inequality arising from the very dynamics of neo-liberal policies, the groups that are excluded from the realms of political economic decision-making and rendered as instruments for winning an election (the peasantry, professionals and formal labour), have sought ways to pursue and develop alternatives. In this vein, the efforts of the activists involved in the ACCs can be taken as an effort to revive and revitalize a public sphere around a common issue – food.

The ACCs, both in discussion and action, share specific features that help us to identify them as a public sphere. The activists involved are careful to allow the participation of different and disparate groups with different political leanings and representing different social standing. The ability to participate in the public meetings organized by the ACCs, attend workshops, and visit and buy from the shops is open to all. Other consumer cooperatives that are currently in operation, or were in the past, served only their members. On the other hand, ACC shops are accessible to all and serve all. One of the major criticisms of the 'public sphere' is that despite the rhetoric of accessibility and openness it is exclusionary in terms of gender and class. The claim on gender does not hold in the case of the ACCs: the majority of the ACC founders are women (the percentage of female founders is between 25 and 100 per cent) (Oba and Ozsoy, 2020). Also, as suppliers, they give priority to female-owned and - managed producer cooperatives and/or female-owned small companies. The majority of the founders are middle-class professionals and university students; blue-collar workers comprise a comparable smaller group. Members of the ACCs are not differentiating themselves from 'others', on the contrary they are trying to embrace marginalized groups in the food provisioning system. And, on an equal basis with the small commodity producers, they collaboratively carry out workshops and seminars that are open to the public. In so doing, it is expected that a space to re-socialize and build counter-communities and that allows connectivity among the excluded groups will be provided. As suggested by the activists, "connectivity at local and national levels would enable them to rebuild socio-economic relations and regain lost positions in the political realm" (interview notes). Although as a common interest these different groups converge on 'food' and 'food politics' (transforming the production and consumption nexus, altering the power relations between producers and consumers, providing pesticide free foodstuff, and establishing a just food system) they are also spaces of freedom for developing and articulating counter-arguments against the populist neo-liberal policies, privatization and capitalism. Finally, the ACCs, as spaces of freedom, provide a milieu where oppositional movement strategies that challenge the existing power relations and practices can be fostered, the legitimacy of the political order is questioned, and criticisms of the state policies are freely expressed.

We also view ACCs as argumentative and experimental spaces. The decisions about the daily operations of the cooperatives are taken in a participative manner with face-to-face discussions, where participants openly express their opinions, ideas and concerns. They can be seen as an experiment in developing an alternative to the representative democracy, an alternative to the prevailing Turkish political culture that is characterized by a culture of obedience and compelled by a milieu of fear (Yaylacı, 2013, p 5). This aspect of the public sphere – consensus-based decision-making and participation – has been criticized for its overemphasis on the lifeworld. For example, Smucker (2014), based on his experiences with Occupy Wall Street, asserts that such spaces are 'indispensable for social movements since they nurture solidarity and commitment' (p 76). Too much emphasis on the lifeworld of the prefigurative group can lead the group to a position where they lose their motivation to bring change. In other words, if the internal life of the group becomes a more important motivator, then the question is, is it possible to accomplish change? Furthermore, Smucker (2014) claims that if prefigurative politics aims to build a lifeworld around the values of the participants and avoids involvement in changing power relations in a wider field, it is only a 'private liberation' (p 81). Prefigurative politics should be expressive and instrumental and for that to happen these spaces should create bridges between themselves and other groups, they must win allies so that they can build collective power. In response to such criticisms, we can develop the following argument: the activists involved in the ACCs experiment and share their experiences not only as related to the inner world of the cooperative but also in the wider realm of food politics. We have seen that they are both expressive and instrumental. Similar to the examples provided by Raeksted and Gradin (2020), they aim towards structural change within the prevailing food provisioning system and to that end they are building alliances with other constituencies and are engaged in awareness-building activities. While they are experimenting and sharing, they are developing and articulating a specific discourse; a discourse that reflects the lifeworld of the group, has concerns about the prevailing food provisioning system, is against managerialism, and stresses the principles of food sovereignty. Activists involved in the ACCs envision a change in the existing power relations, and while they are reconstituting and defending their 'endangered lives' they expect that such change will eventually lead to redistribution.

Alternative consumer cooperatives in the making of a public sphere

In an effort to revitalize a public sphere and voice their political concerns, activists involved in the ACCs utilize direct encounters mediated by their shops (such as public meetings and workshops), the alternative football league and online communications (such as social media and web pages). Direct encounters like talks, workshops and site visits are also announced and shared on their social media accounts. Such communication informs the public, facilitates a different consumption culture, and unveils that 'another world that is possible'. Furthermore, these online and offline communications are instrumental in building networks with other constituencies (the Farmers' Union, producer cooperatives, female-owned producer cooperatives, local people, the public, small farmers and municipalities) so that opinions and actions are organized for a counter-hegemonic struggle. On the way to building networks of opposition, the ACCs organize regular public meetings, trips to the sites of petty commodity producers, street festivals, workshops on food politics and talks by specialists. These activities provide an opportunity to meet others and connect people of diverse backgrounds. They reinforce the values and practices of the group members, facilitate the expansion of movement boundaries, and provide a forum for discussing issues such as the environment, women's rights, economic policies, minorities, and workers resistance. In the following section we offer examples of the various online and offline activities carried out by the members of the ACCs and try to show how ACCs, as prefigurative spaces, play an important role in the articulation of various concerns regarding populist neo-liberal policies and political actions taken by the government, and how they encourage political debate and open avenues for visualizing alternatives.

Direct encounters

In this section of the chapter, we provide a detailed account of the various direct encounter means adopted by the ACCs in the making of a milieu that is expressive of the concerns of the activists and stimulates the interest of the locals. In so doing, we draw on the discourse underlying the premises of the ACCs.

Public meetings: 'The Coop Is Explaining Itself'

Activists are involved in the ACC's experiment with direct democracy and an alternative way of living and culture. Through various activities they show how this is possible and how it can be realized. For example, some of the ACCs organize a public meeting on a regular basis, usually once a month, called 'The Coop Is Explaining Itself'. The notification of the meeting is made via their social media accounts at the shop. These meetings are usually carried out in a public place, in some cases in buildings belonging to the municipality. During the pandemic, from time to time, these meetings were held online: anyone interested in the meeting could send an email to the volunteers of the cooperative who then shared a Zoom link. We participated in some of these offline and online meetings carried out by different ACCs. Although there are some variations in terms of duration and the depth of discussions, all public meetings follow the same format. The meeting is carried out by two cooperative members; both of them are involved in explaining their experiences and answering questions. The meeting usually starts with a detailed explanation of the values and practices of the cooperative, and then, as questions arise from the audience, discussion expands to the AFNs, food sovereignty and, finally, to the policies of the government in relation to agriculture. At the end of the meeting participants are asked whether they would like to join the group as volunteers (Oba and Özsoy, 2020) or, in some cases, are invited to the weekly decision-making meetings of the cooperative. While explaining what the cooperative does, detailed information on the following issues are given to the participants: the work units (such as finance, communication, product representatives and training), how decisions are made, how petty commodity producers are identified and selected, what type of tasks are done by volunteers and how volunteers arrange their work schedule. Additionally, participants are informed about various producers and their products and how co-purchasing networks are formed with the other ACCs and newly formed cooperatives in other districts of İstanbul. In the final part of the meeting, which is devoted to participants questions, a wide range of issues are covered, such as how to grow special foodstuff that is free of pesticide, how the shop is run, and whether the producers are given guidance in their efforts to produce ecologically safe products. Therefore, these meetings are events where old, well-established members, newcomers and the interested public have a chance to interact and exchange opinions and experiences. They function as a prefigurative space where discussions on political/economic issues are held and solidarity with other constituencies are built. Also, these meetings provide a chance to share experiences in direct democracy and participative consensus-based decision-making, and show that 'another world is possible'.

Field trips to production sites

ACCs also occasionally organize trips to the production facilities of petty commodity producers. These visits are open to all, and field notes and videos of the visit are shared on the social media accounts and web pages of the cooperatives. If the visit is arranged by a particular ACC, then the others publicize this visit and share it with their followers. Field notes contain information about the product(s), production methods, labour conditions and distribution. For example, in a site visit to a producer cooperative located in Hatay Vakıflı (the only Armenian village in Turkey), it was explained in detail how orders are distributed among the cooperative members on an equal basis so that everyone in the cooperative earns the same amount. Also, these notes explain how the producers are compensated and how the cooperatives surplus is distributed (to pay for student scholarships, the wages of formal cooperative employees and cooperative expenses).[1] Besides providing information, these field trips are instrumental in assuring transparency of the operations of the cooperative. The field notes also reflect a political position-taking and help the reader to remember the political concerns that have shaped the alternative cooperative movement. For example, in a site visit to the Özçay Tea Production Cooperative in Tirebolu, in the Blacksea region, it was explained that the cooperative was established in response to the privatization efforts that happened after the 12 September 1980 military coup. The government agency Çaykur began to implement quotas for tea purchases in order to promote the swift entry of privately owned companies, and this led to a situation where the producers could not sell all of their tea. The discussions about how to find a solution to this problem resulted in the establishment of a cooperative.[2] The information about these visits is given much like a tourist pamphlet, detailing how long it takes to commute to the site, the historical places visited, the living conditions in and around the site visited, and are presented in an appealing style for those searching for an alternative holiday. For example, the notes on the trip to a cheese producer with whom all the ACCs work, located in Kars in northeastern Turkey, starts with how long it takes to get to Kars by plane, alternative transportation methods, and the historical places and natural beauty spots of the region, as well as notes on the cheese production facilities. Also, woven within this background information about the region and village, detailed information about milk and the various types of cheese is provided. Field notes end with an evaluation of the social issues in relation to the feudal community structure, gentrification and gender that underline the road to be taken.[3]

Talks/documentary screenings

ACCs frequently organize talks on various issues and in some cases they are accompanied by a documentary screening. These events are open to all and are announced on social media. Talks are generally organized on a specific topic, such as foodstuff (for example, cheese, rice, beans, honey or bread), food sovereignty, the history of cooperatives, arts and society (for example, the 1980 coup, alienation, alternatives, ageing and so on). Talks about foodstuff are delivered by the producers where difference between industrially produced food and traditional farming are contrasted in terms of quality, reliability and costs. If applicable, related legislation and the consequences of its application are evaluated. In nearly all such meetings, a reference to the working conditions and empowerment of women is made by the producers. Besides talking about the foodstuff, these events open a setting for discussing local initiatives for combatting the impoverishment of the peasantry, the practices developed by locals for environment friendly, labour-intensive farming, and the economic obstacles faced by the small commodity producers. In some cases, talks extend beyond food to cover academic freedom and activism in academia. Depending on the topic, talks are also accompanied by a practical session where the producer and participants collectively prepare food, that is, make cheese or bread or cook a dish of beans. Recipes are given so that consumers can try to produce their own food at home. As indicated by the activists involved in the ACCs, it is hoped that these meetings with the producers will contribute to the development of awareness on the part of the consumers (especially those who shop in the cooperatives) about production processes and the relationship between human beings and nature. It is commonly stated by ACC members that "consumers can transform the producers and production methods" as they learn more about a specific foodstuff and the production relationship that shapes it. In one of the meetings in which we participated this was explained as such; following a talk by a non-industrial rice producer in Artvin (in northeastern Turkey),[4] consumers' interest in rice grown with local seeds and traditional methods intensified. During the talk it was also explained how villagers worked collectively when planting and harvesting and how the burden on women was reduced by this collective production method. As the demand for rice grown in this village increased, other producers were drawn in and changed their production methods.

During these events, an alternative lifestyle and consumption mode is presented and experimented with. Some other talks/film screenings are related to agriculture, food sovereignty and the cooperative movement. In all these events, participants freely discuss and share their concerns about a common interest on an equal basis. The social and economic distance between small producers in the rural areas and consumers in the urban dissolve, and a climate for developing a common discourse and establishing political alliances is formed.

Workshops

In an effort to revitalize the lost public sphere, the ACCs also arrange a diverse set of workshops. A group of these workshops focuses on various aspects of food politics – ecological farming, consumption without intermediaries, food crises, food sovereignty, privatization and alternative cooperatives. Besides building networks, workshops are spaces of learning and gaining a deeper insight into the topic discussed. This was stated by one of the founders of an ACC: "We are against industrial production; we are on the side of ecological farming. In order to have a more comprehensive understanding of the issue we want to share the knowledge and know-how of those specialized in this field."

These workshops are open to anyone who is interested and are announced on social media so that they can be shared by the followers of the ACC. The announcement also provides a brief description of the workshop, names the lead participants and, in some cases, provides a reading list, with the participants being asked to read at least one of the articles appearing on the list. These workshops can be taken as spheres of critical discussion where the policies and practices of global and local big capital, as well as the government agencies, are assessed. For example, the announcement for the workshop titled 'You Can't Patent Seeds' was posted in the social media account of Kadıköy Kooperatif in 2019 as:

> The ministry of Agriculture and Forestry renewed the legislation that requires the certification of local seeds. With the implementation of this regulation the availability of local seeds and thus their usage by villagers will be limited. This regulation supports big companies rather than the villagers. We will discuss the possible other outcomes of this new legislation and what we can do as organized consumers.

In another workshop on 'Food Politics and Cooperatives', the announcement starts with a question 'How can we establish a new generation of cooperatives that will transform our habits, perceptions and values that will replace the prevailing dominant system of production and consumption?' Then it details cooperatives, their goals, functions, and their difference from private companies in terms of profits and the availability of healthy and affordable food. Participants are given a reading list and, finally, the aim of the workshop is stated. As can be seen from these examples, these events are settings for different constituencies, where, through critical argumentation, alternatives are sought and public opinion is shaped. They are calls for collective reasoning, action and solidarity.

As well as the workshops organized around the problems of food politics, some ACCs organize workshops for building furniture, making household items, and for personal wellbeing, such as music, yoga and meditation. These activities are carried out in collaboration with other alternative, grassroots collectives. For example, in a workshop for building wooden garden furniture, the students and academics from the ACC, described as 'solidaristic, grassroots architects', designed and constructed furniture collectively. Garden furniture built by participants later decorated the garden of the cooperative. These types of workshop are instrumental in providing a space where different activists from different prefigurative spaces and sharing similar political concerns convene.

The shop

> 'Our shop is not a supermarket; it is a shop and a place for friendly chats with our visitors.'
> A volunteer, in the online public meeting 'The Coop Is Explaining Itself', held in March 2022

The shop (sometimes called the *barrack*) is especially important in the creation of the public sphere; it is not only a shop, it is a meeting space where consumers, members of the cooperatives, volunteers and sometimes producers meet, exchange ideas and share their concerns in relation to the prevailing food provision system. At one meeting one of the founding members of an ACC explained that, 'in the shop there are two tables: one for processing the transactions and the other for those shop visitors who would like to learn more about what we are doing'. Through these shop encounters, the members hope to raise awareness among the urban consumers about local seeds, traditional farming practices and ecologically grown foodstuff.

As a shop with 'solidarity shelves', for the products of the disadvantaged producers, with detailed information about the producer of each product and with volunteers ready to explain the various aspects of the items available, the ACCs exemplify a different shopping experience. The shops are rented, but since they are small and have limited and modest display shelves, as opposed to the supermarkets, the rent paid for these shops is reasonable. In some ACCs, the shop's assets (the shelves, tables, chairs, PCs and so on) are provided by the contributions of their members and inhabitants of the district. One ACC, as well as the food shop, houses a bookstore and a café. The café offers breakfast prepared with foodstuff sold in the shop. Since all the work (sales, cleaning, shelf-filling and so on) is done by volunteers, who work as salaried employees in other organizations or are university students, the shops are only open during specific hours. Depending on the size of the ACC, the opening hours of the shop varies: a smaller ACC shop (one that carries out its operations with a small number of volunteers) may open only in the evenings for two hours, while some of the relatively larger ones are able to open the shop for longer periods (between 12 am and 8 pm and even between 9 am and 8 pm).

Since the ACCs work with petty commodity producers that are involved in traditional farming, producing ecologically safe foodstuff, and not exploiting women and child labour, the variety and quantity of the items available at the shop is limited. During an interview, the situation was clarified as follows:

> 'Sometimes a visitor is disappointed that we do not have the stuff s[he] would like to buy. Yes, we do not have everything in the shop and the availability of any foodstuff depends on whether the petty commodity producer with whom we established a relationship (and they are a few) has completed the production process. We do not put pressure on the producers that they have to deliver whatsoever they have in hand.'

It is expected that through pre-orders, social media announcements about the new arrivals and lists of items available in the shop, the buying habits and perceptions of the consumption activity will change. Consumers can develop the habit of evaluating the information provided and thus do not fetishize the product but value the process of production and the labour involved behind it. The ACCs see consumers as an integral part of the solidaristic network and prefer to identify them as collaborative 'prosumers'. One of the interviewees explained this collaboration:

> 'We do not operate a supermarket. For example, someone comes to buy coffee. Although we have coffee in storage, it is not available in the shop. The volunteer shop attendant asks, "Can anyone of you take over the shop so that I will fetch the coffee bags." One of the customers in the shop proposes, "Maybe it is much better if you stay in the shop, and I will go and get them." And s[he] goes and brings in thirty kilograms of coffee to the shop. Our customers know or should know that this is not a supermarket. If we (producers, consumers, activists) collaboratively work, share some responsibility there will be more products available on the shelves.'

The shop also is a venue for bringing in different constituencies, sharing political concerns and discussing public issues. Although the ACCs are keen to preserve their autonomy, they provide a space for those constituencies that have an oppositional stance to the established conventional neo-liberal order. As discussed previously, talks and workshops are organized in the shop. Also, representatives of oppositional political parties (for example, the HDP – People's Democratic Party or the TIP-Turkish Labour Party) visit shops for short ad hoc meetings that are shared on social media. As can be seen from the following social media call, New Year celebrations, brunches, evening meetings, anniversaries are also occasions when a discussion on prevailing food politics and its alternatives can develop.

> Let's meet, taste, and get acquainted – Nowadays it is getting harder and harder to access healthy food. In this context, trustworthy, non-profit, and collaborative alternatives deserve primary importance. Our cooperative tries to realize such an alternative. Its doors are open to everyone; it belongs to all of us. The more volunteers and friends, the more variety in the shop. A more trustful and fair production and consumption that repairs the climate, the nature is possible. Let's meet at the shop of the cooperative.

Karşı lig (the 'alternative' league)

> 'Football is beautiful on the field but not at the stock market.'
> Interview with Metin Kurt[5] and Cenk Caner,
> 'böyledir bizim sevdamız', Göktürk, 2012

Football – 'against industrial football, racism, nationalism and sexism, all kinds of hate speech and discrimination, the alternative league' (Yılmaz et al, 2020, p 217).

The Karşı Lig (the alternative league) was established in 2014 under the leadership of the Yeldeğirmeni and Caferağa initiatives and with the participation of seven teams. Shaped around the spirit of Gezi, the Karşı Lig aims to design and implement a league away from violence and competition, where male and female players can jointly participate. The participants are solidarity groups and unions such as Eğitim Sen (the Education and Science Workers Union), DİSK (the Confederation of Progressive Trade Unions of Turkey) and KESK (the Confederation of Public Workers Unions).[6] Additionally, people from many occupations and fans of the major football teams like Fenerbahçe and Beşiktaş take part in the Karşı Lig. In a documentary by Setenay Gültekin (2015), Fenerbahçe fans mention how industrial football became an expensive sport for them because of the price of season tickets and e-tickets. The alternative league has its own rules: the winning team gets three points, the losing team gets one point and in the case of a draw each team gets two points. According to the Manifesto[7] (Kara and Güngör, 2021) that was collectively drafted, those players who think they are professional players, that the league is an industrial football league, or use sexist discourse and disrupt an honest game are dismissed from the league. The rules of the league are no referees, no cards, no tolerance for the cancellation of matches, and if a player claims that it is a foul, accept it. Teams do not have an owner or administrator. The coordination between the teams and the organization of the league is carried by co-captain groups comprised of a female and a male player from each team (Yılmaz et al, 2020; Kara and Güngör, 2021). Each team has a concept which fits with the spirit of the league, and the logos and uniforms are designed accordingly. Teams are composed of 14 players and a minimum of six must be women. New players are expected to read and accept the Manifesto and be committed to its premises. For the football pitch an agreement with the local Kadiköy municipality was made: the municipality do not charge a fee and in return participants carry out a social responsibility project every year (for example, supporting children from Soma,[8] Beycik village and Diyarbakır with football equipment, or providing resources for animal shelters) (Yılmaz et al, 2020).

Members of the ACCs are active participants of the league. They come together, play football and communicate. It is a meeting point for the activist from various ACCs, AFNs and other constituencies to exchange ideas, to collaborate and plan future activities. It is not only football, but also a space for opposition, for protests or, as stated by Kara and Güngör (2021), a space for those who were distanced from the political public sphere after the Gezi protests, where they can express their political concerns and claims by taking part in the public sphere. These political claims are not only expressed on the field by the rules of the game, but also voiced in public demonstrations carried out by the participants. For example, during the opening ceremony of the league in its first year, a parade for Berkin Elvan[9] was organized. In the same year, a protest was organized in front of a Turkish clothing company that carried out production activities in Bangladesh. After the 2013 Rana Plaza disaster in Bangladesh, a 'fire and workplace safety' agreement was signed by most local and international producers. However, Turkish firms were reluctant to sign the agreement (*Cumhuriyet*, 31 May 2013). During the protest, the company was shown a red card (Yılmaz et al, 2020) and other Turkish clothing companies were asked to undertake the necessary steps for workplace safety. In another event, support was shown for the inhabitants of a district in İstanbul who, for a long time, resisted the decision of the local municipality to demolish (against existing legislation) a public green area for the construction of a mosque. As explained in the book *Yeniden İnşa Et* (Yılmaz et al, 2020), which is collectively authored, the aim of the participants was not only to play football once a week, but to expand their network, to form a new culture, and find new inspiration for empowering those in opposition. In so doing, every week a theme (children rights, discrimination against women, femicide, trans individuals as the target of hate speech, male violence, protecting the environment from gold mines) is chosen and slogans, posters and banners are prepared accordingly. In order to develop a network of resistance, the activists are involved in a variety of activities for refugee children, for workers on strike, for the protection of market gardens; they arrange visits to animal shelters and campaign for supporting village schools by providing books, stationery and furniture (Kara and Güngör, 2021). Also, occasionally, politicians who take an oppositional position, participate in matches and share their concerns with the wider public. For example, during the İstanbul mayoral elections in 2019, when the winning candidate Ekrem Imamoğlu's certificate of election was delayed, the then deputy of HDP, Ahmet Şık, participated in a match with a banner 'give the certificate'. The event was shared in the newspaper *Duvar* (7 April 2019) and on the social media accounts of the Karşı Lig. The activities carried out and the political positions taken by the Karşı Lig are valued by other constituencies and thus these groups are influential in amplifying and converting them to a political position. For example, SES (the Equality, Justice, Woman Platform; esitlikadaletkadin. org) explains that the Karşı Lig is an example where male hegemony is challenged and broken down, and women and men can take part in all aspects of life, in collaboration.

Online communications: social media and websites

Utilizing social media as a medium of communication provides a milieu where participants are not simple listeners but also speakers. This opportunity to speak up, raise concerns, propose solutions and develop arguments is instrumental in integrating individuals and groups into the public sphere.

As discussed by Benkler (2008), such participation in the public sphere can be influential in organizing opinions and actions that can drive the political process. Communications via social media have the capacity to reorient listeners, their observations and evaluations of daily events and shape the positions taken. In other words, citizens can, with a minimum cost, participate in the Internet-mediated public sphere (blogs, social media, web pages) to express their discontents with the agenda of the hegemonic groups and express their own opinions. On the other hand, as discussed by Fuchs (2014, p 89), social media 'in Habermas' terms has the potential to be a public sphere and lifeworld of communicative action' but it is owned by corporations and subject to the state's monitoring of personal data. In other words, state and corporations colonize social media and hamper its capacity to be a public sphere (Fuchs, 2021). The ACCs vigorously use their social media accounts for mobilizing others and, as noted during the interviews, although using corporate-owned social media bears risks of state monitoring, it is an efficient medium of communication. According to Media Ownership Monitor 2021, Turkey is 16th globally in mobile Internet usage, and the most popular sites are Facebook, YouTube and Twitter. Eighty-five per cent of Internet users get news from the Internet, but the most visited sites are usually monitored by the pro-government media. Furthermore, according to the same source, Turkey is 4th globally for the removal of content on Twitter, and the new Social Media Act (5651), passed in October 2020, specifies that social media providers that do not comply can face monetary penalties and restrictions on bandwidth. Given the fact that approximately 79 per cent of the total population are active Internet users and spend more than 7 hours daily on the Internet (Media Ownership Monitor-Turkey, 2021), using Facebook and Instagram to inform, raise awareness, facilitate the development of an alternative consumer culture and expand networks seems to be a viable strategy. The discourse used in the posts reflects the position taken by the activist groups. Regardless of the issue posted, the content always contains political position-taking and facilitates timely and continuous information about the cooperative, organized activities, available foodstuff and other initiatives that they support.

The most common usage of websites and social media by the ACCs is about the foodstuff available in their shops. Weekly foodstuff lists and new arrivals are continuously shared with their followers. As we will discuss in detail in Chapter 6, these posts contain information about the food, the producer and the labour conditions. This information enables the would-be customers to comprehend the differences between the foodstuff available in the ACC's shop and industrially produced products and unveil the conditions under which they are produced. In a way, the ACCs try to overcome commodity fetishism. The common discourse in the posts of all the ACCs concerns social justice, equality, ecological safety and cleanliness (free from pesticides and artificial fertilizers), and, as illustrated in the following examples taken from Facebook posts, reflects a political position-taking:

> In Mexico/Chiapa, Zapatistas produce coffee that is ecologically grown and collectively produced, not for big corporations but for building their lives. Zapatista Kahve Kolektif in İstanbul in a solidaristic tie with the Chiapa delivers this coffee to us. Coffees named Ch'ulcan (meaning the sky) will be available in August.

> Products of the powerful and productive women of Yırcalı (a village in Soma where women protest against mines) are now available in the shop … soaps produced from the oil of olives that stood against bulldozers.

> We have a new producer Tragaia from Trakya. Tragaia works in line with the principles of good agriculture, good hazelnuts, good human beings. Their production process does not destroy the environment and adds value to the local peoples' labour.

> The boss got crazy! Then long live boss-lessness. As the production and living conditions get harder because of the pandemic, Free Kazova still operates without a boss. After sweaters and T-shirts, their bags (hundred percent cotton) are in our shelves. For strengthening solidarity, they are waiting for us.

Some ACCs also share their price list. And for some foodstuff (for example, vegetables, fruit and milk) pre-orders are taken, which in turn enables an efficient usage of shop space, inventories and reduction of waste. These are not simple announcements of available foodstuff but are also a means of developing a counter, ethical consumer culture where consumers' buying choice is based on the conditions and means used in the production of the available foodstuff. By so doing, the consumer assumes an activist position for the establishment and maintenance of social justice and environmental protection. Besides providing information about the available foodstuff, these sites function as a connectivity device: announcements are instrumental in linking community values, concerns and discontents to other groups. They are sites where, through calls for demonstrations and reminders of critical dates and issues, political position-takings are crystallized. Calls for demonstrations concern a diverse set of issues that affect the public in general: for example, the destruction of forests, climate justice, the protection of public and green spaces from private interests, violence against women and the implementation of the İstanbul Convention; while other posts celebrate events such the 25th anniversary of the food sovereignty declaration and the anniversary of the Gezi protests. Also, reminders are posted for local and international critical events such as 'Women Farmers Day', 'International Migration Day', 'the September 12 coup', and 'the October 10 Ankara bombing'.

They are inclusive spaces aiming to reconnect excluded groups, provide an 'alternative' to the prevailing food provisioning system and show their discontent with the economic measures taken in line with the populist neo-liberal policies. For example, when a textile company – Kazavo – was taken over by workers as compensation for their unpaid wages, the ACCs sold their products. The announcement regarding Kazavo sweaters, on the web page of an ACC, stressed that it was a boss-less company. When the government took action to privatize a sugar beet company, activists involved in the ACCs actively protested with various posts on their social media accounts.

> Privatization of sugar beet plants and food sovereignty. The privatization of sugar beet plants violates human rights. We want to open a discussion on this issue from the perspective of petty commodity producers and consumers and evaluate its consequences (public health, public policies…) in line with our food politics.

The ACCs, by participating in and organizing workshops (local and international), conferences and festivals also aim to develop and maintain their connectivity to other groups who have similar stakes. These activities, besides facilitating learning and sharing knowledge, are useful in developing a culture based on solidarity, inclusion and participation.

In conclusion

In this chapter, we have provided an explanation of the various activities and the discourse utilized by the ACCs in the making of a public sphere. To do so, we drew on Jürgen Habermas's concept of the public sphere. From this perspective, we explained how the 'hegemonic neo-liberal' project excluded certain groups – formal labour and the petty commodity producers – from the political process, while others – big capital and pro-government media conglomerates – gained a central position in the political decision-making process. The Labour Law (4857) drafted and accepted in 2003, and the pervasive wave of privatization, laid the ground for the marginalization of formal labour and the weakening of organized labour. And with the implementation of neo-liberal policies, namely the Agricultural Reform Implementation Project (ARIP) that was drafted by the World Bank, the Treasury and the Ministry of Agriculture and Rural Affairs, and the accompanying instruments, such as contract farming, direct income support, the petty commodity producers were proletarianized. While formal labour and the petty commodity producers were marginalized, big capital, through rent-seeking activities, facilitated by financialization and building networks of mutual support with the government cadres, became the main actors in the political sphere.

We argue that the efforts of the ACCs to include the marginalized groups in the political decision-making process contributes to the making of a public sphere where the normative arrangements of the hegemonic, neo-liberal project are challenged and alternative ways of doing things are nurtured. It is a move generated by the legitimation crises where the validity claims of the hegemonic system are questioned, prevailing social norms are interrogated, and alternative governance modes and alternative norms are experienced. In order to explicate this argument, we provided a detailed account of the various methods utilized (the shop, social media, the football league, site visits), the activities carried out in these settings and the discourse employed by ACCs. This public sphere, which incorporates a wide spectrum of activities, is instrumental in raising awareness, questioning and unveiling problems in agriculture, in food provisioning, and in the daily lives of the citizens. Furthermore, it is a space for experimenting with direct democracy and allowing others to be part of it through sharing experiences. And finally, it is a space where political position-takings are crystallized, and the opinions and actions of the marginalized groups are aligned for change.

6

Experimenting with an Alternative to the Capitalist Food Provisioning System

Introduction

The impact of globalization and neo-liberal policies in Turkish agriculture has been marked by the subordination of the petty commodity producers to market forces and their displacement from land and farming tradition. After the 1980 structural adjustment programme, governments with legislative reforms withdrew subsidies, reduced price supports and privatized parastatal organizations which in turn compelled small producers of agricultural products to rely on their own resources in their struggle within local and international markets. The pervasive implementation of neo-liberal policies, especially after 2002, transformed both production and consumption in agriculture.

On the production side, with the increasing dominance of agro-food companies and the commodification of foodstuff, petty commodity producers were driven out of the market. According to the official data of the Social Security Institute (SGK), in the last twelve years the number of insured farmers has dropped by 48.6 per cent (see Figure 6.1) and, in the last eighteen years, the amount of arable land has decreased by 3.150 million hectares (Tuncer, 2019). Small farmers deprived of government subsidies became more reliant on bank loans for the provision of their seeds, pesticides and machinery. As explained by the president of Çiftçi-Sen (the Farmers' Union), the petty commodity producers' debts for agriculture to the banks and credit cooperatives increased 53 times between 2002 and 2020 (Çameli, 2021), while subsidies were reduced by 48 per cent. In this transformation process, as well as increases in input prices, petty commodity producers faced stiff competition from imported foodstuff. However, it is worth noting that, currently, due to foreign currency fluctuations and the Turkish lira losing its value drastically, lowering trade barriers does not work as a viable strategy. In

Figure 6.1: Number of insured in agriculture

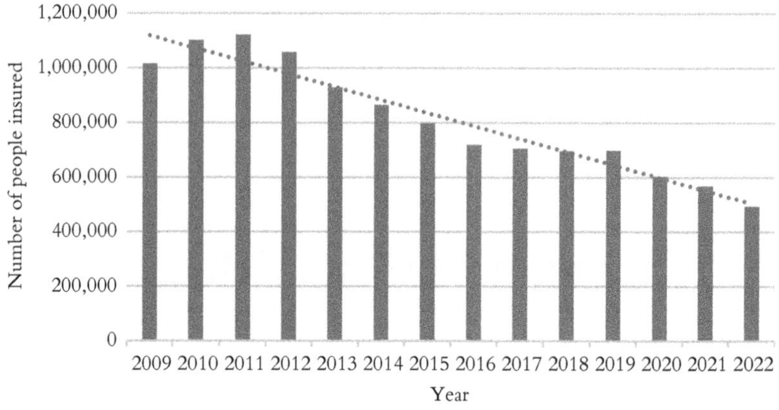

Source: Social Security Institution (www.sgk.gov.tr)

such an economic and political milieu, the petty commodity producers are left with a choice between leaving their farm and/or negotiating contracts with the agro-food companies.

On the consumption side, after 1980, with the implementation of free-market operations and the deregulation of agriculture, a major transformation in the food industry took place; the number of foreign companies increased and major international food processors and retailers entered the Turkish market either as greenfield operations or as joint ventures with local big capital (Yenal, 1999; Atasoy, 2013; Değirmenci, 2021). The investment decisions of these companies were also driven by the size and attractiveness of the emerging urban market. The liberalization of agriculture as an outcome of governmental policies has been marked by the proletarianization and migration of the rural petty commodity producers to the cities. In the 1990s the increasing urban population, composed of migrant smallholders as an informal workforce and a middle class identified with a specific lifestyle and education, was instrumental in the expansion of an urban food market. Initially, the urban middle class was drawn into the consumption of non-traditional foodstuff (such as frozen and processed foods, packaged dairy products) created by the agro-food companies (Yenal, 1999). However, over time, especially after 2000, the middle-class consumers' perceptions of 'good quality food' changed; they lost trust in mass-produced industrial food and were gradually driven away from the corporate-led food provisioning system. This process, as well as worldwide changing trends, was also prompted by the deliberate actions taken and policies developed by the government to promote neo-liberal policies single-handedly, drafting legislation for the betterment of agro-food businesses, without considering the needs of the petty commodity producers and the concerns of the urban consumers. The neo-liberal policies have led to unrest among the middle class, which were dissatisfied with the precarious social conditions, economic uncertainty and the commodification of nature.

In this chapter we aim to provide a deeper understanding of the alternative food provisioning model developed by the ACCs as a response to the populist neo-liberal policies and their authoritarian implementation in present-day Turkey. As discussed in Chapter 3, the neo-liberal project was inclusive for pro-AKP factions and the urban poor, while the middle class and petty commodity producers lost their long-standing dominant position in the face of the implementation of neo-liberal policies; professionals, women and small farmers were marginalized both economically and socially. The ACCs are trying to draft and implement an alternative model, both in production and consumption, of the food provisioning system in Turkey, to overcome the problems instigated by neo-liberal policies. In so doing, we focus on how ACCs appropriate and distribute surplus, develop means to bypass the intermediaries in production and distribution, and demystify commodity fetishism.

The chapter is organized as follows: in the first part the current food provisioning system, which is shaped by capitalism and the populist neo-liberal policies of the AKP, is explained, with an emphasis on its exclusionary and populist approach. This part provides in detail an explanation how petty commodity producers are excluded from the prevailing food system. In so doing, we explain the policies of the government in structuring and restructuring agriculture over three periods: those of state-led developmentalism, the capitalization of agriculture and the full-blown liberalization after 2002. In the second part of the chapter, we explain the model which the ACCs experiment with for re-shuffling the power relations in the prevailing capitalist system. This part is comprised of four sections that explain different aspects of the alternative model: reconstituting peasantry, experimenting with an alternative surplus generation, scaling-up and commodity de-fetishization.

Capitalization of agriculture in Turkey

In the Turkish economic and political landscape, the state had been the major actor in the production and distribution of agricultural products until the 1980 structural adjustment programme. Between 1930 and 1980, in line with the national developmentalist economic policies pursued by the governments of different political factions, agriculture and peasantry were protected from the pressures of commodity and currency markets (Keyder and Yenal, 2011). Through policies such as the provision of inputs, low-priced credit and supporting the formation of parastatal organizations such as the production and sales cooperatives, the state aimed to facilitate the expansion of production in agriculture (Aydın, 2010; Değirmenci, 2017, 2021). This support regime was populist and, as discussed by Güven (2009):

> [the] support schemes symbolized Turkish politicians' acknowledgement of the structurally disadvantaged position of rural producers in the face of rapid capitalist industrialization led by urban elites; they were used, most effectively by right-wing parties and neo-patrimonial leaders, to solicit mass support in return for ameliorating this systemic disparity via regularized interventions in agricultural markets. (p 169)

During this period, the scale and scope of state dominance varied, which in turn was influential in wealth distribution. The 1930–39 period was shaped by *étatism* and was marked by the implementation of a series of legislation that would enable the control of the market for agricultural products. In this vein, Ziraat Bank (the state-owned Agriculture Bank) was given full authority for direct purchases of agricultural products from the producers; the law for the protection of wheat (Buğdayı Koruma Hakkında Kanun) laid the ground for transferring the difference between the payments of the buyers and receipts of villagers to the state; and finally, peasant credit cooperatives were legally recognized (Boratav, 2019). This was a period during which agriculture was a source of revenue for the state. During the Second World War period, two major initiatives of the ruling party – CHP (Republican People's Party) – were the founding of Köy Enstitüleri (Village Institutes) and drafting a legislation for land reform. Köy Enstitüleri aimed to educate young villagers and modernize the then typical Turkish village life. It was a collaborative project, realized by the voluntary participation of local villagers, teachers, students and the state in provisioning resources, building facilities and maintaining them. For education purposes, lecture rooms, workshops, warehouses, kitchens, dining rooms and communication rooms were built. Also, for improving the living conditions of the local villagers, facilities such as Turkish baths, laundries, kitchens, warehouses for crops and water supply systems were developed. Köy Enstitüleri had a distinct approach to education: the curriculum was developed in line with the demands of the students, students had a say and participated in the maintenance of the buildings and, for practice, students and teachers collectively produced agricultural and dairy products, and raised the livestock which were to be used by the students (Güneri, 2004). From 1943 onwards, the ruling party attempted to draft legislation for land reform. The reform aimed to distribute land to villagers who had no land and who had to work as sharecroppers, to support villagers with inputs for agricultural production, to guarantee that the land was cultivated on a continuous basis, and finally to control the size of the arable land (for this an upper and lower limit was determined). Land owned by the state was to be distributed to the landless and if there was a shortage of land then private land would be expropriated and distributed (Karaömerlioğlu, 1998). The main spirit of the legislation was to change the ownership pattern of those big farms which were operated by sharecroppers (Avcıoğlu, 1968). The preparation and the approval the legislation at the General Assembly was marked by tensions between big landholders (some of whom occupied a seat at the Assembly as a parliamentarian), politicians on the opposition front and the Ruling party cadres (Avcıoğlu, 1968; Karaömerlioğlu, 1998). Finally, in 1946, the legislation was accepted by Parliament. However, over time, with the change of government to the 'liberal' Democratic Party (DP), and the pressures of the big landholders that were part of the state, it turned out to be an instrument for the distribution of 'publicly owned and marginal lands to the landless and small landholders' (Aydın, 2010, p 153). Both initiatives, Köy Enstitüleri and the Land Reform, which aimed the betterment of the peasantry and agriculture, were terminated in mid the 1950s by the DP who won the majority of votes in the elections.[1]

The 1947–53 period was marked with a transition to intensive farming and mechanization in agriculture (Aydın, 2010), which in turn transformed the rural class structure and work relations. The 1947 Economic Development Plan, which was prepared for delivering Marshall Aid, gave priority to private investments, financing development by foreign resources and the development of agriculture (Tekeli and İlkin, 1974). The plan identified agriculture as the driver of national development and other sectors, such as transportation and energy, were supposed to provide support for the improvements in agriculture. The plan and the subsequent Marshall Aid aimed to increase productivity and facilitate the mechanization of agriculture and the use of chemical fertilizers and pesticides (Tekeli and İlkin, 1974), which were imported using the financial resources of the Aid and then sold to villagers (Türkiyede Marshall Planı, 1952, 1953). The outcome was a greater increase than had been planned in the use of machinery and equipment and thus in agricultural output (especially cash-crops such as cotton and hemp). The capitalization of agriculture changed the class structure in the rural areas (Keyder, 2005; Değirmenci, 2021): the tenants and sharecroppers became wageworkers on big farms, or they moved to the fringes of the cities, while traditional big landholders, benefiting from favourable credit terms, returned to the rural areas (Aydın, 2010; Koç, 2014). In other words, the mechanization of agriculture as an outcome of Marshall Aid was marked by the proletarianization and migration of the rural population (Aydın, 2010; Değirmenci, 2021).

Between 1960 and 1980, the priority of the state was the capitalization of agriculture by the provision of machinery, inputs, low-cost credit and subsidies to farmers. The results of such a transformation were reflected in wealth distribution: big capital gradually moved from production to the distribution of agricultural products and processed foodstuff (Sönmez, 1987). Furthermore, during this period, a new actor, the multinational companies (MNCs), were included in the traditional connections of state, petty commodity producers, tradesmen and big landholders. As productivity in agriculture and the contribution of agricultural products to the GDP increased, Turkey became attractive for the MNCs. Besides buying agricultural products from Turkish farms, these MNCs started to produce inputs (seeds, fertilizers and pesticides) in Turkey for local and international markets. For example, Cargill with a local partnership in 1960, BASF in partnership with the state-owned enterprise Sümerbank in 1968, and Bayer by establishing a factory in 1966, entered the Turkish market (Değirmenci, 2021). Consequently, the capitalization of agriculture mainly relied on inputs produced by the MNCs and the support provided by the state.

Until the 1980s, agriculture was a priority for the Turkish state, with subsidies, low-priced credit and support pricing, so that productivity increases were secured (Keyder and Yenal, 2011). These policies were popular in maintaining the support of the peasantry, which comprised a high percentage of the population, and were useful in transferring the agricultural revenues to industry. Moreover, the petty commodity producers were supported, rural areas enjoyed welfare gains and dispossession rates were low (Aydın, 2002; Aydın, 2010; Koç, 2014; Boratav, 2019). The structural adjustment programme of the 1980s is characterized by a radical shift in the structuring of agriculture, which in turn shaped the focus of production, the production relations, the role(s) played by the state, and the social composition in the rural and urban areas. With the introduction of neo-liberal policies, the integration of agricultural producers to the world markets gained momentum while the state withdrew its support from agriculture. These neo-liberal policies in agriculture were also shaped by a shift in world agriculture: a shift towards the use of industrial inputs, production of high-value cash-crops and the rise of the agro-food industry. In the 1980s, with the drive of the MNCs, IMF, World Bank and WTO, Turkey, as a late developed capitalist country, changed its agrarian policy with a series of legislation, restructured the institutions of agriculture for free-market operations, and promoted the development of the agro-food industry.

Changes in agrarian policy were carried out through the privatization of state-owned input provisioning and support purchasing organizations. With the privatization of state-owned organizations, the prices of input (fertilizer, seed, gasoline, and so on) were left to the market mechanism. For example, fertilizer prices were determined according to US dollar/ Turkish lira parity in 1984 and two years later trade barriers for imports and exports of fertilizer were removed (Aysu, 2008; Değirmenci, 2021). To obtain some inputs, legal arrangements that enabled joint ventures with foreign companies were drafted. Besides the provision of subsidized inputs, the state gradually narrowed the scope of its support purchases. For example, in 1984, by drafting relevant legislation, the government permitted investors to purchase, process and distribute tea (Değirmenci, 2021), and with the Tobacco Law, the state-owned regulating agency TEKEL was replaced by the Tobacco Board, which was equipped with the authority to privatize the industry (Aysu, 2008; Aydın, 2010; Keskin and Yaman, 2013).

The outcome of the privatization process had distributional effects: privatized organizations were either sold to MNCs or to domestic family-owned holdings. In most cases, domestic holdings took over these organizations by themselves or by forming partnerships with the MNCs. However, as noted by Değirmenci (2021), some of them were later sold to international companies. It can be argued that the privatization wave, as well as the deregulation of agriculture, facilitated the entry of MNCs into Turkey as well the large domestic companies. During the late 1980s, foreign direct investment (FDI) in the food industry increased and the 1990s was a period where big food processing and retailing multinationals started their operations as FDIs in Turkey (Yenal, 1999). Domestic companies were more interested in the production, packaging and distribution of foodstuff rather than the production of agricultural products (Aydın, 2010; Değirmenci, 2021). This trend is reflected in the proliferation of retail chains owned by Turkish and foreign companies in the 1980s (Yenal, 1999; Atasoy, 2013, 2017; Değirmenci, 2021). Initially, these retail chains were established as joint ventures by Turkish holding companies and international retailers (primarily European); later domestically owned supermarkets entered the industry as well. In the latter cases, the role of Saudi finance has been noted by Atasoy (2013). This trend in the retail segment of the agro-food industry was influential in distancing petty commodity producers from the market (Atasoy, 2013).

Although the neo-liberal transformation started in 1980, the 5 April decision in 1994 (limitation of input subsidies for agricultural production, limitations on support purchases by the government, determining the price ranges of agricultural products according to global markets, privatization of state owned enterprises and provision of credits to farmers for purchasing inputs such as seeds and pesticides), in response to the financial crises, was the starting point for a comprehensive restructuring in the agriculture support system (Aysu, 2008, 2015; Aydın, 2010; Değirmenci, 2021). The guidelines of the restructuring were identified in line with the demands of international organizations and particularly the IMF. The aim of the restructuring was to limit support purchasing practices to a few crops (cereals, sugar beet and tobacco) and to limit the power of the state-owned agricultural sales cooperatives by not financing them through the Central Bank. Consequently, prices for agricultural products would be determined according to world markets, input subsidies would be limited, and the privatization of state-owned organizations would be completed (Oral, 2013; Aydın, 2010). Due to elections and changes in the composition of the ruling parties in Parliament, the implementation of the 5 April decisions was not smooth; every newly constituted government revised the programme. On the other hand, the economic crises facilitated a political milieu where bureaucrats prepared legislation for the enactment of free-market institutions that would facilitate the restructuring and transformation of agriculture in line with the recommendations of the IMF, the World Bank and bring harmonization with EU agricultural policy.[2]

With the implementation of neo-liberal policies after 1980, a serious, pervasive and continuous decline began in agriculture and undermined the social and economic position of the peasantry. Turkish agriculture, which was characterized by small farms, drastically changed in terms of ownership and scale of operations (Keyder, 1983; Kaymak, 2011; Boratav, 2019), and small producers that were unable to compete with the national and international big producers were gradually driven out of agriculture. Although from 1980 onwards there were efforts to transform agriculture to free-market operations, the comprehensive liberalization process had started with the 1999 intent letter submitted to the IMF by the then ruling coalition government headed by Bülent Ecevit. After the 2001 financial crises, the transition to a srong economy programme with the IMF was operationalized for restoring fiscal and economic stability. In line with the premises of the programme, in 2001 the Agricultural Reform Implementation Project (ARIP) was drafted by the World Bank, the Treasury and the Ministry of Agriculture and Rural Affairs to facilitate the liberalization of Turkish agriculture (Aysu, 2008; Akder, 2011; Karapınar et al, 2011; Aydın, 2010; Değirmenci, 2017; Değirmenci, 2021). The components of the ARIP were the repeal of subsidies and support purchases, the privatization of parastatals and state-owned agricultural sales cooperatives, and the transition from subsidized agricultural products to alternative crops. It was acknowledged that the losses incurred from the repeal of subsidies and support purchases would be compensated for by a programme of direct income support. The privatization of state-owned organizations had been underway since 1986 through related legislation (Law 3291), which was prepared under the umbrella of the World Bank, but the implementation of the ARIP speeded up the process of privatization. The Alternative Crop Programme suggested that maize, soya beans and sunflowers were to be planted instead of subsidized crops, that is, sugar beet, nuts and tobacco. Although the transformation process in agriculture by the ARIP started during the 2000–01 period, its full-fledged implementation was carried out after the AKP won the elections in 2002.

The liberalization of agriculture

Although the implementation of the ARIP was finalized in 2009, it had already been instrumental in transforming agriculture and the rural areas. In order to have a better understanding of how the ACCs made a difference, we have to discuss direct income support, contractual farming and the privatization of agricultural sales cooperatives as the main pillars of the ARIP. The outcome of these three instruments directly led to changes in ownership patterns, scales of production, production relations and the pricing of agricultural commodities. Furthermore, besides its distributional effects, the ARIP led to a transformation in rural employment patterns. Toward the end of this process, around 2008, agricultural employment dropped 25 per cent, creating a surplus of workers, composed of the younger male generation, in the urban labour market and the aging of the agricultural labour force in the rural areas (İlkkaracan and Tunalı, 2010; Değirmenci, 2017). The process also indicates the proletarianization of the small commodity producers (Çelik, 2017), which gained impetus with privatization and the change from the production of traditional crops. The official data indicates a drastic decrease in the number of insured agriculture workers following this process, as shown in Figure 6.1.

Direct Income Support

With the implementation of the ARIP, the traditional subsidies for agricultural products and inputs (fertilizers, seedlings and gasoline) regressed. Instead of these subsidies, an alternative payment programme, Direct Income Support (DIS), which was based on ownership and the size of the land, was instigated (Akder, 2011; Aydın, 2010; Kandemir, 2011; Boratav, 2019; Şazmaz and Özel, 2019). The aim of DIS was to mitigate the losses of farmers that had increased due to the reduced subsidies. DIS started as a pilot project in a few regions but after 2002 it was implemented countrywide. However, there were problems with its implementation: firstly, payments were to be made to landholders and those who had less than one decare or more than 500 would not be supported (Aydın, 2010; Oral 2013).[3] Consequently, big landowners, in order to be eligible for DIS, transferred their land to other family members and most of the small landholders did not take the trouble to register and apply for the payment (Akder, 2011). Secondly, since a proper register did not exist, especially with regard to small pieces of land, it was difficult to identify the owner, and in some cases absentee landholders, construction cooperatives and land developers registered for the support (Aydın, 2010; Koç, 2014). Also, since DIS was distributed according to ownership of land but no other criteria such as income, production capacity and input use, sharecroppers and tenant farmers were excluded from the system. And finally, after 2002, with the change in government, the system was diluted, and fuel and fertilizer subsidies were included in the DIS. These input subsidies were paid to the owners according to the size of their holding (Akder, 2011; Aydın, 2010). Furthermore, the payment rates for crops were different, as internationally traded alternative cash crops received more support than traditional crops.

DIS was fully supported by big capital and the representative association TÜSIAD clearly expressed that subsidies and support purchases in agriculture should be replaced by the direct income support model (Değirmenci, 2021). Especially after 2002, the DIS project, due to problems in its implementation, diverged from its initial premises and consequently turned out to be a system that favoured big landholders rather than the small farmers, sharecroppers and tenant farmers who were left out. Furthermore, some agricultural products that were cultivated by small farmers were driven out of the market (Aydın, 2010; Kandemir, 2011; Şazmaz and Özel, 2019) while the production of alternative crops was validated (Güven, 2009).

Contract farming

Although contract farming in Turkey started around the late 1960s, it became a pervasive production process after the 2000s. In 1965, in line with a state initiative organizing the production of cereal seeds, state-owned sugar factories (TŞFAŞ) started to implement contract farming (Aydın, 2010). In later years, and especially after 2006 with the Agrarian and Seed Laws, the groundwork was prepared by the state for the pervasive implementation of contract farming (Aysu, 2008; Aydın, 2010). Besides legislation, the state enforced contract farming by incentive schemes whereby a large number of farmers produced agricultural stuff for a specific company. In this later period, the focus shifted to high-value industrial crops and contract farming was mainly utilized by international agro-food companies. The producers of traditional crops were gradually driven out of the market, and they shifted to contract farming those crops that were in demand by the agribusinesses. Soon products such as tomatoes, potatoes, other vegetables and fruit were produced through contract farming. The number of domestic and international companies involved in contract farming increased. The local firms, in general, established partnerships with foreign companies that were involved in seed production and food processing (Aysu, 2008, 2015; Aydın, 2010; Değirmenci, 2021).

Contract farming is based on a pre-purchased agreement between a producer (the agribusiness firm) and farmers, where the producer firm specifies the amount, quality and the price. The producing company decides what has to be sown. Also, the producer provides the seed, fertilizer, pesticides and machinery for which the farmer pays. In this system, the farmers bear the risk – the risk of bad weather conditions, shortage of water, energy supplies, labour shortages – and pay the labour costs, so that if they cannot produce the pre-determined amount, they still have to make the payment for the inputs and machinery.[4] Consequently, this new production relation led to the proletarianization of the farmers and a drop in the number of traditional crop producers.

The privatization of state-owned sales cooperatives

Although the Privatization Master Plan, prepared in line with the premises of the World Bank, was put into operation in 1986 with legislation, the pervasive implementation of the privatization of parastatal organizations started with the ARIP (Aydın, 2010). One of the premises of the ARIP was the privatization of state-owned agricultural sales cooperatives. From the mid-1930s onwards these cooperatives were supported by the state for regulating agricultural markets and supplying agricultural products to domestic and international markets by securing a fair price and crop standardization (Aydın, 2010; Keyder and Yenal, 2011). In 1984, 1985 and 1991, with the implementation of various laws, the groundwork for transforming these cooperatives to corporations was prepared (Oral, 2013). The full transformation process was sped up and completed by the ARIP. The major impact of the ARIP was the restructuring of these cooperatives so that they would be autonomous in governance and independent of state in finance. Also, it was stated that they would not be involved in the production of foodstuff so that the unutilized assets (plant, equipment, and so on) could be privatized. For their governance, a board composed of state-appointed members would be in charge of these transformative decisions (Keyder and Yenal, 2011; Oral, 2013).

The privatization of agricultural sales cooperatives is taken as one of the predecessors of the decline in agriculture. With the withdrawal of state support and the full-fledged implementation of neo-liberal policies, agricultural credit cooperatives and state-owned enterprises (SOEs) that were instrumental in the price-setting of agricultural products like tea, nuts, alcohol, wheat, and so on, were gradually phased out. Finally, tariffs and quotas for the imports of agricultural products were regressed. From 2010 onwards, the AKP cadres, in line with their neo-liberal policies, tried to control price inflation in agriculture through imports and removed tariffs from most of the foodstuff (Akçay, 2017). Consequently, the ratio of agriculture in the GDP dropped drastically, the ratio of agricultural products in exports declined, while the ratio of imports for agricultural products (mainly inputs) increased (Kandemir, 2011; Kaymak, 2011). The choice of the AKP government was to encourage the big, industrial producers and this was a final blow for the petty commodity producers and led to the dissolution of traditional farming. Tuba Çameli (2021), in an interview with the president of Çiftçi-Sen, Ali Bülent Erdem, recalls the words of the former Minister of Agriculture, Mehdi Eker, "Either peasants will turn out to be corporations or the corporations will do agriculture". Eker explains that those farmers that employ contractual farming and use certified seeds produced and sold by the MNCs are supported by the government. Furthermore, the pervasive market logic in the provisioning of inputs drives the petty commodity producers out of agriculture, as they are deprived of resources such as energy and water. The recent announcement made by the chairman of the board of directors of DEDAŞ (the Electricity Distribution Company of Southeast Region) indicates the acuteness of the problem: "those villagers who have not paid their debts will not have electricity … they should not start planting" (*Duvar*, 3 November 2021). As a result of these conditions, poverty among small farmers increased, some of them migrated to the cities as informal labour and those who stayed in their villages reduced their investments, relied on family members (especially women) as the contingent workforce and supported their operations with bank loans. As noted by Değirmenci (2017), with the decrease in government support in agriculture, the petty commodity producers drifted towards bank loans from both local and international banks for the provision of financial resources (bank loans increased 8 times in the14 years following 2002), and a greater number of farmers were unable to repay their debt.

Thus, the liberalization of agriculture by deregulating input prices, withdrawing subsidies and price supports, and privatizing the organizations that supported farmers had serious effects on the ownership patterns, production relations and the position of the actors involved in the system. This is not to say that the state-led system was much better, but to suggest that instead of a full commitment to neo-liberal policies, alternatives could have been researched, evaluated and tried, such as La Via Campesina and the food sovereignty movement, which would integrate petty commodity producers into the markets and be more participatory and transparent in governance. These alternatives would unite small farmers, provide economic and social equity and sustainable agricultural production, where what to produce and how to produce it are decided by the farmers rather than the big firms.

In search of alternatives

'We must take food provisioning out of the market logic. My dream is to show that it can be done in a different way … with reciprocal relations among producers and consumers.'

Interview with a volunteer from
Kadıköy Kooperatif, March 2018

In the mid-2010s, the consequences of the two major transformations in Turkish agriculture – capitalization (which started in the 1950s in line with the premises of Marshall Aid) and liberalization (which started in the 1980s with structural adjustment and gained momentum after 2002) – had devastating effects on the petty commodity producers and traditional subsistence crops. While petty commodity producers drastically lost their position in the production and sales of agricultural stuff, big capital, represented by domestic and international agro-business firms, became dominant in determining the type and price of the commodities to be produced. The dispossession and proletarianization of the petty commodity producers also influenced the shift from the production of subsistence crops to high-value industrial crops. Although subsistence crops and agricultural products produced in small farms are better in terms of quality (no pesticides or chemical fertilizers, and using local seeds), they are more expensive compared to industrially grown foodstuff. Also, the petty commodity producers face difficulties in relating their output to the urban consumers who are left with no alternative than what is offered by the vertically integrated big firms. Alternative consumer cooperatives aim to fill this void and, in an effort to link petty commodity producers to the urban consumers, they develop an alternative surplus generation that enables the consumption of high-quality foodstuff at affordable prices.

Reconstituting peasantry: developing an unmediated relation with producers

On the production side, one of the major problems currently faced in Turkey is the marginalization and de-peasantization (Jacoby, 2008) of the petty commodity producers within the capitalist economy, that is, their displacement from their land, from farming traditions and from rural areas. With the implementation of free trade agreements, imported seeds and foodstuff (vegetables, meat, cereals, and so on) found a place in the supermarkets. 'Food from nowhere' at low prices, produced by a small number of vertically and horizontally integrated firms, and usually imported with zero tariffs, invaded the markets. Petty commodity producers lost their competitive position as they had higher costs. In the case of seedlings, small farmers, using imported seeds, had to use imported fertilizers and pesticides, which turned out to be very costly after the devaluation of the Turkish lira. Furthermore, in order to finance their operations, small producers depended on bank loans, which turned out to be a debt trap. The urban farmers located in various parts of big cities suffered from the populist neo-liberal policies as well. As a consequence of the AKP's attempts to reshape big cities (especially İstanbul), and following gentrification initiatives, urban farms changed hands; they were sold so the land could be used for building mosques, shopping malls, supermarkets, the new airport and TOKİ houses.

In an effort to re-shuffle the production relationship between small and big foodstuff producers, the ACCs developed practices related to two issues: (a) bypassing the intermediaries, and (b) experimenting with a different way of surplus generation and distribution. Bypassing intermediaries and establishing direct relations with the small farmers enables them to control quality and prices. The founders of the ACCs state that, "everyone, no matter their socio-economic status, has the right to healthy and good quality food … we want to sell better quality stuff at a lower price so that the quality and quantity erosion in food provisioning in this country is eroded." This system evokes some indirect contributions too: it supports producers with know-how on agrochemical safe production methods; establishes collaborative networks of producers that facilitates information, know-how and material exchange; supports the production of subsistence crops; and empowers women producers (for example, organizing women farmers around production cooperatives and arranging separate payment accounts for female members of the family). As the activists we interviewed maintained, such an approach "puts the producer [the petty commodity producer] at the centre of the production–consumption nexus and opens the path for new alternatives". On the other hand, since the ACCs are run by consumers and all decisions about what to sell in their shops are made collectively, it enables the consumers to have a right in deciding what they are going to consume.

Establishing an unmediated relationship with petty commodity producers requires the identification of small producers that implement ecologically safe, traditional farming practices. In so doing, all of the ACCs, as shown by their web pages, social media accounts and public talks, approach producers that support the food sovereignty movement, adopt ecological farming methods, use local seeds and do not exploit women or use child labour. The identification and selection of producers is decided upon collectively by all the participants of an ACC, where the product and the price and delivery methods of a specific producer are evaluated. In this way, it is anticipated that the small producers implementing traditional farming methods and using local seeds will be empowered in their struggle for survival against the vertically integrated big industrial producers. Furthermore, female-owned producer cooperatives, producers that belong to disadvantaged groups such as immigrants, the LGBT community, victims of natural disasters, and those who have lost their jobs are given a priority. For example, from time to time, some ACCs sell the sweaters of Kazova, a group of workers who, through resistance, reclaimed their salaries and compensation after the Kazova textile factory went bankrupt. The resistance continued as a factory occupation and currently two workers' cooperatives – Diren (Resist) Kazova and Özgür (Free) – sell textiles produced in the worker-owned factory.[5]

For identifying and selecting the petty commodity producers with whom the ACC will cooperate, a procedure is followed: the potential producer is asked to fill out a form which is available publicly and then the volunteers in the governing bodies of the related ACC consider the eligibility of the candidate. If needed, references from Çiftçi-Sen and other cooperatives that have already established a relationship with the farmer are requested. The relations with the producers are carried out by the volunteers. Each volunteer assumes responsibility for a producer, checks how much of the producer's foodstuff is sold in a week, decides how much is to be ordered and considers whether any complaints from consumers are related to the producer. In order to ensure that the producers meet their commitment, and for transparency purposes, the ACCs visit their farms and organize site excursions that are open to everyone. The records of these visits, encounters with the farmers and the stories of the foodstuff produced by them are displayed on the web pages or social media accounts of the ACCs (details of such site visits are given in Chapter 5). In some cases, the farmers themselves or the consumers of the ACC can appeal to authorities for a laboratory analysis of a foodstuff. If needed, farmers are linked to other farmers so that promises for ecologically grown and healthy foodstuff are met. During the interviews we witnessed many cases similar to the following: an ACC decided to buy tarhana and noodles from a women's cooperative, but they discovered that this producer cooperative used industrial flour as an input. They therefore connected the cooperative to a producer from their list who produced wheat using local seeds and traditional methods.

The ACCs are sensitive to the exploitation of women, children and immigrant labour. If they discover that women are not being involved in the decision-making process and are being oppressed, the ACCs use various mechanisms to change the situation (Kadıköy Kooperatifi Kollektifi, 2020). For example, in Turkey, because of the dominant patriarchal family structure, men usually control the household finances, and rural women witness and live through a pervasive gender-based division of labour and carry most of the production work burden without payment or social security (Yaman, 2019). They are 'unpaid family workers' who do not participate in the decision-making process; men deal with the middlemen, municipalities and banks. Eren (2017), in her study among the mountain villages in the Aegean region, has seen that 'women's money belongs to everyone [husband, children] and men's money belongs to himself' (p 827). Similar results are reported for the Marmara (Yılmaz et al, 2019) and Black Sea regions (Keskin and Yaman, 2013; Karaçimen and Değirmenci, 2019). This gender-biased division of work is also exacerbated by the patriarchal ownership relation, where in most cases women do not have a claim on the ownership of the farmland (Yaman, 2019; Karaçimen and Değirmenci,2019). Men, as the owners of the factors of production, claim the right to make the decisions and control the finances. In an effort to change the position of women as unpaid family workers and promote their inclusion in the decision-making process, the ACCs make direct payments to female members of the farms so that their labour is compensated. If necessary, they encourage women farmers to have their own bank accounts and provide a milieu where they can have a voice in decisions related to the production process (Oba and Ozsoy, 2020).

Experimenting with an alternative surplus generation

The ACCs also experiment with a different approach to surplus generation. Since the ACCs do not aim to generate profit, they are consequently different to conventional cooperatives – they do not distribute profits to their members. According to Kooperatifler Kanunu (Cooperative Law 1163), in Turkey a minimum of 10 per cent of cooperatives' revenues should be accrued as retained earnings and a minimum of 50 per cent of the revenues should be distributed among the cooperative partners. Cooperatives can make interest payments to their partners provided that they are not more than the amount offered by the government bonds (clause no. 4/38). If needed, cooperatives can secure financial resources for establishing and operating organizations that support their partners and employees. On the other hand, on their web pages and social media accounts, the ACCs announce that they are non-profit organizations. Instead, their aims are:

> Building and strengthening a transparent and sustained bond between small farmers and urban consumers so that they will challenge the industrial food producers that aim for profits while undermining the health of human beings. (Salkım Kooperatifi, 2021)

> To support and intensify the food sovereignty movement, all our revenues are to be used to support the food sovereignty movement. (Kadıköy Kooperatif, 2021)

> To inspire others to implement similar consumer cooperatives in districts and workplaces, promote the founding of other consumer cooperatives that will develop solutions to the problems of small producers and consumers, and assure that healthy food (without chemicals) is available to all income groups. (BÜKOOP, 2021)

As non-profit organizations, they set prices without aiming to create a surplus; their priority is to create social value. If a surplus is created, it is used for those groups that struggle for just employment relations, those groups that are excluded because of their sexual choice, and those who suffer gender inequality (BÜKOOP, 2021; Kadıköy Kooperatif, 2021; Salkım Kooperatifi, 2021). For example, on its web page, Kadıköy Kooperatif states that, 'We add 1 per cent for depreciation, 1 per cent for the solidarity fund (that is distributed every four months) and 1 per

cent for cooperative activities over the price of items sold at the shop'
(kadikoykoop.org, 2021).

Also, in the shops of each ACC, one of the shelves, the 'solidarity shelf'
is secured for the products of disadvantaged producers – an immigrant
women, a farmer that lost his/her yield because of a flood, or a civil
servant that lost his/her job for political reasons. The major cost items
are the foodstuff sold, the salary for an accountant (the only staff member
who is not a volunteer), the rent for the shop, expenses for holding a
general assembly (a legal requirement) and tax payments (Oba and Ozsoy,
2020). Recently, especially with the Covid-19 pandemic, some ACCs
started deliveries to households. For example, the Yeryüzü and Nardugan
cooperatives announce their products and price lists on social media sites
and communication apps like WhatApp each week and issue a deadline for
orders; they then deliver the products to the consumers in their district.
Also, besides home delivery and shop sales, some of the coperatives have
a stand at the farmers market organized by the municipality of İstanbul
for supporting small farmers.[6]

The ACCs, when purchasing from the farmers, do not negotiate the
prices, but ask farmers to offer a fair price, a price which will provide them
with an income that enables a decent living (Kadıköy Kooperatifi Kollektifi,
2020; Oba and Ozsoy, 2020). Such a practice, contrary to the capitalist
mode of production, avoids surplus-value in the exploitation of the farmers.
The farmers are paid in cash within two to four weeks after the delivery
(interview notes, https://bukoop.org/). Since bookkeeping and preparing
financial documents such as a balance sheet, income statement and reports
for the evaluation of partners at the general assembly is a legal requirement,
the ACCs employ an independent accountant. Similarly, the general assembly
and the way it has to be organized is a legal requirement and the procedures
are defined by the related legislation, which involves some cost such as the
registration of the assembly, an authorized signature list, and so on.

On the production side, producers have been involved in the development
of the ACCs from the start. Indeed, as noted by Çiftçi-Sen, some producers
like İlhan Koçulu and Ali Ünüvar have supported the formation of the
ACCs. They have participated in the workshops and meetings organized by
BÜKOOP (the first ACC), explaining the possible benefits of alternative
cooperatives both for the consumers and producers. The food provisioning
system developed by the ACCs does not only support and protect the urban
consumers but also protects the petty commodity producers. Producers that
we have interviewed stated that in the beginning there were only a few
cooperatives that purchased their products, but now they have a big portfolio
of buyers, which is useful for expanding their operations. Furthermore, the
expansion of the ACCs has been coupled with the expansion of producer
cooperatives and has changed the attitudes of the small producers towards

the cooperative form of organizing. During an interview, İlhan Koçulu stated that:

> 'a decade ago, when I tried to organize farmers for establishing a producer cooperative, they approached the idea with reservation. They hesitated and thought that they will be defrauded. Now the same people come and ask me to establish a producer cooperative. They have witnessed how the previously established ones survived and became successful.'

Scaling-up or not?

One of the major issues of this alternative model of food provisioning is related to scaling-up. By confining their operations to a district and its inhabitants and adhering to the ideal of remaining small, the ACCs face a dilemma in relation to scaling-up. By scaling-up they can lower costs and supply certain products at affordable prices, but as noted by Little et al (2010) scaling-up can evolve into a different type of organization where volunteer work is replaced by paid work and there is less interaction between producers and consumers. Too much emphasis on scaling-up and profits carries the risk of degenerating into a cooperative that adopts business/market values and practices (Pansera and Rizzi, 2018). Although it is difficult to give an exact number for the ACCs in Turkey,[7] based on our interviews and fieldwork we can say that the number of ACCs, especially in İstanbul, are rapidly increasing. During the past year, new ACCs have been established in different districts of İstanbul (for example, Yeldeğirmeni, Maltepe, Bostancı, Kozyatağı, Kuzguncuk, Ataşehir, Nardugan and Arı Köy) and in other cities such as Ankara, Eskişehir, İzmir and İzmit.

The objective of the ACCs is not only to provide healthy food at affordable prices but also to raise awareness and direct attention to the problems in agriculture and other environmental issues. This entails a close relationship with producers and consumers and enables them to exchange knowledge. In line with their initial ideals, the ACCs stay small and confine their operations to a district, but they also provide guidance and know-how whenever a group of consumers consider establishing a new cooperative. So, the existing ones inspire activists and dwellers from other neighbourhoods of the city and share their knowledge and experiences. As stated by a founder of the Beşiktaş Kooperatif:

> 'First, we called a friend from Kadıköy Kooperatif. He told us the political aspects of this type of organizing. When we achieved a group of 6–7 volunteers, we learned from them what we could do collectively with our neighbours. Then we went through some reading ourselves. We had also got the reading lists of Kadikoy Kooperatif.'

Besides sharing knowledge and experiences, the ACCs encourage the establishment of replicas in different districts of the city. They freely share information about the newly established cooperatives, even if they are located very close to theirs. For example, at a public meeting organized by one of the ACCs, in which we participated, the volunteers who were running the meeting announced that a new ACC in a nearby district was going to be formed. For those participants who were interested in the new cooperative, they also shared the names and email adresses of the founders so that, as consumers and volunteers, they could join them. Through such cooperation and knowledge-sharing, the ACCs opt for 'horizontal' scaling-up. In so doing, they experiment with two contrasting approaches. One approach is to support the establishing of new ACCs in other districts of İstanbul and in other cities. During the interviews this was explained as follows: "some interested groups asked us whether we will permit them to be our branches, we are not for subsidiaries, but if they want to establish an independent ACC, we can support them with our knowhow and network." The founding partners of each newly established ACC are different and so are the volunteers who work for the cooperative. This approach can be instrumental in expanding the ACC network and in establishing closer relations with the neighbourhood. Since most of the founders and volunteers are from a specific district, they have a better understanding of the locals' concerns, they will be more devoted to providing a solution for local problems and can establish closer relations with the locals. The other approach, in contrast, aims to establish branches in different districts. For example, Yer Deniz Kooperatif, has branches in the districts of Kuzguncuk, Göztepe and Yeldeğirmeni, and the founder of these cooperatives gave the following explanation:

'Operating with branches is instrumental to cutting costs; we only pay for one accountant, carry out only one general assembly for all the branches, so general assembly costs are minimized. Each branch is run by a group of local volunteers; they are autonomous and independent from the other branches in decision-making.'

For vertical scaling-up, all of the ACCs have developed alliances to facilitate bulk purchases from small producers and producer cooperatives that produce environmentally friendly, ecologically safe foodstuff. For example, a group of ACCs and AFNs (sixteen altogether) located in İstanbul made a joint order of 1.5 tons of lentils from a producer in Kars (in the far east of Turkey). In this way they were able to pay less for transportation and thus charge lower prices. Just four years ago, when there were only a few ACCs, this amount was only about 500 kilograms. Such collaboration is useful not only in reducing the prices but enables the existing petty commodity producers to scale-up and also encourages new producers to join the network.

De-fetishization of foodstuff

On the consumption side of the food provisioning system, the ACCs have developed practices to change the power relationship between consumers and the small producers. As an alternative to the dominant logic, the ACCs supply only seasonal products so that consumers have to be satisfied with what is available in the shop. The prevailing capitalist system supports consumption by facilitating the purchase of anything without knowing its origin and without knowing the producer and the production conditions. Emphasis on the exchange-value of agricultural products disguises two things: as consumers we disregard their use-value, that is, we no longer see them as products that satisfy a need and serve a specific function; and secondly, we do not see them as the products of a farmers' labour, nor consider what is involved in their production, that is, somehow, we are not aware of the labour power used, the time needed to produce a specific item and the relationship between different producers. In other words, for an urban consumer who has no chance of experiencing the specific conditions under which wheat is produced, there will be no difference, except the price, between the credentials of industrially grown and traditionally grown wheat. The same consumer will not even consider the value of labour involved in its production and may even equate the labour of industrially grown and traditionally grown wheat. Fetishized exchange value blinds the consumer; they think that the value of the wheat arises from its exchange value but not the labour that has produced the wheat. In a capitalist society, it is assumed that commodities possess a value that is attributed to the characteristics of the commodity but not the labour conditions required to produce it. The capitalist system, by relying on money in the exchange process, conceals the social relationship; the value of a commodity is evaluated according to its price, and the social relationship between individuals takes the form a relationship that exists between things. For example, in the farmers market, the producers and consumers meet but communicate only during the exchange process where both of them are represented by the commodities they can offer (the consumer with the money she/he can pay and the farmer with the product of her/his labour). The labour and social relationships that enable the production of the commodity are hidden in the exchange process. Price determines the value of a commodity, and the farmer thinks and believes that the 'market' makes her/his labour valuable rather than understanding that the market is made by the collective labour of various others. This leads to a situation where exploitation in surplus generation is veiled and, with the acceptance of the dominated, opposition is silenced.

> It is precisely this finished form of the world of the commodities – the money form – which conceals the social character of private labour

and the social relations between the individual workers, by making those relations appear as relations between material objects, instead of revealing them plainly. (Karl Marx, 1990, pp 168–9)

Providing information about the origin of the food and about the producers can provide a solution to commodity fetishism (Allen and Kovach, 2000; Goodman and DuPuis, 2002). The ACCs, in various ways (labelling products with information about the producer, production methods and location of the producer, providing excursions to production sites, and so on), attempt to de-fetishize the agricultural commodities. They use their social media accounts to announce the arrival of new products and, in so doing, always identify the producers and direct attention towards the social and political conditions the producers face. For example, instead of announcing a special commodity and its price, they announce that foodstuff from the Ovacık cooperative (a cooperative founded by the Ovacık municipality, the only Marxist municipality in Turkey) has arrived or that chickpeas from a producer who has lost his/her academic job due to political reasons has arrived in the shop. These announcements provide information about the producers and the products offered by those producers. As a buyer, we are informed about who the produces are, the conditions of production, what type of production methods are used and how the product is certified as safe. If available, the interview notes of the producers, where they explain the conditions of production and labour involved, is added to these announcements. For example, in an interview with a milk producer, detailed explanations of how the animals are fed, what type of food they are given and what methods of hygiene are used are provided, while the daily operations on the farm and the workload of farm workers are also explained in detail. In another announcement, the producers explained that, 'Nut paste was established by two women who aim to provide good and affordable food. The nuts and dates used in our products are grown without pesticides and fertilizers.' In their announcements about the products and producers, the ACCs, in line with their aim of supporting women's labour, pay special attention to revealing their contribution, and incorporate such statements as 'the women cooperative, the women entrepreneurs, the women farmers, the women shepherds'.

In a similar vein, some ACCs, before the Covi-19 pandemic, organized site visits to the farms of the producers in their network. These visits (discussed in detail in Chapter 5) are announced on their web pages and are open to all who are interested. Site notes and videos are posted on the web pages and social media accounts. Such a practice is useful in disclosing information about the producers, the conditions of production and it also raises the consumers' awareness. It is commonly stated by ACC members that 'consumers can transform the producers and production methods' as they learn more about a specific foodstuff and the production relations that shape it. Similarly, some producers were invited to deliver a public speech where they explained their production methods and associated problems. For example, in such a meeting, a non-industrial rice producer from Artvin (on the eastern Black Sea coast) was invited by BÜKOOP. During the talk he described the labour conditions, the traditional farming practices employed and the problems that the petty rice producers encountered. He also outlined how the villagers worked collectively when planting and harvesting and how the burden on women was reduced by this collective production method. After the talk, the consumers' interest in how rice was grown with local seeds and traditional methods was intensified. As the demand for rice grown in this village increased, other producers were drawn in and changed their production methods. As previously noted, some ACCs jointly organize workshops, such as cheese-making, bread-making, and so on, with their producers. These workshops are open to the public, are free of charge and are carried out at the ACC's shop. In the cheese workshop, where one of us participated, the cheese producer provided a detailed explanation about the various types of cheese produced in Turkey, how they are produced, and the differences between industrially produced and traditionally produced cheese; and in the second half of the workshop he demonstrated a simple method for producing cheese at home. These practices, labelling that contains information about the producer and product, excursions, social media posts, workshops, have a dual function: on the one hand, they are attempts to de-fetishize agricultural commodities; on the other, they aim to raise the awareness of the urban consumers. Consumers are not only informed about the availability and price of a specific commodity but also develop an appreciation of the labour conditions that enables their presence in the market. These practices are also instrumental in linking petty commodity producers to the politicized urban consumers and establishing an ethical, trust-based relationship.

In conclusion

In this chapter we discussed the transformation of the smallholders in Turkey as the result of the capitalization and liberalization policies implemented by governments. With the abandonment of government support after the state-led developmentalist period, capitalization and liberalization waves removed the traditional production and consumption nexus in agriculture, leaving petty commodity producers to the forces of free-market operations. Since the structural adjustment programme of the 1980s, the production and consumption nexus in agriculture has gone through a pervasive restructuring, where market risks, for both inputs and outputs, are not mitigated by the government and agro-food producers and retailers have gradually dominated the market for foodstuff. This restructuring through contract farming, direct income support and privatization of the parastatal organizations has resulted in the petty commodity producers becoming informal workers in the cities or the proletariat of the agro-food companies in the rural areas. As peasantry and farming became dependent on the dynamics of free-market operations, safe agrochemical production methods dwindled, farmers had to rely on off-farm jobs for a subsistence living, farming traditions dissolved, and the role of agro-food processors and intermediaries (both domestic and international) in the food provisioning system increased. In many cases, land was commodified, lost its value as a site for farming and was utilized for housing and tourist hotels. The same process influenced the consumption patterns of the urbanites, especially the middle class. Initially, during the 1990s, the demand for processed, packaged foodstuff increased but, over time, middle-class consumers lost trust in industrially produced foodstuff and started to look for alternatives to the corporate-led food provisioning system. This search also coincided with the thrust of neo-liberalism in agriculture and its authoritarian implementation in the political realm after the mid-2000s.

The main argument of this chapter is that ACCs are influential in creating an alternative model to the capitalist food provisioning system and they can be the drivers of change in food politics. They have a transformative capacity and manifest potential economic and organizational alternatives. We have noted that ACCs are examples of the transforming of urban middle class and rural petty commodity producers as economic and political subjects that experiment with an alternative food provisioning system shaped by non-capitalist activities. It is a process that aims to reconstitute peasantry by trying an alternative surplus generation model, by refusing scaling-up and by involving politicized urban consumers. The activists involved in the ACCs, by imagining, desiring and experimenting with non-capitalist ways of producing, distributing and consuming, have created an alternative space for the unfolding of an unmediated relationship with producers, the de-fetishization of foodstuff and a different surplus generation. This space has also promoted a milieu where solidaristic bonds are nurtured for the construction of an alternative, inclusive community. This community enables the exchange of know-how between petty commodity producers on agrochemical safe production methods, promotes an awareness on the consumption of subsistence crops and thus supports their production, and empowers women by giving priority to the foodstuff produced by them on the shelves of the shops. In so doing, the practices developed and experimented with are in line with the goals of the ACCs; they are not for profit; they do not aim to scale-up. Their priorities are to create social value and expand the alternative surplus generation model to other districts of İstanbul and other cities in Turkey so that they will be heard by wider audiences. Also, by various practices, such as providing information about the producer and the production methods employed, consumers' awareness on labour conditions, labour power and the duration of production is fostered. The de-fetishization of agricultural products influences the buying behaviour of the urban consumers – what they consume is not only the foodstuff but also the process through which it is produced. By choosing certain products and producers over others they can reinforce some labour practices and production methods (non-capitalist forms) and reject others (capitalist forms) which entails consumers' choice as a political act.

7

The Governance of Alternative Consumer Cooperatives

Introduction

The activists involved in the ACCs are against authoritarianism; they value participation, solidarity and equality. As discussed in Chapter 3, the hegemonic neo-liberal project deliberately excluded some groups (women, the secular middle class and people with a specific political orientation) from economic and social life. As a consequence of the implementation of neo-liberal policies, after 2001 most of the activists became precariat; they deliberately refused the governing principles of investor-owned companies and the managerialism underlying them. Being against authoritarianism, neo-liberal policies and the politically exclusionist attitude of the ruling groups, the activists aimed to develop an alternative governance based on the principles of equality, inclusion and participation.

Experimenting with democratic and dialogic decision-making practices, they decided to get rid of the hierarchical relationship in the newly formed cooperatives. Using a diverse economy approach as a framework (Gibson-Graham 2006; Gibson-Graham et al, 2013) we analysed the work practices of the ACCs that are based on 'zero-hierarchy' and 'consensus-based collective decision-making'. By experimenting with various practices negotiated among their members, activists involved in the ACCs aim to prefigure a post-capitalist society that is just, democratic and egalitarian.

This chapter explains the 'alternative' governance model which the ACCs experimented with. In so doing, we examine how various practices of this governance model are developed and how conflicts that arise from this new governance model are handled. The chapter is composed of three parts: performance measures, form of organization and volunteer work.

In search of an alternative governance model

The roots of the ACCs and the prefigurative strand taken by activists can be traced back to the Gezi protests and the underlying values and practices that were developed in the subsequent 'park forums' and Occupy houses. Gezi was an occasion where the discontents of the hegemonic neo-liberal project – the white-collar workers, professionals and students, had a chance to experiment with an alternative model shaped by solidarity, direct democracy, participation, mutuality, consensus and cooperation. As stated by a food activist, "Gezi was a 'call', where people who were seen as a political, insensitive to societal and ecological issues came together to build a future society that is inclusive, democratic and egalitarian." The book *Yeniden İnşa Et* (Yılmaz et al, 2020), collectively written by the activists involved in the first neighbourhood ACC, considers their cooperative as one of the outcomes of Gezi, with its governance model shaped around horizantalism, participation and autonomy (Yılmaz et al, 2020). In an attempt to challenge the prevailing, deep-rooted inequalities, the activists are trying to align their daily practices in the cooperative with their political and ethical commitments. Through experimenting and learning they are attempting and trying to construct an alternative way of organizing that can challenge power inequalities in the capitalist system and authoritarianism prevalent in Turkish society and workplaces. In order to avoid the trap of being conditioned by the capitalist logic and the authoritarian culture that they aim to change, the activists are involved in a continuous process of learning and experimenting. In so doing, they read, contact international organizations, host speakers from other countries, translate books/texts and hold discussion groups. In other words, they share their experiences and knowledge, and learn and experiment. They plan activity programmes and arrange workshops to discuss a diverse range of topics such as ecological farming, developing and sustaining mutual initiatives, solidarity economies, food politics and alternative cooperatives. As noted by the activists during this 'collaborative learning process', the topics to be scrutinized, guest speakers to be invited, resources to be utilized are determined collectively. In this way, activists from diverse backgrounds bring their expertise and knowledge and build up a rich knowledge-base. As one volunteer stated:

'I come from the ecology movement, someone else comes from a leftist organisation, and someone else is interested in healthy nutrition. We are learning from each other not only about a certain topic but also how to get organized. We all share our knowledge and experiences. This is wealth accumulated and distributed on an equal basis.'

During this learning process, participants assume an equal role and there is no hierarchy, no distance. As one activist puts it:

'[It is] a horizontal kind of relationship where nobody is the teacher. Everyone is a teacher, and everyone is a learner depending on the issue tackled. What I learned and experienced in a month cannot be achieved in five years.'

Through 'collaborative learning' and experimentation the ACCs have become sites where mutuality, consensus-based decision-making, horizantality and self-organizing is practised.

Solidarity but not profits

Two major characteristics of the ACCs that are contrary to the capitalist economic logic: they are not-for-profit and do not aim to scale-up. In other words, their performance is not measured and evaluated in terms of profits and strategic tools that lead to profit maximization (a detailed explanation of these issues is provided in Chapter 6). Instead, the ACCs are organized around the ethics of solidarity (Gibson-Graham, 2003, 2008), where decisions about which products are to be sold, how petty commodity producers are to be paid, the allocation of the workload, and the terms and conditions of volunteer work are taken through the full participation of all the concerned parties. They are open to discussion that reflects past experiences and future expectations.

The ACCs deliberately stay small and operate in a specific neighbourhood of the city. Since they do not aim to scale-up and aim to limit their operations within a specific district, they are able to practise consensus-based decision-making and an organizational structure shaped by the premises of horizantality. In other words, the distinction between ends and means of the ACCs dissolves, and organizing becomes expressive of the ends and, in turn, shapes the nature of future political action to be followed. Limiting the scale of operations to a district (neighbourhood) is a compromise for scaling-up and profitability but, on the other hand, it enables the development of communal spaces where what is aspired to can be experimented with and validated. Thus, we view the ACCs as 'laboratories for a post-capitalist future' (Kokkinidis, 2014, p 849), trying to experiment with a non-capitalist economic model and organizational practices.

Developing communal spaces in the neighbourhoods ('neighbourhood solidarity initiatives', as the activists call them) is a new practice in the realms of Turkish politics and society. Previous examples of 'solidarity networks' were organized around being *hemşehri* (people from the same hometown) (Hersant and Toumarkine, 2005; Ayata, 2008), belonging to the same Islamic sect (Kaya, 2015; Akpınar, 2017), or belonging to an ethnic group (Çelikpala, 2006). These types of networks are very common, especially among those who have migrated from rural areas and smaller cities to the peripheries of the big cities. These *hemşehri*, religious and ethnic enclaves are instrumental in providing resources (such as housing and finance), information and knowledge to their in-group members and are also effective in preserving the norms, practices and lifestyles of the group. They are 'closed' networks where only certain groups from similar, ethnic, religious or provincial backgrounds are accommodated. On the other hand, the newly emerging neighbourhood solidarity initiatives are inclusive of all those residing in a specific district, no matter their occupation, religious choice, ethnic group political choice or lifestyle. Moreover, neighbourhood solidarity can be seen as the nucleus of a mobilization, a powerful starting point. Indeed, wider audiences could be reached if locals see and are convinced that a different future is possible. In *Yeniden İnşa Et* (Yılmaz et al, 2020), the activists stressed the importance of organizing in the neighbourhood as,

> utilizing the dynamics of Gezi, we try to develop an organization that will be inclusive of all in the district, regardless of their religion, ethnic identity and sexual choice. If we start this process from our own street, we can establish common ground and long-lasting relations with our district, city, and country. (p 266)

Organizing in the neighbourhood, and forming solidarity groups, was also useful in the development of a 'we' feeling and overcoming the fear of expressing concerns publicly as an individual. Neighbourhood solidarity initiatives breed hope among the inhabitants and mobilize them for realizing their dreams about a new future. A volunteer explained:

> 'The neighbourhood is the initial place that surrounds us, that shapes our lifestyles. During the Gezi protests we rediscovered the importance of neighbourhood. We all felt that our street, our neighbourhood should be part of this movement. This is how we started to restore streets, houses in Kadıköy, organized solidarity with local tradespeople, organized festivals for children, tried to revitalize the city garden, organized a collective kitchen. And all was done with the cooperation of the neighbours.'

Prefigurative organizing in the ACCs

The governance system experimented with by the ACCs can be considered as a solution to the capitalist logic of competition, profit maximization and self-interest. In the capitalist system, market forces – the competition for buyers – make for-profit companies reduce costs and develop management techniques that will enable efficiency and profit maximization. In these companies, an organizational structure based on the division of labour, specialization and a chain of command enables efficiency in time, labour and financial resources. Furthermore, such a structure creates a division of work, between the planning and the execution, that is, between those who make decisions – the managers – and those who do production – the labourers (Atzeni and Vieta, 2014). Since ACCs are not-for-profit and their performance is not measured in terms of profitability and growth, they have tried to develop an organizational structure without a chain of command, division of labour and specialization. Instead, they experiment with organizational practices shaped with the premises of self-organization, mutuality and direct democracy.

Decision-making

In a hierarchical, bureaucratic organization, operating with a capitalist logic, people at the top are assumed to have all the knowledge that is necessary to make the 'right' decisions for the entire organization. However, according to Peter Kropotkin, hierarchies are not effective since people at the top do not have the knowledge and information necessary for making a decision (De Geus, 2014). On the contrary, people who are affected, who have been part of a specific issue, can have more detailed information and are capable of making decisions without the guidance of people occupying higher positions in the hierarchy. Taking others' expertise, knowledge and opinions seriously contributes to the empowerment of people and enables active participation on how things should be done.

The organizing practices of the ACCs are based on collective decision-making with full consensus, no specialization, a flexible organization structure and a governing body shaped by the values of 'equal work, equal voice' and 'solidarity'. ACCs aim to be, and are designed as, non-hierarchical, horizontal organizations, based on equality, transparency, participation and trust (Aysu, 2019; Kadıköy Kooperatifi Kolektifi, 2020). This view was noted by an activist: "We all are around the same table. No one is higher or lower than others. We are all responsible to each other." Decisions about the daily activities of the cooperative are made during the regular weekly meetings; they are announced on the social media accounts of each cooperative and are open to everyone. The items on the agenda are predetermined, depending on the demands of the work groups. Meetings are carried out in line with the forum tradition formed during Gezi and park forums. The ACCs reject voting in the decision-making process as they assume that it will lead to inequalities, that is, the outcomes can favour the majority and the voices of the minority can be unheard. Thus, for the inclusion of all, and for securing equality among all, the decision-making process is based on the right to speak and the obligation to listen without judgement. This was illustrated by an interviewee as follows:

'We're people who grew up in hierarchies without realizing it. We have teachers, we have parents. We have seniority at work and bosses. Here, in the cooperative, one word is no more important than the other. Or in case of conflict, there is no one to intervene, we try to find egalitarian solutions.'

At the beginning of the meeting one of the participants takes the role of the moderator. The role of the moderator is to give all participants the chance and time to voice their ideas. Decisions are made with full consensus; in most cases, even volunteers, whether they are members of the cooperative or not, have a say in the decision-making. Depending on the distinct features of the district where a particular ACC is located, there can be slight differences in the practices employed. It is expected that, as long as they adhere to the main principles and values of the ACCs, these divergent practices will have a positive contribution in terms of outputs. For example, in the Kadıköy Kooperatif, the decision-making group, called 'the kitchen', meets every Thursday, with the full and equal participation of all interested. The format of these meetings was explained as follows by one of the interviewees:

'It's a similar version of the horizontal relationship at the forums that were going on here, and everyone in the kitchen – like in the forum – gets an equal say. No one is superior. The people involved in the cooperative since its foundation and newcomers have an equal say, an equal chance for a proposal.'

During the meeting, if a full consensus is not reached and only a few participants are not convinced, to use time more efficiently they are asked whether they agree with the 'fall-back' option. If this is not possible, the issue is put aside for reconsideration at a workshop that is run regularly every week. During these workshops, the issue in question is examined in depth and outcomes are presented at the next meeting.

Dividing work and rotation

While experimenting with direct democracy, the ACCs also prioritize developing an organizational form that is based on equality and egalitarianism; participants try to divide the work of the cooperative in a fair way so that inequalities based on gender, education and socio-economic standing will be avoided. In so doing, some organizational mechanisms, in line with the premises of non-hierarchy, are used. One of these mechanisms is 'work units', which are formed around the tasks to be performed in the daily operation of the cooperative. The identification of these work units and their scope of activities is determined collectively according to the needs of each ACC. The work units are designed according to the principles discussed and determined during the weekly meetings. Any modification to the existing practices and rules has to be made after consulting all the parties involved. In general, we have seen that all the ACCs have work units such as finance, technical, organization-building, training, research, relations with producers, communication, women, archiving and social media. None of these work units is positioned at the centre or higher in the hierarchy. Work units are not decision-making bodies but are equipped with full authority for implementing the decisions made collectively during the regular weekly meetings. Work is done by volunteers and volunteers choose the work unit they would like to be in. In this way, it is expected that there will be room for individual autonomy and collective unity can also be maintained.

The other organizational mechanism developed for a more equal distribution of tasks is rotation. It is expected that, by rotation, diversity can be assured and the distinction between more 'valuable' and less 'valuable' work can be levelled. Accordingly, no work can be done by a specific person or group for a long time and the duration of work rotation is determined collectively by each ACC during their weekly meetings. Rotation is also considered to be useful for learning: having an idea of how things are carried out in the cooperative enables members to identify problems and formulate solutions. In order to promote this collective learning environment and secure continuity in the daily life of the cooperative, the 'buddy system', which is based on the premise of egalitarian knowledge and experience-sharing, is utilized. The buddy system is helpful in transferring the values and the routines of the cooperative as well as their political foundations. The work rotation system also eliminates information asymmetry among group members and, at least partially, avoids knowledge-based inequalities. Furthermore, it endorses a locality where volunteers, in line with the values of sharing and collective work, are supplied with all the knowledge needed for the management of the cooperative.

Discussion on prefigurative organizing in the ACCs

These decision-making practices of the ACCs tackle the problems posed by representative forms of democracy that are incapable of addressing the concerns of workers in capitalist forms of organizing. With an emphasis on continuity and stability, representative democracies promote a milieu where a few people are given voice to raise concerns, to resolve conflicts. Such an approach in the workplace creates a stratum that leads to a divide between representatives and the workers. The direct democracy practices employed by the ACCs, on the other hand, are an effort at reclaiming power for making decisions that will affect the daily activities of the cooperative. By implementing consensus-based decision-making with the participation of all, managers and representatives are de-centred, and the ruler and ruled distinction is avoided. In so doing, the alternative world based on the premises of non-hierarchy and horizantality that limit power inequalities will be prefigured. As discussed by Sitrin (2012), horizantality or 'horizontalidad' can be a way of direct democracy; it is both a tool and a goal to establish a new social relationship that is egalitarian, autonomous and non-hierarchical. As the crises of capitalism has intensified, as the everyday practices of capitalist organizations have given way to inequalities, and a few people have come to dominate the decisions taken in the name of participative democracy, there has been more emphasis on searching and experimenting with alternative structures for more equality and participation through direct democracy. For example, the contributions of horizantality to direct democracy is discussed in relation to the recaptured factories in Argentina (Vieta, 2010), the solidarity initiatives in Greece (Daskalaki and Kokkunidis, 2017), the social centres in Barcelona (Yates, 2015), the Midtown Alternative Consensus (MAC) in the UK (Ready et al, 2016) and the anti-globalization movement (Maeckelbergh, 2011, 2014). However, such a focus has also led to evaluations and discussions of the limitations of horizantality. These limitations, which are sometimes criticized, are the lack structure, the overemphasis on expressive politics and informal hierarchies. In the 'The Tyranny of Structurelessness' Jo Freeman (2013), in reference to the USA women's liberation movement, explains that the idea of structurelessness through time became 'a goddess in its own right' (p 5); it was taken as the only alternative to oppression. In other words, avoiding a formal structure does not mean that informal structures, with their elites, can prevent a 'star' system from emerging, with power limited to those who know the rules or those in the public eye acting as a spokesperson. Thus, Freeman argues that 'structurelessness' masks power (p 1). During the interviews, we have seen similar concerns raised by the activists; it was mentioned that personal conflicts from time to time block the smooth running of the meeting and divert the agenda from the problems of the cooperative. In the participative milieu of the meetings, some participants subverted the discussions towards personal preferences, likes and dislikes, which hindered the democratic mechanism.

Furthermore, in the collectively written chapter by Kadıköy Kooperatif Kolektifi (2020), it is stated that, in a society like ours, where interpersonal relations are produced and reproduced over hierarchy and a gendered structure, it is expected that such issues will be reflected in the daily lives of the cooperative members. They admit that there have been opposing wings and supremacy of some dominant characters over the collective. However, it is learning process (Maeckelbergh, 2014), and as stated by Graeber (2002) for the anti-globalization movement, it is not refuting the need for organization, but creating new forms of organization. For example, as we noted previously, the ACCs, in order to prevent the dominance of a few people in the decision-making process, have developed a mechanism: with the permission of the participants, such issues are discussed in a separate meeting (the 'long meeting') which is held once in a month on Sundays. Also, some ACCs have drafted detailed guidelines for the smooth running of meetings so that blockages in the decision-making process will be avoided: for example, the moderator of the meeting ensures that everyone's contribution is equal in terms of time, while those who are silent are asked to voice their opinion, no one is interrupted, and judgmental attitudes are avoided.

Another criticism about prefigurative organizing, consensus-based decision-making and non-hierarchy is related to informal inequalities. According to critics, in the process of direct democracy, people with less socio-economic means and those who are not familiar with participative democracy (Polletta, 2005; Polletta and Hoban, 2016) can be isolated from the decision-making process. For example, Soborski (2018), argues that consensus-based decision-making is almost a utopian concept due to informal inequalities among the activists, as more privileged, affluent, and well-educated people dominate the group. Similarly, Smucker (2017) suggests that the main reason for the failure of the Occupy Wall Street (OWS) movement was the consensus based decision-making processes; though, these processes are beneficial in strengthening group identity and solidarity, it is utopian and is not viable on a much larger scale. On the other hand, Cornell (2011) views the Movement for a New Society (MNS) as a successful example of 'antiauthoritarian social movements' with skilfully applied non-hierarchical, consensus-based decision-making processes. In order to empower people, they developed training programmes and workshops (for democratic group processes, direct action, and strategic campaigns), and skill-sharing manuals. However, Cornell (2011) also points out that many other groups adopted the practices developed and utilized by MNS without evaluating how these practices evolved and how the shortcomings were resolved. Based on these criticisms of prefigurative organizing, it can be argued that the governance practices (consensus-oriented, participatory decision-making, task rotation and dividing work) can be developed in such a way that informal inequalities and hierarchies arising from differences in education and gender should be eliminated; activists besides 'creating formally equal decision-making structures ... must also address informal and indirect hierarchies and inequalities' (Raekstad and Gradin, 2020, p 60). Prefigurative organizing based on equality requires commitment to develop and experiment with practices that will minimize the gap in knowledge, social and economic status, gender, and prior experience with a non-hierarchical way of organizing. Such gaps may exist in organizations shaped by consensus-based decision-making and non-hierarchy, but acknowledging their existence, talking about them, and trying to develop and experiment with alternative means to overcome them should be the major concern of the activists.

When we evaluate these concerns in relation to the ACCs, we have seen that, in terms of educational background, socio-economic class and gender, the activists involved are similar: young, middle class and mainly women. However, people who have responsibilities at home, such as supporting children, doing housework, looking after the elderly, are not able to participate in the activities of the ACCs. The heavy work burden at home excludes certain groups – mainly women with children and single parents – from joining the ACCs; only those who can devote their time to decision-making meetings, which may take many hours, can afford to be an ACC member. During the interviews it was stated that the decision-making process and the volunteer work are domains where the ACCs deal with the informal inequalities pervasive in the Turkish context. In order to solve these informal inequalities the ACCs do not offer training programmes but utilize different strategies: for orienting newcomers they rely on the 'buddy system'. The buddy system, as discussed earlier, is also used for work rotation, and for newcomers it facilitates a smooth introduction to the daily life of the cooperative. We have also seen that some ACCs utilize 'The Coop Is Explaining Itself' meetings (discussed in Chapter 5), which are open to the public, as a means to familiarize potential members with the ideals, values and practices of the cooperative and invite interested participants to join the regular weekly decision-making meeting.

During our field studies and interviews we identified two problems that in some cases lead to informal inequalities and conflicts that are difficult to reconcile: the gap between the older and younger generations and the lack of a repertoire on collective decision-making. These problems are deeply rooted in Turkish culture in general and Turkish management culture specifically, with its patriarchy, high power distance and less emphasis on individualism (Ataca et al, 2005; Hofstede et al, 2005). Patriarchal norms render gender equality by assuming that the primary responsibility of women is family and home as caregivers. Consequently, the presence of women in the public sphere and workplace is limited to those who opt for and strive to change the prevailing conditions. As indicated by Hofstede (1991), high power distance in the workplace reproduces hierarchical structures, unreachable managerial cadres and a workforce that follows the directions of the superiors. Low scores in individualism indicate that loyalty to a group is important and conflicts are to be avoided. So, Turkish work values are characterized by values of dependency and hierarchy. In organizational settings, superiors are often inaccessible and ideal managers have a paternalistic approach towards their subordinates. There is a concentration of power at the top that is accepted and followed both by managers and subordinates. A top-down control system is acceptable and communication within the organizations are very formal and indirect (Hofstede, 1991; Hofstede et al, 2005). Furthermore, less powerful members in workplaces accept unequal power relations; they accept it as 'normal'. While preparing students for prospective jobs, the school system also perpetuates the existing societal values, as teachers and administrators are considered father figures who the students must obey (Yıldırım, 2009). Given this background to Turkish culture, we have seen volunteers have difficulty in adopting and experiencing horizontality and consensus-based decision-making. It is new, different from home, school and office. This was illustrated by an interviewee as follows:

'For the first time, I am involved in a horizontal organization. I did not understand it at first; this is a system I am not used to. How do you make decisions at home? Parents talk, they profess. We are having a tough time in the Coop because no one declares anything. Consensus may be our core principle, but it will slow down the process. There is an 18-year-old person here, and there is also a 50-year-old person. Their experiences, their way of looking at life, their way of sustaining life and their core principles are not the same.'

In cultures of patriarchy and high in power distance like Turkey, older members of the family or senior members in the workplace are given the right to make the first comment and their opinions are taken with the utmost importance. In the past, there have been conflicts among the older and younger activists, which have led to a split and the founding of another ACC. As we have discussed previously, the majority of activists involved in the ACCs are young, professional precariat who are in some way excluded from workplace identities and, by developing alternative organizations, are creating spaces that cultivate collective identity through friendship and shared lifestyles. One activist emphasized the importance of friendship:

'We now sympathise with each other so much that we're all friends. We went to college in different places but now I have a new group of friends, people I did not know until I was thirty have become a group of friends now. We went on a holiday with Irem. We did a workshop planning with Ezgi for weeks. We worked together till 1–2 am. We went for a farm visit with Özden. I'm going to visit Güneş's house in Çeşme. Umut can call me in the middle of the night. I do not mind a lot of things they do because they are my friends. If these are done by someone else, I might have been uncomfortable.'

However, friendship, especially in cultures where belonging to a group and being loyal to the in-group members, is a double-edged sword: on the one hand, friendship nurtures collective identities but, on the other hand, it can lead to tensions among different friendship-based cliques. In the absence of written rules and mechanisms for handling complex problems, these cliques can dominate the decision-making process, which consequently supports the ideas of a specific group:

> [S]ome problems were subverted, aborted, or ignored. Norms of friendship overwhelmed norms of solidarity … favouring a friends' opinion, treating friends unequally led to the dissolution of solidarity principles … as the spirit of acting together disappeared some members left. (Yılmaz et al, 2020, pp 197–9)

Volunteer work and volunteer recruitment

In line with their goal 'not profits but providing good quality food stuff at reasonable prices to urban consumers by supporting petty commodity producers', all the work in the ACCs is undertaken by volunteers. Since the ACCs experiment with a non-capitalist form of work, rooted in the premises of solidarity, activists claim that if people are forced to do certain tasks, their freedom will be limited and without freedom to decide what to do, solidarity cannot be achieved. Volunteers are comprised of students, academics, professionals, housewives, white-collar workers and small business owners and, in most cases, they have strong ties with unions, professional bodies, environmentalist organizations and feminist initiatives. Depending on the demographic characteristics of the neighbourhood, devoted volunteers are either young single professionals (for example, Kadıköy Kooperatif), or retired people (for example, Koşuyolu Kooperatif). People from diverse backgrounds work together collectively. Their priorities are also different from one another as they have different political backgrounds. Though volunteer work requires a significant amount of time and energy, being a part of cooperative motivates them. For example, feminist activists are powerful in various ACCs and their major concern, besides food provisioning, is maintaining a solidarity network among women.

The shops are run by volunteers: they do the cleaning, labelling, shelving and sales. Some of the ACCs, depending upon the availability of volunteers, open their shop during weekdays as well as weekends. In most cases the shops are open between 7 pm and 9 pm on weekdays and between 10 am and 6 pm at the weekends. Every evening after work or school (university), volunteers come to the shop, sign in the duty roster, open the shop, count the cash and start selling. If a new package from a producer has arrived, they open it and place the products onto the shelves. In the early days, sales were recorded manually, but nowadays they have computerized systems. Besides handling the daily operations of the shop, volunteers are involved in explaining the cooperative (values, practices) to their customers and visitors: "In the shop there are two tables: one for the processing the transactions and the other for those shop visitors who would like to learn more about what we are doing", said one of the activists during a public meeting. These shop encounters provide an opportunity to raise awareness among the urban consumers about local seeds, traditional farming practices and ecologically grown foodstuff.

Responsibilities of the volunteers are not limited to the daily activities and chores of the cooperative. They attend the regular weekly meetings and express their ideas concerning the practices and policies of the cooperative. Volunteers are expected to join these meetings; if due to family or employment-related problems they cannot join a meeting, they have to inform the group and be given permission. In smaller ACCs volunteers must perform more than one duty or committee responsibility. Moreover, as one of the activist stated, those who have much more free time can spend much more time in the ACCs:

'When I was working in a company I had only one shift in the cooperative. Now, I do not have a permanent job, I have more time to devote to the coop, so I am working full-time here. I am working in two units now. The communications department is dealing with the website's co-op mail and social media. We are also updating the organization model.'

In every ACC, a volunteer is assigned as a product/producer representative. Representatives act as a bridge between the petty commodity producers and the cooperative; they check the stock, place orders after a decision has been made at the weekly meeting, and, from time-to-time, visit the production site to verify the quality claims of the producer. Apart from offering their labour, in some cases, volunteers contribute to the operations of the ACCs by offering their cafés and houses as places for meetings (both formal and informal) and, if needed, as storage spaces.

In terms of member recruitment, training, placement and job rotation, the ACCs have developed some unique mechanisms. Volunteers join the ACCs through informal networks and open calls. Public meetings (such as the Coop Is Explaining Itself), organized in public spaces or through videocalls and announced on social media accounts, are settings for volunteer recruitment. After each meeting, potential members from among the interested attendees are called in for training, which is an information sharing session to explain the details of the work. After training, volunteers work as interns in the shop and are assigned a volunteer partner (the buddy) from the cooperative. Training is usually done in the shop at a time decided on by the buddy and the volunteer. The volunteers determine their own training schedule and decide when they are ready to work alone in the shop.

Discussion on volunteer work in the ACCs

As we have tried to show, the ACCs strive to bring together people with diverse backgrounds and concerns around a common issue and create an egalitarian work system that will avoid inequalities between these diverse groups. Building such collaborative communities and maintaining commitment devoid of tensions and frustrations is not possible. We have seen that the major problems faced by the ACCs in relation to volunteer work is the availability of sufficient volunteers to run the cooperative, the ability to complete the tasks volunteered for, and the development of 'labour hierarchies'. In the long term, the success of the ACCs depends on the availability of a sufficient number of volunteers to take on the tasks associated with collective work. The participatory mechanisms employed by the ACCs in relation to volunteer work shapes their identity and consolidates the formation of a collective. Such involvement in the cooperatives affairs makes work more meaningful and brings satisfaction, satisfaction that what they visualized is becoming real. As explained by a volunteer, 'empathy' is the most important motive for involvement:

> 'It may sound very romantic, but I feel it. When we ask why you are coming … Why would a person give up all her/his comforts and come here and give 2 or 3 hours a week? Why during their leisure time, they have to work in the cooperative? It is about emotions. That is what we have been missing for a long time. We do not promise anything.'

The participatory practices employed by the ACCs, the chances of having a voice and being listened to, makes volunteers feel that they are valuable and provides a sense of connectedness, a situation that is described as 'disalienation' by Kociatkiewicz et al (2021). However, even if the volunteers are highly motivated, volunteer work can be very exhausting, and volunteers can experience physical, mental and emotional burnout (see, for example, Hibbert et al, 2003; Fourat et al, 2020). The workload of volunteers in the ACCs is demanding in terms of time and energy. Although it is an aspiration that the workload should be allocated equally for all, some volunteers are less able to devote their time to the cooperative. So, volunteers differ in how much work they contribute. Sometimes, it is inevitable that tensions arise, some members leave and managing the cooperative becomes much harder.

So, it is critical to avoid volunteer burnout and maintain egalitarian relationships. On the other hand, if every member is expected to put in the same amount of labour, that is, attending all the meetings, taking part in the committees, and having the same number of shop shifts, those who have more commitments at home (such as married women with children) and at the office will automatically be excluded. This could be considered a double-edged sword because the ACCs want to include people from diverse backgrounds, however only those who have enough time and energy may be part of them. Though the ACCs claim to implement the 'equal work–equal voice' principle, the equal division of labour, at best, turns out to be partial. Although the ACCs try to organize work around 'collective work and inclusiveness', in some ACCs, especially in the smaller ones, some volunteers have a greater workload than the others. Those who contribute more with their work claim much more authority in the decision-making process. This leads to tensions: they are accused of exercising a 'labour hierarchy' that blocks democratic governance structures, and more devoted volunteers accuse the less-involved members of 'free-riding'. In a similar vein, work and work units are not taken as equal: some tasks that require more physical labour (such as cleaning, carrying the foodstuff, and so on) are less popular among most of the volunteers. On the other hand, there is always more enthusiasm for tasks (such as organizing events, workshops or running the public meetings) that will improve the visibility of the participants on social media. Furthermore, when there is an uneven division of work among volunteers, those who perform more gain more knowledge, which creates an information asymmetry that prevents a democratic governance structure. However, within the available literature, there is no simple solution to the problem of balancing an equal distribution of labour, avoiding a heavy workload and being inclusive of people from diverse backgrounds and priorities (Ashforth and Reingen, 2014). As stated by the activists involved in the ACCs, the critical issue is to be aware of the problems, talk about them and deliberately experiment with alternative ways so that their impact will be minimized. For example, some ACCs are currently discussing whether to pay a symbolic hourly amount for the shifts in the shop and hire part-time workers. They are aware that employing paid staff could decrease the commitment of the volunteers and affect group cohesion, and that there would be less information about the daily operations and the information necessary for decision-making might be lost. In other words, as indicated in studies on collectivist-democratic decision-making practices (see, for example, Chen, 2009; Lee, 2014; Leach, 2016), hiring paid staff brings professionalization, increases efficiency but also hinders consensus-based decision-making, as well as potentially leading to the re-enactment of hierarchies and more powerful group membership.

In conclusion

The viability and sustainability of the practices developed by the ACCs can be questioned. They are the products of activist strategies developed for and experienced in a specific context at a specific period. These strategies do not intend to replace the prevailing practices of organizing, governance and work but instead confront them by unveiling some alternative practices. The activists involved in the ACCs have different ideals to the managerialist perspective; they experiment with alternative practices and forms with the expectation of transforming the dominant logic and the prevailing power structure. Therefore, a cooperative is not an end for the activists who want to create an alternative future for themselves; what they propose is to commit to the principles of direct democracy, mutuality and solidarity.

ACCs that are based on consensus-based decision-making and zero-hierarchy have strong ties with social movements that are proposing a new way of life by radically transforming society. Thus, their intentions go beyond food provisioning and aim to create alternative livelihoods by prefiguring a future society that is egalitarian, just and inclusive. Organizing in a neighbourhood, activists define local spaces and everyday life as the basis of politics. The neighbourhood is considered a political entity to be activated. The ACCs involve themselves in local problems and they try to translate local politics and relations to a macro level. The activists stated that if the ACC that they are involved in collapses they are ready to rebuild it. For them, the basic thing needs to be a sense of hope, reciprocity and trust. Although they are organized around alternative food provisioning, their ideals go beyond food politics. They are actively involved in many other solidarity-based organizations and initiatives that intend to build a future society. In so doing, they have opened their minds and hearts to a dream of an alternative future.

8

Instead of a Conclusion

The alternative consumer cooperatives (ACCs) studied in this book strive to transform the prevailing food production and consumption nexus by re-positioning the petty commodity producers and bridging the gap between the urban middle class and the rural areas. In so doing, the ACCs have introduced fundamental changes such as bypassing the middlemen, de-fetishising foodstuff and experimenting with zero-hierarchy and consensus-based decision-making that challenge the capitalist forms of organizing and doing business. They are not driven by the profit motive and growth-pursuing strategies but instead develop and promote solidarity, collective action and mutuality among and within the urban middle class and rural small producers that have been excluded from the economic realm by the authoritarian implementation of neo-liberal policies. The ACCs are transforming the long-established socio-economic rural–urban relations in agriculture and invite other constituencies (municipalities and professional groups like architects, designers, software engineers and actors) to participate in the diffusion of alternative ways of organizing. The actions taken, tools developed and positions taken are important in understanding this transformation process and assessing its future trajectories. Thus, in this study we have tried to understand and describe how and why the ACCs evolved and how they challenge capitalist logic in food provisioning by experimenting and re-organizing their practices as problems are encountered.

The ACCs are grassroot organizations initiated by petty commodity producers, their representative organizations and the urban middle class who are excluded from the economic and social realm by the implementation of neo-liberal policies. As discussed in Chapter 4, the initiation of the ACCs is marked by the collaboration of petty commodity producers and urban middle-class citizens. As small producers, individual producers (for example, İlhan Koçulu and Ali Ünüvar) that had prior experience with producer cooperatives, Kibele (a producer cooperative) and Çiftçi-Sen (Farmers' Union) were actively involved in the founding of the ACCs. The association Tohum-İzi Derneği (formerly KEÇİ–Solidarity Initiative between Urbanites and Farmers) and the academic and administrative staff of Boğaziçi University were the initial representatives of the consumers. The dominant values that inspired and guided these groups were rooted in the premises of La Via Campesina. Accordingly, as stated by Bingöl (founder of KEÇİ and Tohum-İzi Derneği and La Via Campesina Europe Policy Development Officer) in an interview conducted by Büyükyılmaz (2020), they take food,

'not as a commodity, it is a human right, part of identity and culture. Within this framework, food systems serve a public purpose and encompass various dimensions related to ecology, culture, health, welfare, economy and politics. As an urban consumer, to purchase a foodstuff, to decide which food to buy, and through which channels to bring it to our home, to our table, means that we are part of the production process ... Food consumption is a vital need; thus, it is important to identify the political stance with which this activity is carried.'

Given this background, which reflects the dominant premises that underpin the practices and political stance of the ACCs, the first alternative consumer cooperative, BÜKOOP, was established in 2009 (Al, 2020). The founders of BÜKOOP, in collaboration with the producers, made several public meetings with an expectation to expand the idea of the ACCs in other universities in İstanbul. At these meetings, the ideals, values and experiences, as well as the information for forming a cooperative, were shared with the participants. However, the impetus for the proliferation of the ACCs gained momentum after the Gezi protests. During our talks and interviews, we have seen that this prefigurative activism is rooted in the democratic and communal practices experienced during the Gezi protests in the summer of 2013. Gezi influenced the emergence of the ACCs in various ways: it was an occasion where people with similar values and beliefs but previously disconnected were able to exchange their ideas and experiences. They saw that it was possible to invent alternative ways of living without being subject to Turkey's dominant cultural, social and economic framework. A group of citizens, using their individual democratic experiences as activists, aimed to experiment with an alternative form of organizing and food provisioning system that could challenge the status quo. Democratic decision-making processes, collective work for daily chores and horizontality experienced during the Gezi protests, and following the park forums, have raised hopes that there is an opportunity for direct democracy and a non-capitalist form of organizing. The activists express the pivotal role of the Gezi protests in the formation of the ACCs as follows:

'We divided the Gezi Park area into various neighbourhoods; each represented a district in İstanbul. There were seven separate forums in each district, and seven of them held a joint forum to discuss shared problems. We talked about how to maintain the Park spirit in the future, about the state, the causes of the problems encountered and possible solutions … We discussed social justice, better and just education and housing … We tried to develop alternative solutions to the current problems of the country … Gezi provided a milieu where people without a 'wall' can bring in whatever they want and a social structure where the only control would be over action.'

Over time, groups of urban consumers, in response to the domination of the agro-food companies in production, distribution and thus less availability of good quality foodstuff at affordable prices, joined the ACCs. Thus, the ACCs became a site where locals from a neighbourhood could meet and discuss what could be done to solve the problems of the prevailing food provisioning system, how an alternative system could be created and how a non-hierarchical, participatory, inclusive governance system where everyone could express their opinion was developed. Activists involved in the ACCs take food consumption as a political issue; as adherents of the food sovereignty movement and following the path of La Via Campesina, they privilege those petty commodity producers who produce foodstuff with local and heirloom seeds and do not use chemicals. Moreover, they are sensitive about the production process and support producers that employ non-exploitative labour relations. Such an approach not only secures safe and good quality food for the urbanites but also is a step for transforming the dominant capitalist logic underlining the agricultural policies and foodstuff provisioning system where petty commodity producers are distanced from agricultural production and traditional farming knowledge, and agroecological know-how becomes redundant. From a political and social perspective, such an attempt opts for the inclusion and re-positioning of the petty commodity producers marginalized in the capitalist food provisioning system. It is an alternative for transforming the production–consumption nexus embedded in the capitalist logic through mutuality, solidarity and dialogue between the urban middle classes and small producers. With shop encounters, social media posts, regular public meetings, and workshops conducted in the shops with small producers, the ACCs reclaim public space for raising awareness and building alliances with other marginalized constituencies.

Borrowing from Gibson-Graham (2014), the ACCs are communities developed by the urban middle class and petty commodity producers of foodstuff and characterized by cooperation, mutuality and togetherness. Everyday decisions and activities in the ACCs are shaped by their ethical concerns about how to distribute surplus justly and be engaged in ethical transactions with each other. The activists involved in the ACCs through direct democracy try to co-create an alternative way of organizing that is shaped by an understanding and appreciation of interdependency between all those who are part of their community. Thus, we view them as sites of transformation, evolving in and around their everyday activities where economic activities are re-socialized and re-politicized. The ACCs are sites that prefigure a non-capitalist food provisioning system and transform the prevailing hegemonic market-driven nexus of production and consumption. In this transformation process, the inclusion and equal participation of all constituencies involved are asserted. This assertion does not stay as a claim: it is substantiated by various means developed to promote direct democracy and a just food provisioning system. In other words, instead of claiming that some groups (for example, the urban middle class and petty commodity producers) are excluded in the capitalist food provisioning system because of the authoritarian implementation of neo-liberal policies, they provide opportunities and means for the inclusion of these groups. It is prefigurative activism grounded on values and immediate, direct action for a more just and inclusive future that is exemplified in the actions taken and methods developed in the present. Practices developed by the ACCs in surplus generation and distribution have the potential to transform the existing production–consumption nexus towards a more inclusive socio-economic system. Similarly, their practices for the de-fetishization of foodstuff have the capacity to transform the transactions between buyers and sellers from a market-based logic to an ethics-based logic that thrives on trust and solidarity. Finally, governance practices developed and experimented with by the ACCs promise a transformation for more equitable, inclusive and participatory organizing.

The practices employed by the ACCs are also politicized: ideas around anti-capitalism, solidarity, egalitarianism in work and decision-making and a just food system is experienced, demonstrated and communicated by the activists. As Yates (2015) noted with regard to Barcelona's social centres, these practices also have a politicizing power which is experienced through public meetings, excursions to producer sites, shop encounters, workshops and social media sites. These are spaces and occasions where political values underlining the practices are shared with wider constituencies. These spaces enable communication among different constituencies. Furthermore, by sharing their experiences and knowledge, activists can establish relations with other groups who share similar political ideas, concerns and values and who would like to initiate similar alternative forms of organizing. Thus the political and politicized practices employed by the ACCs are diffused and construct solidarity between diverse collectivities.

In the Turkish cooperative (both producer and consumer) movement, the ACCs provide a divergent example of grassroots, non-hierarchical, democratically governed organizations initiated by urban consumers who have an oppositional stance against neo-liberal policies and their authoritarian implementation. They differ in various aspects from state-led conventional cooperatives. Earlier, conventional cooperatives in Turkey were limited to providing cheap, quality products to their members, and they have been managed under the strict surveillance of the governments. Unlike these conventional 'closed' cooperatives, the ACCs are autonomous: they are established without financial support from the state cadres and thus can bypass any intervention in their governance. Furthermore, they are not instrumentalized, like the conventional cooperatives, by the state for political support, especially during elections. Also, their financial autonomy allows them to experience a space of freedom for experimenting with an alternative provisioning system and governance model with a transformative capacity. As opposed to the state-led, 'closed' conventional cooperatives, the ACCs are 'open'; they offer their services not only to the cooperative members but to all those interested and willing to purchase their foodstuff. They deliberately opt to be open and create a public sphere by organizing public meetings, workshops and festivals. Such an 'openness' enables them to reach wider audiences, build alliances and raise awareness for their struggle against the hegemony of the existing system. The means developed for the maintenance of openness (meetings, social media posts, shop encounters, and so on) have a dual function: they reinforce solidarity among in-group members and facilitate the inclusion of newcomers and, thus, the enlargement of the movement. The events provide a space where old, well-established members and newcomers have a chance to interact and exchange opinions and experiences without hierarchy, and signify the bonding of people with similar value orientations and lifestyles who are devoted to prefigurative ideas.

The ACCs originated and still operate as grassroots organizations promoting food sovereignty, an anti-capitalist stance and striving for social benefit as opposed to capitalist accumulation. They aim to develop solutions for the prevalent problems in agriculture and the neo-liberal policies that promote the emergence and perseverance of these problems. In so doing, they experiment with and try to develop an alternative to challenge the economically, politically and socially exclusionary approach that the state has adopted as a consequence of the deep-rooted commitment to the capitalization of agriculture. As grassroots organizations, the ACCs can identify and highlight needs, draft alternatives and experiment with them locally. By confining their activities to the local, the ACCs are able to re-establish the connection between rural and urban around foodstuff and re-embed petty commodity producers and urban consumers to the economy through dialogue which improves their knowledge about food and the conditions of production (both labour and ecological), and ensures the continuation of a food consumption culture. Being and staying local by promoting bulk purchases can shorten the distance between producers and consumers and can facilitate the development and maintenance of alternative supply chains that function in a different logic to that of the conventional corporate-controlled chains. Furthermore, as a local initiative, the ACCs are able to experiment with direct democracy: in small groups, decision-making with full consensus is easier to implement. Similarly, in such communities, developing and maintaining a cultural milieu where relations are shaped around norms of reciprocity, solidarity and direct democracy is a possibility.

While implementing their values and premises, the ACCs did not transpose or translate a specific alternative cooperative model developed in another location to local conditions. The development of the various practices employed by the ACCs is an experimenting and learning process. Although the ideals, values and premises that shaped their formation persevere and guide their decisions and activities, the practices employed are developed in response to the problems encountered. For example, during the early days of the alternative cooperative movement, the idea was to work with organic food producers. However, through time, the activists have seen that getting an organic certificate is expensive for small farmers. Such a certification system empowers some organizations endowed with the right to certify. In a way, it creates a hierarchy within the food provisioning system. Also, the ACCs favour heirloom seeds that are not included in organic food certification. So, with the guidance of Çiftçi-Sen, the activists started to search for other sources of healthy foodstuff and came up with a solution – to target those small farmers that use traditional farming knowledge to fulfil her/his household demand. It was also envisioned that such producers would not use chemicals and pesticides. In order to achieve this, the activists identified such producers (in this regard, Çiftçi-Sen and Tohum-İzi Derneği were supportive in providing the information), and approached and convinced those producers to supply the ACCs. Then, in collaboration with the producers, some tools that would facilitate this system were developed. One such tool was the 'product information form', which was used to select the producers and develop a producer repository. Another example was visiting producer sites to establish direct links between the producers and consumers, eventually leading to the de-fetishization of food and raising awareness.

Similarly, in their initial stages, nearly all of the ACCs relied on pre-orders announced on their web pages or social media accounts. Although by taking pre-orders it was possible to reduce inventory costs, shop space and the risk of not selling, operating a shop was always an attractive option. Shop encounters are valuable and are always a priority for the ACCs. As discussed in Chapter 5, the shop is more than a simple shop; it is a venue, a meeting place for consumers, producers and cooperative members. However, running a shop needs more labour and the solution in the early days to this problem was volunteer work. As the number of volunteers increases, a cooperative shop is able to open its doors for longer periods of the day. However, due to the housing crises and escalating rentals (112 per cent annual increase as stated by a BETAM report), the ACCs are facing a dilemma: to keep the shop and increase the price of the foodstuff sold or close down the shop and resort to pre-orders. For example, the Koşuyolu cooperative has announced that it is closing their shop due to high rentals. In their announcement on social media, they explain how keeping the shop open will lead to high prices and is against their ideals of 'just', clean food. They are resorting to the pre-order system, which they have implemented previously. There have been various trials related to volunteer work as well.

In this book, we described how alternative consumer cooperatives can be critical actors in implementing transformative strategies by politicizing the food production–consumption nexus and extending the struggle to other domains of the economy while providing examples of alternative economic possibilities. We show that there are alternatives and that these alternatives can be initiated and carried out by diverse group of people (sharing similar concerns, values and ideals), through prefiguration. We know that studies on alternative organizations are inclined to romanticize the involved parties' values and achievements. However, analysing the practices, values and motives of such alternative organizations in building a direct democracy, horizontal relations and an alternative surplus generation and distribution system needs to be documented. The efforts of the activists provide ample evidence to emphasize the role of alternative cooperatives in developing and challenging the capitalist relations in agriculture through experimenting with various practices and re-positioning the excluded groups, that is, the rural petty commodity producers and urban consumers. We think that the ACCs and their experiences offer an alternative way of existence that has to be approached neither with distrust about their survival, nor by glorifying their current achievements.

Although the consumers and producers involved in the ACCs are aware of their limited impact in bringing a significant change to the prevailing system, they are not pessimistic. During our shop encounters and participation in various meetings and interviews, we have seen that what keeps these consumer and producer groups together is not pessimism in the face of problems but, instead, insistence and persistence in developing solutions, as expressed by Özlem Öz in an interview conducted by Kaynak and Barçın (2016):

> Pessimism about ACCs is centred around the arguments 'that start with an assumption that capitalism is pervasive and unbeatable, alternatives will not work, and sooner or later, they will disappear'. However, it is not like that. You know, most probably read the literature, there are alternative economies. They have a potential to have a stronghold. To make them more visible, to organise solidarity among them … when a firm goes bankrupt nobody thinks that capitalism collapsed.

The producers and consumers involved in the ACCs have the potential to create an alternative: practices such as not buying from industrial food producers, bypassing the middlemen, buying from petty commodity producers involved in ecological food production, giving priority to women producers and their cooperatives, providing information about the foodstuff and producers involved in its production, being 'open' in offering their services, and valuing local and direct democracy still persist. Newly founded ACCs follow them in these respects. These practices transform the producers as well as the consumers. Furthermore, the petty commodity producers are interested in forming producers' cooperatives that bring together farmers using traditional knowledge, and more women farmers have joined the food provisioning system. Although limited in number, the consumers prefer direct links with the producers they have information about. Also, the locals who participate in the ACCs as volunteers and shoppers are able to expand their knowledge of the capitalist form of organizing agriculture and experience direct democracy. Furthermore, we have seen that some municipalities run by the oppositional party have consulted activists involved in the alternative cooperative movement, and initiated similar food provisioning systems. Currently, some municipalities in İstanbul and Bodrum operate farmers' markets where petty commodity producers using traditional farming knowledge and producing clean (free of chemicals and pesticides) foodstuff offer their products.

The transformative capacity of the ACCs is also rooted in the incorporation of prefigurative politics to the development of specific practices and an organizational form. Activists involved in the ACCs emphasize the primacy of action guided by their values/ideals (doing, experimentation) over planning and theorizing. This is important in explaining how new practices and forms emerge, since in prefiguration means and ends are linked to each other (Maeckelbergh, 2011): for example, the practice of zero hierarchy represents an alternative to a power system where managers are empowered. This correlation between doing and the activists' values/ideals provides consistency in practice and improves the transformative capacity of the ACCs. Their values/beliefs are infused in their daily practices, and the political concerns underlying these practices become more visible. The practices developed in the ACCs exemplify the alternative to their own members and to outsiders. This is particularly important in explaining the diffusion process and displacement of the old form with the new. The everyday practices of the ACCs has enabled the expression of a specific set of values, imbued with political meanings, and have been helpful in establishing connections with various other constituencies.

Given these outcomes, studying the values and various practices of the ACCs, and sharing their experiences, is vital for nurturing an alternative way of understanding the economy and citizenship rights. The ACCs are not only spaces of 'hope', they are also 'spaces of possibility' (Gibson–Graham et al, 2013, p 163) for a more just, ethical and inclusive alternative. They are spaces of resistance to the prevailing food provisioning system. However, they still operate within the capitalist system they resist, which makes them precarious. There is no guarantee about the advancement of their transformative efforts: it all depends on how the activists involved and the practices developed contribute to a shift in the pessimism or maybe 'hopelessness' underlying the trial of something 'different' and 'new'.

Notes

Chapter 2

[1] Fındıkoğlu (1967), based on the annual reports of some cooperatives, provides evidence about the high level of profits realized. For example, in the report of the İstanbul Memurlar İstihlak Kooperatifi (İstanbul Civil Servant Consumer Cooperative) in one year, when the war ended and the cooperative was not supported by the government with the essential items, profits dropped from 48,886 lira to 4,191 lira.

[2] Details of this Colombain report can be found in Memioğlu (2017).

[3] A detailed documentation of these plans and cooperatives are given in Bilgin and Tanıyıcı (2008).

Chapter 5

[1] See https://bukoop.org/11-kasim-2019-vakifli-kooperatifi-ziyaret-notlari/

[2] See http://yerdenizkooperatifi.org/index.php/2021/11/12/ozcay-kooperatifi-uretici-ziyareti

[3] See http://yerdenizkooperatifi.org/index.php/2021/11/09/koculu-peynircilik-ziyaretimiz-2/

[4] In Artvin, there were fourteen villages involved in rice production and twelve of them vanished after the construction of a dam in the region. Gradually, being a farmer lost its position, and villagers sold their land and migrated to cities.

[5] A prominent football player who worked for the rights of the football players, established a sports workers' union, and was a deputy candidate in 2011 of the TKP (Turkish Communist Party).

[6] A detailed account of the karşı Lig can be followed in the short documentary by Setenay Gültekin, Bahçeşehir Üniversitesi. See https://vimeo.com/11852917

[7] Based on the information provided by Kolektif (2020), Kara and Güngör (2021) and the social media account of the Karşı Lig, the contents of the Manifesto can be summarized as: no room for professional players, no need for referees, no tolerance for hate speech and discrimination, solidarity and sharing are the main reasons for existence, the players in the opponent team are not rivals but are comrades, winning or losing is not important, stands with differences in gender and sexual choice, not for pluralism but pluralist, direct democracy should be applied in all the decisions taken.

[8] A disaster where 301 miners lost their lives due to the cost-cutting strategies of the firm running the mine.

[9] A 15-year-old boy who was hit in the head by a tear-gas canister fired by police during the Gezi protests and lost his life.

Chapter 6

[1] A detailed explanation about the role played by big landholders and the DP leaders in the abandoning of these two initiatives is given in *Türkiye'nin Düzeni* by Doğan Avcıoğlu (1968).

[2] Details of this restructuring can be seen in the Seventh Five Year Plan (1996–2000).

[3] As indicated by Oğuz Oyan (2013), 51 per cent of DIS was distributed to big landowners who comprised 17 per cent of all farmers. The amount paid to big landowners was 3.5 times more than the amount paid to petty commodity producers who constituted 83 per cent of the farming population.

[4] As explained by Abdullah Aysu (2008), in the prevision version of contract farming the main providers of inputs were state-owned organizations and, at the harvest, the yield was sold either to a state-owned organization that did support purchases or to a private company. With the income generated, farmers paid their debts.

[5] Berk Mete's (2017) MA thesis provides a detailed account on the movement and its outcomes.

[6] The municipality of İstanbul operates a farmers' market in Kadıköy, where small farmers and farmer cooperatives that use traditional methods of production can have a stall. Stalls are allocated by the municipality after evaluating the production methods and usage of local seeds. Currently, 150 producers and 38 producer cooperatives have stalls in the market (see www.ibb.istanbul).

[7] The difficulty mainly arises from bureaucratic reasons: the accessible data base is kept by the Ministry of Trade (koopbis.gtb.gov.tr). However, this data base does not differentiate between consumer cooperatives in terms of for-profit/non-profit and their scope of operations (that is, serving only members or everyone), and this renders difficulties when identifying ACCs.

References

Adaman, F. and Akbulut, B. (2020) 'Erdoğan's three-pillared neoliberalism: authoritarianism, populism and developmentalism', *Geoforum*, 124(3): 279–89.

Adaman, F., Arsel, M. and Akbulut, B. (2019) 'Neoliberal developmentalism, authoritarian populism and extractivism in the countryside: the Soma mining disaster in Turkey', *The Journal of Peasant Studies*, 46(3): 514–36.

Ahmad, F. (1968) 'The Young Turk revolution', *Journal of Contemporary History*, 3(3): 19–36.

Ahmad, F. (1988) 'War and society under the Young Turks, 1908–18', *Review (Fernand Braudel Center)*, 11(2): 265–86.

Ahmad, F. (2008) *From Empire to Republic: Essays on the Late Ottoman Empire and Modern Turkey*, İstanbul: İstanbul Bilgi University Press.

Akbaş, K. (2013) 'Sınıf ve orta sınıf tartışmaları arasında yaldızlı yakalılar: avukatlar işçileşiyor mu?', *Praksis*, 32(2): 115–44.

Akbulut, B. (2020) 'Cooperative economies as commons', in D. Özkan and G.B. Büyüksaraç (eds) *Commoning the City: Empirical Perspectives on Urban Ecology, Economics and Ethics*, New York: Routledge, pp 193–206.

Akçay, Ü. (2017) '*Tarımda yerli üretimin tasfiyesi*', *Gazete Duvar*, Available from: https://www.gazeteduvar.com.tr/yazarlar/2017/12/11/tarimda-yerli-uretimin-tasfiyesi (Accessed 20 November 2021).

Akcay, Ü. (2018) 'Neoliberal populism in Turkey and its crisis', Working Paper, No. 100/2018, Hochschule für Wirtschaft und Recht Berlin, Berlin: Institute for International Political Economy (IPE).

Akçay, Ü. (2021) 'Authoritarian consolidation dynamics in Turkey', *Contemporary Politics*, 27(1): 79–104.

Akder, H. (2011) 'How to dilute an agricultural reform: direct income subsidy experience in Turkey (2001–2008)', in B. Karapinar, F. Adaman and G. Ozertan (eds) *Rethinking Structural Reform in Turkish Agriculture: Beyond the World Bank's Strategy*, New York: Nova Science Publishers, pp 47–62.

Akdoğan, Y.M., Küçükkiremitçi, İ., Başargan, S., Akça, M. and Yılmaz, E. (2020) 'Gima: Türkiye'nin ilk ulusal süpermarket zinciri', Abdürrahim Özer, HIST 200–1 Series, 10, Ankara: Bilkent University Publications.

Akpinar, P. (2017) 'Challenges to Islamic solidarity: the case of Turkish HNGOs', *Caucasus International*, 7(2): 35–48.

Akser, M. (2018) 'News media consolidation and censorship in Turkey: from liberal ideals to corporatist realities', *Mediterranean Quarterly*, 29(3): 78–97.

Aksoy, A.D. and Günay, G. (2018) 'Türkiye'de kadın kooperatifçiliği', *Third Sector Social Economic Review*, 53(1): 77–90.

Akyazı, P. E. and Ertör, I. (2012) 'BÜKOOP Katılımcı Sertifikasyon Çalıştayı-Katılımcı Garanti Mekanizmaları', Available from: www.karasa ban.net/bukoop-katilimci-sertifikasyon-calistayi-katilimci-garanti-mekani zmalari (Accessed 15 June 2023).

Akyüz, A.A. and Demir, A.Y. (2016) 'The role of a civil society organization in the development of the domestic organic market in Turkey', *İ.Ü. Siyasal Bilgiler Fakültesi Dergisi*, 54: 43–61.

Al, İ.S. (2020). 'The nascent march of "new-generation" food initiatives in the emerging struggle for food sovereignty in Turkey', Unpublished dissertation submitted to the Graduate School of Social Sciences and Humanities of Koç University, İstanbul.

Allen, P. (2010) 'Realizing justice in local food systems', *Cambridge Journal of Regions, Economy and Society*, 3(2): 295–308.

Allen, P. and Kovach, M. (2000) 'The capitalist composition of organic: the potential of markets in fulfilling the promise of organic agriculture', *Agriculture and Human Values*, 17(3): 221–32.

Alonso, C.R. (2015) 'Gezi Park: a revindication of public space', in I. David and K.F. Toktamış (eds) *Everywhere Taksim: Sowing the Seeds for a New Turkey at Gezi*, Amsterdam: Amsterdam University Press, pp 231–48.

Alonso-Fradejas, A., Borras Jr, S.M., Holmes, T., Holt-Giménez, E. and Robbins, M.J. (2015) 'Food sovereignty: convergence and contradictions, conditions and challenges', *Third World Quarterly*, 36(3): 431–48.

Arıkan, Z. (1989) 'İzmir'de ilk kooperatifleşme çabaları', *Tarih İncelemeleri Dergisi*, 4(1): 31–42.

Armstrong, E.A. and Bernstein, M. (2008) 'Culture, power, and institutions: a multi-institutional politics approach to social movements', *Sociological Theory*, 26(1): 74–99.

Ashforth, B.E. and Reingen, P.H. (2014) 'Functions of dysfunction: managing the dynamics of an organizational duality in a natural food cooperative', *Administrative Science Quarterly*, 59(3): 474–516.

Ataca, B., Kagitcibasi, C. and Diri, A. (2005) 'The Turkish family and the value of children: trends over time', in G. Trommsdorff and B. Nauck (eds) *The Value of Children in Cross-Cultural Perspective: Case Studies from Eight Societies*, Lengerich: Pabst, pp 91–119.

Atalan-Helicke, N. and Abiral, B. (2020) 'Alternative food distribution networks, resilience, and urban food security in Turkey during the COVID-19 pandemic', *Journal of Agriculture, Food Systems, and Community Development*, 10(2): 89–104.

Atasoy, Y. (2013) 'Supermarket expansion in Turkey: shifting relations of food provisioning', *Journal of Agrarian Change*, 13(4): 547–70.

Atasoy, Y. (2017) 'Agrifood systems and supermarketization', in Y. Atasoy (ed.) *Commodification of Global Agrifood Systems and Agro-Ecology: Convergence, Divergence and Beyond in Turkey*, London: Routledge, pp 1–35.

Atış, T.N. (2022) 'Food at the intersection of sovereignties: tracing the loss of food sovereignty for Turkish state and farmers', Unpublished dissertation, submitted to Middle East Technical University (METU), Ankara.

Atzeni, M. and Vieta, M. (2014) 'Between class and the market: self-management in theory and in the practice of worker-recuperated enterprises in Argentina', in M. Parker, G. Cheney, V. Fournier and C. Land (eds) *The Routledge Companion to Alternative Organization*, Abingdon: Routledge, pp 71–87.

Avcıoğlu, D. (1968) '*Türkiye'nin Düzeni (Dün-Bugün-Yarın)*', Ankara: Bilgi Yayınevi.

Ayalp, E. (2021) 'Alternatif gıda ağları ve Türkiye'de yurttaş temelli gıda inisiyatifleri', *İdealkent*, 12(33): 965–1005.

Ayata, S. (2008) 'Migrants and changing urban periphery: social relations, cultural diversity, and the public space in Istanbul's new neighborhoods', *International Migration*, 46(3): 27–64.

Aydin, Z. (2002) 'The new right, structural adjustment and Turkish agriculture: rural responses and survival strategies', *The European Journal of Development Research*, 14(2): 183–208.

Aydin, Z. (2010) 'Neo-liberal transformation of Turkish agriculture', *Journal of Agrarian Change*, 10(2): 149–87.

Aysu, A. (2008) *Küreselleşme ve Tarım Politikaları*, İstanbul: Su Yayınları.

Aysu, A. (2015) *Gıda krizi: Tarım, ekoloji, ve egemenlik*, İstanbul: Metis Yayınları.

Aysu, A. (2019) *Kooperatifler: Yemek Politik Bir İştir*, İstanbul: Yeni İnsan Yayınevi.

Babalık, N. (2003) 'Türkiye komünist partisinin sönümlenmesi sözlü tarih araştırması', Unpublished dissertation submitted to Ankara Üniversitesi, Sosyal Bilimler Enstitüsü, Ankara.

Bahçe, S. (2013) 'Orta sınıf miti ve mühendisin nemesisi', *Praksis*, 32(2): 145–64.

Barros, M. and Michaud, V. (2019) 'Worlds, words, and spaces of resistance: democracy and social media in consumer co-ops', *Organization*, 27(4): 578–612.

Bartu-Candan, A.B. and Kolluoğlu, B. (2008) 'Emerging spaces of neoliberalism: a gated town and a public housing project in Istanbul', *New Perspectives on Turkey*, 39: 5–46.

Başkaya, F. (2011) 'Seksen öncesi/sonrası veya rejimin niteliği', in E. Başer, N. Koçyiğit and M. Öziş (eds) *Bugüne bakmak, 1980 sonrasinda Türkiye'de yaşanan toplumsal değişim süreçleri*, İstanbul: Karaburun Bilim Kongresi, DipNot Yayınları, pp 13–31.

Batuman, B. (2019) 'Neoliberal islamism and the cultural politics of housing in Turkey', in K. Kılinç and M. Gharipour (eds) *Social Housing in the Middle East: Architecture, Urban Development, and Transnational Modernity*, Bloomington, IN: Indiana University Press, pp 88–115.

Benkler, Y. (2008) *The Wealth of Networks*, New Haven, CT: Yale University Press.

Bergmann, C. and Tafolar, M. (2014) 'Combating social inequalities in Turkey through conditional cash transfers (CCT)?', Conference Proceeding, the 9th Global Labour University Conference, Inequality within and among Nations: Causes, Effects, and Responses, Berlin School of Economics and Law, Available from: http://global-labour-university.org/wp-content/uploads/fileadmin/GLU_conference_2014/papers/Bergmann_Tafolar.pdf (Accessed 31 August 2021).

Bernstein, H. (2014) 'Food sovereignty via the "peasant way": a sceptical view', *Journal of Peasant Studies*, 41(6): 1031–63.

Bezmez, D. (2008) 'The politics of urban waterfront regeneration: the case of Haliç (the Golden Horn) Istanbul', *International Journal of Urban and Regional Research*, 32(4): 815–40.

Bilewicz, A. and Śpiewak, R. (2015) 'Enclaves of activism and taste: consumer cooperatives in Poland as alternative food networks', *Socio.hu*, 15(3): 145–66.

Bilgin, N. and Tanıyıcı, Ş. (2008) 'Türkiye'de kooperatif ve devlet ilişkilerinin tarihi gelişimi', *KMU İİBF Dergisi*, 10(15): 136–59.

Boggs, C. (1977) 'Marxism, prefigurative communism, and the problem of workers' control', *Radical America*, 11(6): 99–122.

Bora, T. (2021) 'Herkes işsiz ama seninki farklı: Türkiye'de beyaz yakalı işsizliğine genel bir bakış', in T. Bora, A. Bora, N. Erdoğan and İ. Üstün (eds) *'Boşuna mı Okuduk?' Türkiye'de Beyaz Yaka İşsizliği*, İstanbul: İletişim Yayinları.

Boratav, K. (2013) 'Korkut Boratav yanıtlıyor: Gezi direnişi sınıfsal bir başkaldırı mı?', *Scopbülten* [online] 20 June, Available from: www.e-skop.com/skopbulten/korkut-boratav-yanitliyor-gezi-direnisi-sinifsal-bir-bas kaldiri-mi/1352 (Accessed 6 June 2023).

Boratav, K. (2016) 'The Turkish bourgeoisie under neoliberalism', *Research and Policy on Turkey*, 1(1): 1–10.

Boratav, K. (2019) *Türkiye İktisat Tarihi, 1908–2015*, Ankara: İmge Kitabevi.

Boratav, K. and Yeldan, E. (2006) 'Turkey, 1980–2000: financial liberalization, macroeconomic (in)-stability, and patterns of distribution', in L. Taylor (ed.) *External Liberalization in Asia, Post-Socialist Europe, and Brazil*, Oxford: Oxford University Press, pp 417–55.

Breines, W. (1989) *Community and Organization in the New Left, 1962–1968: The Great Refusa'*, New Brunswick, NJ: Rutgers University Press.

Brunori, G., Rossi, A. and Guidi, F. (2012) 'On the new social relations around and beyond food: analysing consumers' role and action in Gruppi di Acquisto Solidale (Solidarity Purchasing Groups)', *Sociologia Ruralis,* 5(1): 1–30.

Buğra, A. (1994) *State and Business in Modern Turkey: A Comparative Study*. New York: State University of New York.

Buğra, A. (2007) 'Poverty and citizenship: an overview of the social-policy environment in Republican Turkey', *International Journal of Middle East Studies*, 39(1): 33–52.

Buğra, A. and Candas, A. (2011) 'Change and continuity under an eclectic social security regime: the case of Turkey', *Middle Eastern Studies*, 47(3): 515–28.

Buğra, A. and Keyder, Ç. (2006) 'The Turkish welfare regime in transformation', *Journal of European Social Policy*, 16(3): 211–28.

Busa, J.H. and Garder, R. (2015) 'Champions of the movement or fair-weather heroes? Individualization and the (a) politics of local food', *Antipode*, 47(2): 323–41.

Büyükyılmaz, M. (2020) 'Dünyayı besleyen yüz milyonlarca çiftçinin küresel hareketi La Via Campesina ne için mücadele ediyor?', *Turkish Independent*, Available from: https://www.indyturk.com/node/236671/haber/dünyayı-besleyen-yüz-milyonlarca-çiftçinin-küresel-hareketi-la-campesina-ne-için (Accessed 15 June 2023).

Çalışkan, K. (2008) 'Çiftçi-Sen', Available from: https://www.birgun.net/haber/ciftci-sen-13391 (Accessed 15 June 2023).

Çalışkan, K. (2018) 'Toward a new political regime in Turkey: from competitive toward full authoritarianism', *New Perspectives on Turkey*, 58: 5–33.

Çameli, T. (2021) 'Tarımda 2020–2021 manzarası: üç basit soru ve çoban ateşleri', *1+1 Express*, Available from: https://birartibir.org/uc-basit-soru-ve-coban-atesleri/ (Accessed 20 November 2021).

Çelik, A. (2015) 'Turkey's new labour regime under the Justice and Development Party in the first decade of the twenty-first century: authoritarian flexibilization', *Middle Eastern Studies*, 51(4): 618–35.

Çelik, Ç. (2017) 'Kırsal dönüşüm ve metalaşan yaşamlar: Soma havzası'nda işçileşme süreçleri ve sınıf ilişkileri', *Praksis: Special Issue on the Problems of Agriculture*, 43: 785–810.

Çelik, E. (2015) 'Negotiating religion at the Gezi Park protests', in I. David and K.F. Toktamış (eds) *Everywhere Taksim: Sowing the Seeds for a New Turkey at Gezi*, Amsterdam: Amsterdam University Press, pp 215–29.

Çelikpala, M. (2006) 'From immigrants to diaspora: influence of the north Caucasian diaspora in Turkey', *Middle Eastern Studies*, 42(3): 423–46.

Cameron, J. and Gibson-Graham, J.K. (2003) 'Feminising the economy: metaphors, strategies, politics', *Gender, Place and Culture: A Journal of Feminist Geography*, 10(2): 145–57.

Chen, K.K.-N. (2009) *Enabling Creative Chaos: The Organization behind the Burning Man Event*, Chicago, IL: University of Chicago Press.

Cheney, G., Santa Cruz, I., Peredo, A.M. and Nazareno, E. (2014) 'Worker cooperatives as an organizational alternative: challenges, achievements and promise in business governance and ownership', *Organization*, 21(5): 591–603.

Çiçek, Ö. (2017) 'Türkiye tarımında sendikalaşma mücadelesi: Çiftçi sendikaları konfederasyonu örneklemi', Proceedings of the Institutions, National Identity, Power, and Governance in the 21st Century, paper submitted to the 8th International Conference of Political Economy, Belgrade, Serbia.

Civelekoğlu, I. (2015) 'Enough is enough what do the Gezi protestors want to tell us? A political economy perspective', in I. David and K.F. Toktamış (eds) *Everywhere Taksim: Sowing the Seeds for a New Turkey at Gezi*, Amsterdam: Amsterdam University Press, pp 105–18.

Cizre-Sakallioglu, U.M. and Yeldan, E. (2000) 'Politics, society and financial liberalization: Turkey in the 1990s', *Development and Change*, 31(2): 481–508.

Claeys, P. (2015) *Human Rights and the Food Sovereignty Movement: Reclaiming Control,* London: Routledge.

Cornell, A. (2011) *Oppose and Propose!: Lessons from Movement for a New Society*, Oakland, CA: AK Press.

Coşkun, G.B. (2020) 'Media capture strategies in new authoritarian states: the case of Turkey', *Publizistik*, 65(4): 637–54.

Crossley, N. (2003) 'Even newer social movements? Anti-corporate protests, capitalist crises and the remoralization of society', *Organization*, 10(2): 287–305.

Daskalaki, M. and Kokkinidis, G. (2017) 'Organizing solidarity initiatives: a socio-spatial conceptualization of resistance', *Organization Studies*, 38(9): 1303–25.

David, I. (2016) 'Strategic democratisation? A guide to understanding AKP in power', *Journal of Contemporary European Studies*, 24(4): 478–93.

David, I. and Toktamış, K.F. (2015) 'Gezi in retrospect', in I. David and K.F. Toktamış (eds) *Everywhere Taksim: Sowing the Seeds for a New Turkey at Gezi*, Amsterdam: Amsterdam University Press, pp 15–22.

De Geus, M. (2014) 'Peter Kropotkin's anarchist vision of organization', *Ephemera: Theory & Politics in Organization*, 14(4): 853–71.

Değirmenci, E. (2017) 'Türkiye tarımında neoliberal dönüşüm ve metalaşma', *Praksis: Special Issue on the Problems of Agriculture*, 43: 765–84.

Değirmenci, S. (2021) *Türkiye'de tarım kapitalistleşirken; talepler ve Yasalar*, İstanbul: SAV Yayinları.

Dışişleri Vekaleti Milletlerarası İktisadi İşbirliği Teşkilatı Genel Sekreterliği (1952) 'Türkiye'de Marşal planı', No. 12 Ankara.

Dışişleri Vekaleti Milletlerarası İktisadi İşbirliği Teşkilatı Genel Sekreterliği (1953) 'Türkiye'de Marşal planı', No. 14 Ankara.

Doğançayır, C.M. (2022) 'Geziden bugüne yerel demokrasi deneyimlerinin seyri', *Istanbul Kent Araştırmaları ve Düşünce Dergisi*, 7: 14–19.

Dural, A.B. (2017) 'Genç Osmanlı döneminde ulusal iktisat politikaları-proletarya-köylü sınıfları ve Ethem Nejat Bey', Sosyal Araştırmalar Proceedings, pp 178–86.

Durukanoğlu, Ç. (2019) 'Kriz ve hayatta kalma/savunma araçlarından biri olarak kooperatifler', Available from: https://www.demokrathaber.org/yasam/kriz-ve-hayattakalmasavunma- (Accessed 2 April 2022).

Edelman, M. (2014) 'Food sovereignty: forgotten genealogies and future regulatory challenges', *Journal of Peasant Studies*, 41(6): 959–78.

Emre, A.C. (1960) *İki neslin tarihi*, Ankara: Hilmi Kitabevi.

Ercan, F. and Oğuz, Ş. (2015) 'From Gezi resistance to Soma massacre: capital accumulation and class struggle in Turkey', *Socialist Register*, 51(1): 114–35.

Eren, Z.C. (2017) 'Köylülüğün itibar kaybı: Bakırçay havzası dağ köylerinden kadınların anlatıları ve kırsal dönüşüm', *Praksis: Special Issue on Problems of Agriculture*, 43: 811–38.

Erkek, M.S. (2010) 'II. Meşrutiyet döneminde milli iktisat fikri ve Ethem Nejat Bey'in iktisadi görüşleri', Paper Presented at the II. İktisat Tarihi Kongresi, Elazığ.

Fairbairn, B. (1994) 'The meaning of Rochdale: the Rochdale pioneers and the co-operative principles, centre for co-operative studies', occasional paper series, University of Sakatchewan (No. 1755-2016-141554).

Fairbairn, B. (2017) 'Raiffeisen as social innovator', *Annals of Public and Cooperative Economics*, 88(3): 425–48.

FAO, IFAD, UNICEF, WFP and WHO (2021) *The State of Food Security and Nutrition in the World 2021: Transforming Food Systems for Food Security, Improved Nutrition and Affordable Healthy Diets for All*, Rome: FAO.

Farmanfarmaian, R., Sonay, A. and Akser, M. (2020) 'Turkish media structure in judicial and political context: an illustration of values and status negotiation', *Middle East Critique*, 27(2): 111–25.

Figueroa, R.M. and Alkon, A. (2017) 'Cooperative social practices, self-determination and the struggle for food', in A. Alkon and J. Guthman (eds) *The New Food Activism: Opposition, Cooperation, and Collective Action*, Oakland, CA: University of California Press, pp 181–205.

Filibeli, T.E. and İnceoğlu, Y.G. (2018) 'From political economy of the media to press freedom: obstacles to the implementation of peace journalism in Turkey', *Conflict & Communication*, 17(1): 1–11.

Fındıkoğlu, Z. (1967) *Kooperasyon Sosyolojisi Nazari ve Tatbiki Kooperatifçilik Denemesi*, No. 1206, İstanbul: İstanbul Üniversitesi Yayını.

Fırat, B.Ö. (2022) 'Kriz, pandemic ve mahalle dayanışma ağları: çuvallayan dayanışmalar', *1+1 Express*, Available from: https://birartibir.org/cuvalla yan-dayanismalar (Accessed 22 March 2022).

Flecha, R. and Ngai, P. (2014) 'The challenge for Mondragon: searching for the cooperative values in times of internationalization', *Organization*, 21(5): 666–82.

Fonte, M. and Cucco, I. (2017) 'Cooperatives and alternative food networks in Italy: the long road towards a social economy in agriculture', *Journal of Rural Studies*, 53: 291–302.

Fourat, E., Closson, C., Holzemer, L. and Hudon, M. (2020) 'Social inclusion in an alternative food network: values, practices and tensions', *Journal of Rural Studies*, 76: 49–57.

Franks, B. (2010) 'Anarchism and the virtues', in B. Franks and M. Wilson (eds) *Anarchism and Moral Philosophy*, Basingstoke: Palgrave Macmillan, pp 135–60.

Franz, M., Appel, A., and Hassler, M. (2013) 'Short waves of supermarket diffusion in Turkey', *Moravian Geographical Reports*, 21(4): 50–63.

Freeman, J. (2013) 'The tyranny of structurelessness', *Women's Studies Quarterly*, 41(3/4): 231–46.

Fuchs, C. (2014) 'Social media and the public sphere', *TripleC: Communication, Capitalism & Critique. Open Access Journal for a Global Sustainable Information Society*, 12(1): 57–101.

Fuchs, C. (2021) 'The digital commons and the digital public sphere: how to advance digital democracy today', *Westminster Papers in Communication and Culture*, 16(1): 9–26.

Gibson-Graham, J.K. (1996a) *The End of Capitalism (As We Knew It): A Feminist Critique of Political Economy*, Minneapolis, MN: University of Minnesota Press.

Gibson-Graham, J.K. (1996b) 'Querying globalization', *Rethinking Marxism*, 9(1): 1–27.

Gibson-Graham, J.K. (2003) 'Enabling ethical economies: cooperativism and class', *Critical Sociology*, 29(2): 123–61.

Gibson-Graham, J.K. (2006) *A Postcapitalist Politics*, Minneapolis, MN: University of Minnesota Press.

Gibson-Graham, J.K. (2008) 'Diverse economies: performative practices for 'other worlds', *Progress in Human Geography*, 32(5): 613–32.

Gibson-Graham J.K. (2010) 'Forging post-development partnerships', in A. Pike, A. Rodriguez-Pose and J. Tomaney (eds) *Handbook of Local and Regional Development,* London: Routledge, pp 226–36.

Gibson-Graham, J.K. (2014) 'Rethinking the economy with thick description and weak theory', *Current Anthropology*, 55(9): 147–53.

Gibson-Graham, J.K. and Dombroski, K. (2020) 'Introduction' in J.K. Gibson-Graham and K. Dombroski (eds) *Handbook of Diverse Economies: Inventory as Ethical Intervention,* Cheltenham: Edward Elgar Publishing, pp 1–25.

Gibson-Graham, J.K. and Roelvink, G. (2011) 'The nitty gritty of creating alternative economies', *Social Alternatives*, 30(1): 29–33.

Gibson-Graham, J.K., Cameron, J. and Healy, S. (2013) *Take Back the Economy: An Ethical Guide for Transforming Our Communities*, Minneapolis, MN: University of Minnesota Press.

Goglio, S. and Leonardi, A. (2010) 'The roots of cooperative credit from a theoretical and historical perspective', Euricse Working Papers, N.011/10.

Goodman, D. and DuPuis, E.M. (2002) 'Knowing food and growing food: beyond the production–consumption debate in the sociology of agriculture', *Sociologia Ruralis*, 42(1): 5–22.

Goodman, D. and Goodman, M. (2009) 'Alternative food networks', in R. Kitchin and N. Thrift (eds) *International Encyclopedia of Human Geography*, Oxford: Elsevier, pp 208–20.

Goodman, D., DuPuis, M. and Goodman, M. (2012) *Alternative Food Networks: Knowledge, Practice, and Politics*, London: Routledge.

Gordon, U. (2008) *Anarchy Alive!: Anti-Authoritarian Politics from Practice to Theory*, London: Pluto Press.

Göktürk, Y. (2012) 'Metin Kurt ve Cenk Caner, böyledir bizim sevdamız', *Bir+Bir*, 16(2): 42. Available from: https://birartibir.org/dergi/birbir-16-2012-02/ (Accessed 25 July 2023).

Gradin, S. (2015) 'Radical routes and alternative avenues: how cooperatives can be non-capitalist', *Review of Radical Political Economics*, 47(2): 141–58.

Graeber, D. (2002) 'The new anarchist', *New Left Review*, 13(6): 61–73.

Grasseni, C. (2020) 'Direct food provisioning: collective food procurement', in J.K. Gibson-Graham and K. Dombroski (eds) *Handbook of Diverse Economies*, Cheltenham: Edward Elgar Publishing, pp 223–9.

Grasseni, C., Forno, F. and Signori, S. (2015) 'Beyond alternative food networks: Italy's solidarity purchase groups and the United States' community economies', in P. Utting (ed.) *Social and Solidarity Economy: Beyond the Fringe*, London: UNRISD and Zed Books, pp 185–201.

Gritzas, G. and Kavoulakos, K.I. (2016) 'Diverse economies and alternative spaces: an overview of approaches and practices', *European Urban and Regional Studies*, 23(4): 917–34.

Güneri, M. (2004) *Hasanoğlu köy enstitüsü kurulurken, 1941–1951*, İstanbul: Türkiye Ekonomik ve Toplumsal Tarih Vakfı.

Guthman, J. (2007) 'The Polanyian way? Voluntary food labels as neoliberal governance', *Antipode*, 39(3): 456–78.

Guthman, J. (2008) 'Neoliberalism and the making of food politics in California', *Geoforum*, 39(3): 1171–83.

Gültekin, S. (2015) 'Karşı Lig short documentary', Available from: https://vimeo.com/11852917 (Acessed 20 January 2021).

Güven, A.B. (2009) 'Reforming sticky ınstitutions: persistence and change in Turkish agriculture', *Studies in Comparative International Development*, 44(2): 162–87.

Güven, A.B. (2019) 'Political economy', in A. Özerdem and M. Whiting (eds) *The Routledge Handbook of Turkish Politics*, London: Routledge, pp 151–62.

Habermas, J. (1981) *The Theory of Communicative Action, Lifeworld and System: A Critique of Functionalist Reason*, Boston, MA: Beacon Press.

Habermas, J. (1987) *The Theory of Communicative Action, Vol 1 & 2*, Boston, MA: Beacon Press.

Habermas, J. (1989) *The Structural Transformation of the Public Sphere: An Inquiry into a Category of Bourgeois Society*, Cambridge, MA: MIT Press.

Habermas, J. (2021) 'Public space and political public sphere: the biographical roots of two motifs in my thought', *The Journal of Philosophy of Disability*, 1: 105–15.

Haug, C. (2013) 'Organizing spaces: meeting arenas as a social movement infrastructure between organization, network, and institution', *Organization Studies*, 34(5–6): 705–32.

Healy, S. (2009) 'Alternative economies', *International Encyclopedia of Human Geography*, Oxford: Elsevier, pp 338–44.

Heras-Saizarbitoria, I. (2014) 'The ties that bind? Exploring the basic principles of worker-owned organizations in practice', *Organization*, 21(5): 645–65.

Hersant, J. and Toumarkine, A. (2005) 'Hometown organizations in Turkey: an overview', *European Journal of Turkish Studies: Social Sciences on Contemporary Turkey*, 2, Available from: doi.org/10.4000/ejts.397 (Accessed 3 August 2023).

Hibbert, S., Piacentini M. and Dajani, H.A. (2003) 'Understanding volunteer motivation for participation in a community-based food cooperative', *International Journal of Non-profit and Voluntary Sector Marketing*, 8(1): 30–42.

Hinrichs, C.C. (2000) 'Embeddedness and local food systems: notes on two types of direct agricultural market', *Journal of Rural Studies*, 16(3): 295–303.

Hofstede, G. (1991) *Cultures and Organizations: Software of the Mind*, London: McGraw-Hill.

Hofstede, G.H., Hofstede, G.J. and Minkov, M. (2005) *Cultures and Organizations: Software of the Mind*, Maidenhead: McGraw-Hill.

Holloway, L., Kneafsey, M., Venn, L., Cox, R., Dowler, E. and Tuomainen, H. (2007) 'Possible food economies: a methodological framework for exploring food production-consumption relationships', *Sociologia Ruralis*, 47(1): 1–19.

İlkkaracan, İ. and Tunalı, I. (2010) 'Agricultural transformation and the rural labor market in Turkey', in B. Karapinar, F. Adaman and G. Ozertan (eds) *Rethinking Structural Reform in Turkish Agriculture: Beyond the World Bank's Strategy,* New York: Nova Science Publishers, pp 105–48.

İnce, A. and Kadirbeyoğlu, Z. (2020) 'The politics of food', in D. Özkan and G.B. Büyüksaraç (eds) *Commoning the City: Empirical Perspectives on Urban Ecology, Economics and Ethics*, New York: Routledge.

İstanbul Kent Bostanları Çalışma Grubu (2021) *Tarım Yapana Kent İstanbul: Bugünden Yarına Müşterek Hayatlar,* İstanbul: İstanbul Kent Konseyi Yayını.

Jacoby, T. (2008) 'The development of Turkish agriculture: debates, legacies and dynamics', *The Journal of Peasant Studies*, 35(2): 249–67.

Jansen, K. (2015) 'The debate on food sovereignty theory: agrarian capitalism, dispossession and agroecology', *Journal of Peasant Studies*, 42(1): 213–32.

Jarosz, L. (2008) 'The city in the country: growing alternative food networks in metropolitan areas', *Journal of Rural Studies*, 24: 231–44.

Jarosz, L. (2011) 'Defining world hunger: scale and neoliberal ideology in international food security policy discourse', *Food, Culture & Society*, 14(1): 117–39.

Jarosz, L. (2014) 'Comparing food security and food sovereignty discourses', *Dialogues in Human Geography*, 4(2): 168–81.

Kadıköy Kooperatifi Kollektifi (2020) 'Kadıköy kooperatifi deneyimi', in F.S. Öngel and U.D. Yıldırım (eds) *Krize Karşı Kooperatifler; Deneyimler, Tartışmalar, Alternatifler,* İstanbul: Notabene, pp 153–82.

Kadirbeyoğlu, Z. and Konya, N. (2017) 'Alternative food initiatives in Turkey', in F. Adaman, B. Akbulut and M. Arsel (eds) *Neoliberal Turkey and Its Discontents: Economic Policy and the Environment under Erdoğan*, London: I.B. Taurus, pp 207–27.

Kahraman, M.D. (2022) 'Demokrasinin ön koşulu kent meydanları ve Gezi direnişi', *Istanbul Kent Araştırmaları ve Düşünce Dergisi*, 7: 30–4.

Kandemir, O. (2011) 'Tarımsal destekleme politikalarının kırsal kalkınmaya etkisi', *Ekonomi Bilimleri Dergisi*, 3(1): 103–13.

Kara, K. and Güngör, N. (2021) 'Karşı lig: Mücadele ve direnişin alt kültürel bir oluşumu', *Türkiye İletişim Araştırmaları Dergisi*, 38: 261–81.

Karaçimen, E. and Değirmenci, E. (2019) 'Kuşaktan kuşağa çay tarımında kadın emeği', in Ö. Şendeniz (ed.) *Aramızda Kalmasın; Kır, Kent Ve Ötesinde Toplumsal Cinsiyet,* İstanbul: Toplumsal Cinsiyet Araştırmaları Derneği Yayını, pp 69–85.

Karakaya, E. (2016) 'Agro food system transitions? Exploring alternative agro food initiatives in İzmir, Turkey', Unpublished doctoral dissertation submitted to the Graduate School of Engineering and Sciences of İzmir Institute of Technology, İzmir.

Karaömerlioğlu, M.A. (1998) 'Bir tepeden reform denemesi: Çiftçiyi topraklandırma kanunu'nun hikayesi', *Birikim*, 107: 31–47.

Karapınar, B., Adaman, F. and Özertan, G. (2011) 'Introduction: rethinking agricultural reform in Turkish agriculture', in B. Karapınar, F. Adaman and G. Özertan (eds) *Rethinking Structural Reform in Turkish Agriculture: Beyond the World Bank's Strategy*, New York: Nova Science Publishers, pp 1–11.

Kardam, A. (2020) *Mustafa Suphi, Karanlıktan Aydınlığa*, İstanbul: İletişim Yayinları.

Kaya, A. (2015) 'Islamisation of Turkey under the AKP rule: empowering family, faith, and charity', *South European Society and Politics*, 20(1): 47–69.

Kaya, Ç. (2019) 'Sosyal iş modelleri ve sosyal girişimcilik: Boğaziçi Üniversitesi tüketim kooperatifi örneği', *İşletme Araştırmaları Dergisi*, 11(3): 1433–49.

Kaynak, S. and Barçın, B. (2016) 'Türkiye'de kooperatifçilik ve BÜKOOP deneyimi (1/2)', Available from: https://dortyuzbes.com.kooperatif-1/ (Accessed 30 December 2022).

Kaymak, M. (2011) '1980 öncesinin sorunsalindan hareketle 1980 sonrası Türkiye tarımı', in E. Başer, N. Koçyiğit and M. Öziş (eds) *Bugüne Bakmak, 1980 sonrasinda Türkiye'de yaşanan toplumsal değişim süreçleri*, İstanbul: Karaburun Bilim Kongresi, DipNot Yayınları, pp 123–42.

Keskin, N.E. and Yaman, M. (2013) *Türkiye'de tütün: Reji'den TEKEL'e, TEKEL'den Bugüne*, İstanbul: NotaBene Yayınları.

Kessler, G. (1948) 'Zonguldak ve Karabük'teki çalışma şartları', *İstanbul Üniversitesi İktisat Fakültesi Mecmuasi*, 9: 173–96.

Keyder, Ç. (1993) *Türkiye'de devlet ve sınıflar*, İstanbul: İletişim Yayinları.

Keyder, Ç. (2005) 'The cycle of sharecropping and the consolidation of small peasant ownership in Turkey', in T.J. Byres (ed.) *Sharecropping and Sharecroppers*, London: Routledge, pp 131–46.

Keyder, Ç. and Yenal, Z. (2011) 'Agrarian change under globalization: markets and insecurity in Turkish agriculture', *Journal of Agrarian Change*, 11(1): 60–86.

Keyder, Q. (1983) 'Paths of rural transformation in Turkey', *Journal of Peasant Studies*, 11(1): 34–49.

Knupfer, A.M. (2013) *Food Co-Ops in America: Communities, Consumption, and Economic Democracy*', New York: Cornell University Press.

Koç, Y. (2014) 'Türkiye'de kırsal kesimde mülksüzleşme (Osmanlı'dan günümüze)', in A. Aysu and M.S. Kayaoğlu (eds) *Köylülükten Sonra Tarım-Osmanlı'dan Günümüze Köylünün Ilgası ve Şirketleşme*, Ankara: Epos Yayınları, pp 125–94.

Kocabaş, Ö.Y. (2003) 'Türkiye'de kooperatifçilik düşüncesinin gelişimi', *Tarım Ekonomisi Dergisi*, 8(1): 15–24.

Kocabaş, Ö.Y. (2011) 'Türkiye'de kooperatifçilik hareketinin düşünsel boyutu', paper presented at the 20th International Congress on Türk Kooperatifçilik Kongresi, Türk Kooperatifçilik Kurumu, Available from: https://ticaret.gov.tr/data/5d41d91713b87639ac9e0235/408dc506e fa12cd18863b3d13b93038f.pdf (Accessed 15 June 2023).

Kocagöz, U. (2016) 'Kır araştırmaları ve paradigma sorunu', *Karasaban.net*, Available from: https://www.karasaban.net/kir-arastirmalari-ve-paradi gma-sorunu-umut-kocagoz/ (Accessed 15 June 2023).

Kocagöz, U. (2018) 'The commons politics of food', in E. Erdoğan, N. Yüce and Ö. Özbay (eds) *The Politics of the Commons: From Theory to Struggle*, İstanbul: Sivil ve Ekolojik Haklar Derneği, pp 132–49.

Kociatkiewicz, J., Kostera, M. and Parker, M. (2021) 'The possibility of disalienated work: being at home in alternative organizations', *Human Relations*, 74(7): 933–57.

Kokkinidis, G. (2014) 'Spaces of possibilities: workers' self-management in Greece', *Organization*, 22(6): 847–71.

Konda Research Centre (2014) 'Toplumun 'Gezi parkı olayları' algısı Gezi parkindakiler kimlerdi?', Available from: https://konda.com.tr/rapor/67/ gezi-raporu (Accessed 15 June 2023).

koopBülteni (2011) Boğaziçi Üniversitesi Mensupları Tüketim Kooperatifi Aylık Bülteni, No. 2, Available from: https://bukoop.org/wp-content/uplo ads/sites/2/2015/03/BuKoop_Bulten_Sayi_2.pdf (Accessed 15 June 2023).

Kurtuluş, G. (2019) 'Türkiyede yeni kooperatifçilik hareketinin sosyal ve dayanışma ekonomisi kapsaminda incelenmesi', MA Thesis submitted to the Social Sciences Institute of Sıtkı Koçman University, Muğla.

Kus, B. (2014) 'The informal road to markets: neoliberal reforms, private entrepreneurship and the informal economy in Turkey', *International Journal of Social Economics*, 41(4): 278–93.

Kus, B. (2016) 'Financial citizenship and the hidden crisis of the working class in the "New Turkey"', *Middle East Report*, 278, 40–8.

Kuyucu, T. and Ünsal, Ö. (2010) '"Urban transformation" as state-led property transfer: an analysis of two cases of urban renewal in Istanbul', *Urban Studies*, 47(7): 1479–99.

Lambru, M. and Petrescu, C. (2014) 'Surviving the crisis: worker cooperatives in Romania', *Organization*, 21(5): 730–45.

Le Velly, R. (2019) 'Allowing for the projective dimension of agency in analysing alternative food networks', *Sociologia Ruralis*, 59(1): 2–22.

Leach, D.K. (2013) 'Prefigurative politics', in D. Snow, D. della Porta, B. Klandermas and D. McAdam (eds) *The Wiley-Blackwell Encyclopedia of Social and Political Movements*, Malden, MA: Wiley, pp 1004–6.

Leach, D.K. (2016) 'When freedom is not an endless meeting: a new look at efficiency in consensus-based decision making', *The Sociological Quarterly*, 57: 36–70.

Lee Caroline, W. (2014) 'Walking the talk: the performance of authenticity in public engagement work', *The Sociological Quarterly*, 55(3): 493–513.

Little, R., Maye D. and Ilbery, B. (2010) 'Collective purchase: moving local and organic foods beyond the niche market', *Environment and Planning A*, 42: 1797–813.

Lockie, S. and Halpin, D. (2005) 'The "Conventionalisation" thesis reconsidered: structural and ideological transformation of Australian organic agriculture', *Sociologia Ruralis*, 45(4): 284–307.

Lovering, J. and Türkmen, H. (2011) 'Bulldozer neo-liberalism in Istanbul: the state-led construction of property markets, and the displacement of the urban poor', *International Planning Studies*, 16(1): 73–96.

Maeckelbergh, M. (2011a) 'Doing is believing: prefiguration as strategic practice in the alterglobalization movement', *Social Movement Studies*, 10(1): 1–20.

Maeckelbergh, M. (2011b) 'The road to democracy: the political legacy of '1968', *International Review of Social History*, 56(2): 301–32.

Maeckelbergh, M. (2014) 'Social movements and global governance', in M., Parker, G. Cheney, V. Fournier and C. Land (eds) *The Routledge Companion to Alternative Organization,* London: Routledge, pp 345–58.

Mais, K.A. (2013) *Food Coops in America: Community, Consumption and Economic Democracy*, Ithaca, NY: Cornell University Press.

Martin, F., Appel, A. and Hassler, M. (2013) 'Short waves of supermarket diffusion in Turkey', *Moravian Geographical Reports*, 21(4): 50–63.

Marx, K. (1990) *Capital, Vol. 1*, Harmondsworth: Penguin Books.

Maye, D. and Kirwan, J. (2010) 'Alternative food networks', *Sociology of Agriculture and Food*, 20: 383–89.

Maye, D. Holloway, L. and Kneafsey, M. (2007) 'Introduction: alternative food geographies', in D. Maye, L. Holloway and M. Kneafsey (eds) *Alternative Food Geographies: Representation and Practice*, Amsterdam: Elsevier, pp 1–23.

McCarthy, J.D. and Zald, M.N. (1977) 'Resource mobilization and social movements: a partial theory', *American Journal of Sociology*, 82(6): 1212–41.

McMichael, P. (2014) 'Historicizing food sovereignty', *Journal of Peasant Studies*, 41(6): 933–57.

McMichael, P. and Schneider, M. (2011) 'Food security politics and the millennium development goals', *Third World Quarterly*, 32(1): 119–39.

Melis, O. and Tok, E. (2011) 'Gentrification as a blanket concept: a tale of resisting and contesting neoliberal urbanization programmes', 51st Congress of the European Regional Science Association: 'New Challenges for European Regions and Urban Areas in a Globalised World', 30 August–3 September 2011, Barcelona: European Regional Science Association (ERSA) Louvain-la-Neuve.

Melucci, A. (1985) 'The symbolic challenge of contemporary movements', *Social research*, 52(4): 789–816.

Memioğlu, Y. (2017) 'Türk kooperatifçiliğinin dönemsel analizi (1950–1960 Dönemi)', *Üçüncü Sektör Sosyal Ekonomi*, 52(4): 897–921.

Mete, B. (2017) 'Türkiye'de ışçilerin özyönetim deneyimi: Diren Kazova Kooperatifi ve Özgür Kazova Tekstil Kolektifi', Unpublished master's thesis, Social Sciences Institute of Maltepe Üniversitesi, İstanbul.

Moragues-Faus, A. (2017) 'Emancipatory or neoliberal food politics? Exploring the "politics of collectivity" of buying groups in the search for egalitarian food democracies', *Antipode*, 49(2): 455–76.

Mülayim, Z.G. (1982) 'Atatürk'ün kooperatifçilik konusundaki görüşleri', Paper presented at a conference delivered at Uludağ University, Faculty of Economic and Social Sciences, Bursa, Available from: http://193.140.245.211/bitstream/11452/20453/1/3_1_17.pdf (Accessed 15 June 2023).

Mülayim, Z.G. (1999) *Kooperatifçilik*, Ankara: Yetkin Basin Yayin ve Dağıtım.

Oba, B. and Özsoy, Z. (2019) 'Consumer-initiated cooperatives (CICs) of İstanbul as an alternative to capitalist food provisioning system', Paper presented at the 11th International Conference in Critical Management Studies: Precarıous Presents, Open Futures, Open University, UK.

Oba, B. and Özsoy, Z. (2020) 'Unifying nature of food: consumer-ınitiated cooperatives in Istanbul', *Society and Business Review,* 15(4): 349–72.

Oksay, K. (1979) 'Büyük mağazacılık ve tüketim kooperatifçiliği', *Türk Kooperatifçilik Kurumu*, 41, Ankara: Türk Kooperatifçilik Kurumu,.

Öktem, K. and Akkoyunlu, K. (2016) 'Exit from democracy: illiberal governance in Turkey and beyond', *Southeast European and Black Sea Studies*, 16(4): 469–80.

Olcan, Anıl (2020) 'Yerel dayanışma ağları I-IV', Available from: https://birartibir.org/ne-sadaka-ne-lutuf-hal-hatir/ (Accessed 25 July 2023).

Oluç, M. (1954) 'Migros-Türk', *İstanbul Üniversitesi İktisat Fakültesi Mecmuası*, 16: 213–49.

Önder, İ. (2011) 'Emperyalizmin Türkiye'yi dönüştürme etkisi: 1980 sonrasi politikalar', in E. Başer, N. Koçyiğit and M. Öziş (eds) *Bugüne Bakmak, 1980 Sonrasinda Türkiye'de Yaşanan Toplumsal Değişim Süreçleri*, İstanbul: Karaburun Bilim Kongresi, DipNot Yayınları, pp 31–59.

Öngel, F.S. (2020a) 'Sendika-Kooperatif ilişkisi ve özgün bir deneyim olarak T. Maden-İş'in Mites-Migsan-Mipaş Deneyimi', in F.S. Öngel and U.D. Yıldırım (eds) *Krize Karşı Kooperatifler; Deneyimler, Tartışmalar, Alternatifler*, İstanbul: NoteBene.

Öngel, F.S. (2020b) 'Sendika-Kooperatif ilişkilerive sendikaların yatırım faaliyetleri', in F.S. Öngel and U.D. Yıldırım (eds) *Krize Karşı Kooperatifler; Deneyimler, Tartışmalar, Alternatifler*, İstanbul: NoteBene.

Oral, N. (2013) 'Tarım ve gıdada çokuluslu şirketlerin egemenliği', in N. Oral (ed.) *Türkiye'de Tarımın Ekonomi Politiği, 1923–1913*, Ankara: NotaBene Yayınları, pp 159–200.

Örs, İ.R. and Turan, Ö. (2015) 'The manner of contention: pluralism at Gezi', *Philosophy & Social Criticism*, 41(4–5): 453–63.

Oyan, O. (2013) 'Tarımda IMF-DB gözetiminde 2000li yıllar', in N. Oral (ed.) *Türkiye'de Tarımın Ekonomi Politiği, 1923–1913*, Ankara: NotaBene Yayınları, pp 111–30.

Öz, Ö. and Aksoy, Z. (2019) 'Challenges of building alternatives: the experience of a consumer food co-operative in Istanbul', *Food, Culture & Society*, 22(3): 299–315.

Öz, Ö. and Ünüvar, A. (2016) 'Türkiye'de Kooperatifçilik ve BÜKOOP Deneyimi' (2/2), Available from: https://dortyuzbes.com/kooperatif-2/ (Accessed 15 June 2023).

Özdemir, A.M. and Yücesan-Özdemir, G. (2006) 'Labour law reform in Turkey in the 2000s: the Devil is not just in the detail but also in the legal texts', *Economic and Industrial Democracy*, 27(2): 311–31.

Özden, A. and Bekmen, A. (2015) 'Rebelling against neoliberal populist regimes', in I. David and K. Toktamis (eds) *Everywhere Taksim: Sowing the Seeds for a New Turkey at Gezi*, Amsterdam: University of Amsterdam Press, pp 89–104.

Özden, B., Akça, İ. and Bekmen, A. (2017) 'Antinomies of authoritarian neoliberalism in Turkey: the Justice and Development Party era', in C.B. Tansel (ed.) *States of Discipline: Authoritarian Neoliberalism and the Contested Reproduction of Capitalist Order,* London: Rowman & Littlefield, pp 189–210.

Özden, F. (2020) 'Gıda etiği bağlamında topluluk destekli tarım modeli üzerine bir inceleme', *Türkiye Biyoetik Dergisi*, 7(3): 84–98.

Özsoy, Z. and Oba, B. (2022) 'How can digital entrepreneurship adress social issues? The case of EkoHarita in fighting ecological disruption', in E. Vinogradov, B. Leick and D. Assadi (eds) *Digital Entrepreneurship and the sharing economy,* London: Routledge, pp 109–27.

Özsoy, Z., Demir, Y. and Oba, B. (2018) 'From Resistance to Solidarity: Kadıköy Consumption Cooperative', Paper presented at the Organization Studies Summer Workshop: Responding to Displacement, Disruption, and Division: Organizing for Social and Institutional Change, Samos, Greece.

Öztan, G.G (2013) 'Gezi direnişi ile kurulan otantik kamusallık ve dayanışma ruhu', *Praksis: Special Issue: Gezi İle Gelen Uzun Haziran, Sözü Aşan İçerik*, pp 165–81.

Özveren, E., Erkek, M.S. and Ünal, H.S. (2016) 'Unity and diversity in the Ottoman school of national economy: a reappraisal of Ziya Gökalp and Ethem Nejat', in E.S. Reinert, J. Ghosh and R. Kattel (eds) *Handbook of Alternative Theories of Economic Development*, Cheltenham: Edward Elgar, pp 194–211.

Pansera, M. and Rizzi, F. (2018) 'Furbish or perish: Italian social cooperatives at crossroads', *Organization*, 27(1): 17–35.

Parker, M. (2017) 'Alternative enterprises, local economies, and social justice: why smaller is still more beautiful', *Management*, 20(4): 418–34.

Parker, M., Cheney, G., Fournier, V. and Land, C. (eds) (2014) *The Routledge Companion to Alternative Organization,* London: Routledge.

Parker, M., Fournier, V. and Reedy, P. (2007) *The Dictionary of Alternatives: Utopianism and Organization,* London: Zed Books.

Parlak, D. (2013) 'Gezi direnişi bağlaminda başka bir siyasallığın olanaklılığı üzerine', *Praksis: Special Issue: Gezi İle Gelen Uzun Haziran, Sözü Aşan İçerik,* pp 135–43.

Patmore, G. and Balnave, N. (2018) 'Controlling consumption: a comparative history of Rochdale consumer co-operatives in Australia and the United States', in G. Patmore and S. Stromquist (eds) *Frontiers of Labor: Comparative Histories of the United States and Australia,* Champaign, IL: University of Illinois Press.

Pinarcioğlu, M. and Işik, O. (2008) 'Not only helpless but also hopeless: changing dynamics of urban poverty in Turkey, the case of Sultanbeyli, Istanbul', *European Planning Studies,* 16(10): 1353–70.

Polat, H. and Tayanç, T. (1973) '*Cumhuriyetimizin 50. yılinda tüketim kooperatifleri ve sorunları*', *Türk Kooperatifçilik Kurumu Yayını,* 35, Ankara: Şark Matbaası.

Polletta, F. (1999) 'Free spaces in collective action', *Theory and Society,* 28(1): 1–38.

Polletta, F. (2005) 'How participatory democracy became white: culture and organizational choice', *Mobilization: An International Quarterly,* 10(2): 271–88.

Polletta, F. and Hoban, K. (2016) 'Why consensus?', *Journal of Social and Political Psychology,* 4(1): 286–301.

Prinz, M. (2002) 'German rural cooperatives, Friedrich Wilhelm Raiffeisen and the organization of trust', 8th International Economic History Association Congress, Buenos Aires, 54: 1–28, Available from: http://citeseerx.ist.psu.edu/viewdoc/download?doi=10.1.1.538.4312&rep=rep1&type=pdf (Accessed 18 July 2021).

Raekstad, P. and Gradin, S.S. (2020) *Prefigurative Politics: Building Tomorrow Today,* Cambridge: Polity Press.

Rakopoulos, T. (2014) 'The crisis seen from below, within, and against: from solidarity economy to food distribution cooperatives in Greece', *Dialectical Anthropology,* 38(2): 189–207.

Reed, D. (2015) 'Scaling the social and solidarity economy: opportunities and limitations of fair-trade practice', in P. Utting (ed.) *Social and Solidarity Economy: Beyond the Fringe,* London: UNRISD and Zed Books, pp 100–15.

Reedy, P., King, D. and Coupland, C. (2016) 'Organizing for individuation: alternative organizing, politics and new identities', *Organization Studies,* 37(11): 1553–73.

Rehber, E. (2000) 'Vertical coordination in the agro-food industry and contract farming: a comparative study of Turkey and the USA', Food Marketing Policy Center Report (No. 052), Storrs, CT: University of Connecticut, Department of Agricultural and Resource Economics.

Rehber, E. (2011) *Kooperatifçilik*, Bursa: Ekin Yayınları.

Reinecke, J. (2018) 'Social movements and prefigurative organizing: confronting entrenched inequalities in Occupy London', *Organization Studies*, 39(9): 1299–321.

Renting, H., Marsden, T.K. and Banks, J. (2003) 'Understanding alternative food networks: exploring the role of short food supply chains in rural development', *Environment and Planning*, 35(3): 393–411.

Robbins, M.J. (2015) 'Exploring the "localisation" dimension of food sovereignty', *Third World Quarterly*, 36(3): 449–68.

Şaşmaz, M.Ü. and Özel, Ö. (2019) 'Tarım sektörüne sağlanan mali teşviklerin tarım sektörü gelişimi üzerindeki etkisi: Türkiye örneği', *Dumlupınar Üniversitesi Sosyal Bilimler Dergisi*, 61: 50–65.

Şener, M.Y. (2016) 'Conditional cash transfers in Turkey: a case to reflect on the AKP's approach to gender and social policy', *Research and Policy on Turkey*, 1(2): 164–78.

Sevinç, M. (2022) 'Gezi ve park forumları geleceğin yönetim biçimidir', *İstanbul Kent Araştırmaları ve Düşünce Dergisi*, 7: 20–3.

Shaw, D.J. (2007) *World Food Security: A History since 1945*, New York: Palgrave Macmillan.

Sitrin, M.A. (2012) *Everyday Revolutions: Horizontalism and Autonomy in Argentina*, London: Zed Books.

Slocum, R. (2006) 'Anti-racist practice and the work of community food organizations', *Antipode*, 38(2): 327–49.

Smucker, J.M. (2013) 'Occupy: a name fixed to a flashpoint', *The Sociological Quarterly*, 54(2): 219–25.

Smucker, J.M. (2014) 'Can prefigurative politics replace political strategy?', *Berkeley Journal of Sociology*, 58: 74–82.

Smucker, J.M. (2017) *Hegemony How-to: A Roadmap for Radicals*, Oakland, CA: AK Press.

Soborski, R. (2018) *Ideology and the Future of Progressive Social Movements*, London: Rowman & Littlefield.

Soydemir, C.O. and Erçek, M. (2022) 'The resurrection of earlier imprints post mortem: explaining the Turkish agricultural cooperative movement with an imprinting theory lens, 1888–1937', *Annals of Public and Cooperative Economics*, 1–34, Available from: https://doi.org/10.1111/apce.12398.

Sönmez, M. (1987) 'Türkiye'de tarım ve büyük burjuvazi', *11. Tez, Türkiye'de Tarım Sorunu*, İstanbul: Uluslararası Yayıncılık Ltd. Şti, pp 230–8. Available from: https://filedn.eu/lpwTKmJuSKCLNjzDCWvh2dm/11-tez/11-tez-07.pdf (Accessed 25 July 2023).

Sözeri, C. (2019) 'The transformation of Turkey's Islamic media and its marriage with neo-liberalism', *Southeast European and Black Sea Studies*, 19(1): 155–74.

Srnicek, N. and Williams, A. (2015a) 'The future isn't working', *Juncture*, 22(3): 243–47.

Srnicek, N. and Williams, A. (2015b) *Inventing the Future: Postcapitalism and a World without Work*, London: Verso Books.

Suphi, M. (2021) *İlk yazılar*, trans. F. Ersin, B. Coşkun and H. Erdem, Sosyal Tarih Yayınları, İstanbul: TÜSTAV.

Tansel, C.B. (2018) 'Authoritarian neoliberalism and democratic backsliding in Turkey: beyond the narratives of progress', *South European Society and Politics*, 23(2): 197–217.

Tekeli, İ. and İlkin, S. (1974) 'Savaş sonrası ortamında 1947 Türkiye İktisadi Kalkınma Planı', Middle East Technical University Publication, No. 24, Ankara: The Graduate School of Social Sciences of Middle East Technical University.

Tilly, C. (1978) 'Did the cake of custom break?' *CRSO Working Paper,* No. 189, Ann Arbor, MI: Center for Research on Social Organization.

Toktamış, K. (2019) 'Now there is, now there is not: the disappearing silent revolution of AKP as re-entrenchment', *British Journal of Middle Eastern Studies*, 46(5): 735–51.

Toktamış, K. and David, I. (2015) *Everywhere Taksim: Sowing the Seeds for a New Turkey at Gezi*, Amsterdam: Amsterdam University Press.

Toprak, Z. (1995) *Milli iktisat-milli burjuvazi*, Tarih Vakfı Yurt Yayınları, No. 14, İstanbul: Türkiye Araştırmaları.

Tuğal, C. (2009) *Passive Revolution: Absorbing the Islamic Challenge to Capitalism*', Stanford, CA: Stanford University Press.

Tuğal, C. (2013) 'Resistance everywhere: the Gezi revolt in global perspective', *New Perspectives on Turkey,* 49: 157–72.

Tuğal, C. (2015) 'The elusive revolt: the contradictory rise of middle-class politics', *Thesis Eleven*, 130(1): 74–95.

Tuğal, C. (2016) *The Fall of the Turkish Model: How the Arab Uprisings Brought Down Islamic Liberalism*, London: Verso.

Tuğal, C. (2017) 'The uneven neoliberalization of good works: Islamic charitable fields and their impact on diffusion', *American Journal of Sociology*, 123(2): 426–64.

Tuğal, C. (2021) 'Urban symbolic violence re-made: religion, politics and spatial struggles in Istanbul', *International Journal of Urban and Regional Research*, 45(1): 154–63.

Tuncer, G. (2019) 'Tarımda gerçekten neler olduğunu gösteren altı tablo', *Independent Türkçe* [online] 1 March, Available from: https://www.indyt urk.com/node/17431/ekonomi/tarımda-gerçekten-neler-olduğunu-göste ren-6-tablo (Accessed 6 June 2023).

Tunç, A. (2018) 'All is flux: a hybrid media approach to macro-analysis of the Turkish media', *Middle East Critique*, 27(2): 141–59.

Turan, E. (2015) 'Gardens of resistance: Urban agriculture in the Yedíkule Market Gardens, Istanbul', Unpublished doctoral dissertation submitted to the Social Sciences Institute of İstanbul Bilgi University, İstanbul.

Ültanır, M.S. (2019) 'Türkiye'de kooperatifçiliğin tarihsel seyri: Devlet inisiyatifi-kalkinma ideali', Unpublished MA thesis, Social Sciences Institute of Hacettepe University, Ankara.

Unsal, B.O. (2015) 'State-led urban regeneration in Istanbul: power struggles between interest groups and poor communities', *Housing Studies*, 30(8): 1299–316.

Utting, P. (2015) 'Introduction', in P. Utting (ed.) *Social and Solidarity Economy: Beyond the Fringe*, London: UNRISD and Zed Books, pp 1–37.

Uysal, A. (2017) *Sokakta Siyaset: Türkiye'de Protesto Eylemleri, Protestocular ve Polis'*, İstanbul: İletişim Yayinları.

Van de Sande, M. (2013) 'The prefigurative politics of Tahrir Square – an alternative perspective on the 2011 revolutions', *Res Publica*, 19(3): 223–39.

Vieta, M. (2010) 'The social innovations of autogestion in Argentina's worker-recuperated enterprises: cooperatively reorganizing productive life in hard times', *Labor Studies Journal*, 35(3): 295–321.

Warner, J. (2013) 'The new refeudalization of the public sphere', in E. West and M.P. McAllister (eds) *The Routledge Companion to Advertising and Promotional Culture*, pp 293–305, Abingdon: Routledge.

Whatmore S, Stassart, P. and Renting, H. (2003) 'What's alternative about alternative food networks?', *Environment and Planning*, 35: 389–91.

White, C., Shopov, A. and Ostovich, M. (2015) 'An archaeology of sustenance: the endangered market gardens of Istanbul', *Archaeology for the People: Joukowsky Institute Perspectives*, 29–38.

Williams, C.C. (2014) 'Non-commodified labour', in M. Parker, G. Cheney, V. Fournier and C. Land (eds) *The Routledge Companion to Alternative Organization*, Abingdon: Routledge, pp 105–19.

Wilson, A.D. (2013) 'Beyond alternative: exploring the potential for autonomous food spaces', *Antipode*, 45(3): 719–37.

Yaman, M. (2019) 'Tarımsal üretimde kadin emeği: tarihte kısa bir gezinti', in Ö. Şendeniz (ed.) *Aramızda Kalmasın; Kır, Kent Ve Ötesinde Toplumsal Cinsiyet*, Panel Presentations and Workshop Outputs, Istanbul: Toplumsal Cinsiyet Araştırmaları Derneği Yayını, pp 57–62.

Yaman-Öztürk, M. and Ercan, F. (2012) '1979 krizinden 2001 krizine Türkiye'de sermaye birikimi süreci ve yaşanan dönüşümler', *Praxis*, 19: 55–93.

Yates, L. (2015) 'Everyday politics, social practices and movement networks: daily life in Barcelona's social centres', *The British Journal of Sociology*, 66(2): 236–58.

Yates, L. (2021) 'Prefigurative politics and social movement strategy: the roles of prefiguration in the reproduction, mobilisation and coordination of movements', *Political Studies*, 69(4): 1033–52.

Yaylacı, S. (2013) 'Reclaiming the public sphere in Turkey: Arendtian and Habermasian interpretation of forums', *Centre for Policy and Research on Turkey*, 2(8): 11–18.

Yenal, Z. (1999) 'Food TNCs, intellectual property investments and post-Fordist food consumption: the case of Unilever and Nestlé in Turkey', *International Journal of the Sociology of Agriculture and Food*, 8: 21–34.

Yeşil, B. (2018) 'The fifth estate: attacking and coopting the Turkish media', in C. Rodríguez-Garavito and K. Gomez (eds) *Rising to The Populist Challenge: A New Playbook for Human Rights Actors*, Bogotá: Dejustica, pp 81–91.

Yıldırım, K. (2009) 'Values education experiences of Turkish class teachers: a phenomonological approach', *Eurasian Journal of Educational Research* (EJER), 35.

Yılmaz, E., Özdemir, G., Oraman, Y., Unakitan, G. and Konyali, S. (2019) 'Tarımsal üretimde kadınların karar alma süreçlerine katılımı ve kooperatiflerden beklentileri', *Tekirdağ Ziraat Fakültesi Dergisi*, 16(1): 71–81.

Yılmaz, A., Toydemir, B., Keskin, C., Yıldırım, C., Kocabıçak, E., Elhan, E. et al (2020) *Yeniden İnşa Et: Caferağa ve Yeldeğirmeni Dayanışmaları Yatay Örgütlenme Modeli*, İstanbul: NotaBene Yayınları.

Zitcer, A. (2015) 'Food co-ops and the paradox of exclusivity', *Antipode*, 47(3): 812–28.

Zitcer, A. (2017) 'Collective purchase: food cooperatives and their pursuit of justice', in A. Alkon and J. Guthman (eds) *The New Food Activism: Opposition, Cooperation and Collective Action*, Oakland, CA: University of California Press, pp 181–205.

Websites

BÜKOOP (2021) Available from: https://bukoop.org

Cooperative Law 1163, Available from: https://mevzuat.gov.tr/mevzuat?MevzuatNo=1163&MevzuatTur=1&MevzuatTertip=5

Cumhuriyet newspaper, Available from: https://www.cumhuriyet.com.tr/haber/kana-bulanmamis-giysi-turklerin-de-hakki-425012

Kadıköy Kooperatif (2021) Available from: https://kadikoykoop.wordpress.com/

Karşı Lig, Short Documentary of Setenay Gültekin, Bahçeşehir Üniversitesi, Available from: https://vimeo.com/11852917

Kooperatifler Kanunu (2022) Available from: https://www.mevzuat.gov.tr/mevzuatmetin/1.5.1163.pdfKooperatifler

Media Ownership Monitor in Turkey (2021) Available from: https://turkey.mom-rsf.org/

OECD Employment Outlook, Available from: https://www.oecd.org/employment-outlook/2019/

Salkım Kooperatifi (2021) Available from: https://salkimkooperatifi.org/

SES (Equality, Justice, Women Platform), Available from: http://esitlikadaletkadin.org/baska-turlu-bir-futbol-mumkun-karsi-ligin-kadinlari/

Index